D1733289

DISCOVERING THE BASIS OF LIFE
AN INTRODUCTION TO MOLECULAR BIOLOGY

ANN ROLLER

McGraw-Hill Book Company

New York   St. Louis   San Francisco   Düsseldorf   Johannesburg
Kuala Lumpur   London   Mexico   Montreal   New Delhi   Panama
Rio de Janeiro   Singapore   Sydney   Toronto

DISCOVERING THE BASIS OF LIFE
an introduction to molecular biology

123456789   M A M M   9876543

This book was set in Uranus by University Graphics, Inc. The editors
were William J. Willey, Hiag Akmakjian, and James R. Belser; the
designer was Jo Jones; and the production supervisor was Ted Agrillo.
The drawings were done by Vantage Art, Inc.
The Maple Press Company was printer and binder.

Library of Congress Cataloging in Publication Data

Roller, Ann.
Discovering the basis of life.

Bibliography: p.
1. Molecular biology. 2. Life (Biology)
I. Title. [DNLM: 1. Molecular biology. QH506
R749d 1974]
QH506.R63   574.8'8   73-12028
ISBN 0-07-053564-7

CONTENTS

1793382

PREFACE

Molecular biology is in the public eye. The cornerstone of molecular biology, the structure of DNA, is described in lead articles of major magazines, whose covers are adorned by the DNA double helix. The breakthroughs of molecular biologists, because they concern the origin of life, an eventual cure for cancer, and the nature of life, death, and disease, are highlighted in the newspapers.

"Walter, explain DNA just once more and I promise I won't ask you again."

The purpose of this book is to permit students, including those with no training in biology or chemistry, to participate in the current excitement in molecular biology. To that end, Chaps. 1 to 3 and 6 include the essentials of evolutionary theory, cell biology, chemistry, and genetics; also, specialized vocabulary is avoided as far as possible.

The achievements of molecular biology are the result of experiments, and many are here described in considerable detail. These include not only the classics of molecular biology but also recent experiments which are on the frontiers and still of uncertain significance. It is hoped that this experimental approach will enable students to appreciate the methods, the ingenuity, and the thrill of research.

Both friends and strangers have contributed generously to this book. Many have supplied photographic material, for which I am extremely grateful; they are specifically acknowledged with each figure. I would also like to thank the publishers and authors who have given me permission to reproduce illustrations; the origin of such material is given in each case.

It is a pleasure to acknowledge the help of those who have read and criticized the manuscript. In particular, throughout its preparation R. Jeener offered excellent suggestions and much-appreciated encouragement; the detailed criticisms of Francis Crick and René Thomas were of great help in eliminating errors and, in some cases, simplifying the text; and, finally, thanks go to my two youthful critics, Elaine Roller and Christopher Darnell, for their innumerable helpful suggestions. Most of the comments of these and other critics have been incorporated into the text. Any faults which remain are entirely my own.

Ann Roller

THE CHARACTERISTICS OF LIFE

Fish and fowl, bird and beast, tree and grass, and insect and algae—the diversity of the living organisms which inhabit the earth is staggering. In, on, and above the land and seas of our planet dwell more than 300,000 species of plants and more than 1 million species of animals. Diversity would seem to be, and indeed is, a characteristic of life.

Paradoxically, another equally fundamental, though less obvious, characteristic of life is a profound similarity of living organisms. Bit by bit, over a period of several hundred years, biologists have accumulated the evidence for this similarity.

The first step was the classification of plants and animals according to their similarities. John Ray (1627–1705) distinguished a number of families of plants and published the first systematic arrangement of animals, based mainly on a comparison of fingers, toes, and teeth. The great classifier, Carolus Linnaeus (1707–1778), developed the formal system of classification and nomenclature which is still in use today.

The microscope, invented in 1590 (by Zacharias Janssen) and gradually perfected during the following centuries, vastly extended man's knowledge of the world around him. Improved microscopes ultimately made possible the formulation in the nineteenth century of a fundamental and amazing generality—that all living creatures, plant or animal, are put together from similar, small, living building blocks, the *cells*.

Figure 1-1 Carolus Linnaeus (1707–1778), remarkable Swedish botanist who enunciated principles for classifying the plants and animals, making use of the binomial system of nomenclature still in use today. Linnaeus included man in his categories, baptizing him *Homo sapiens. (Courtesy the Linnean Society of London.)*

THE CELLULAR BASIS OF LIFE

Robert Hooke (1635–1703) was the first to observe cells. Looking through his microscope at thin slices of cork (the bark of the cork oak tree), he saw "little boxes or cells . . . in the manner of a honeycomb, but not so regular." Anton van Leeuwenhoek (1632–1723) made a great impression on his contemporaries with his myriad discoveries. Leeuwenhoek was the first to see living cells—protozoans (single-celled animals), spermatozoa, red blood corpuscles, and even the much tinier bacteria.

But the significance of the cells observed in wood, in stagnant water, and in blood could not yet be appreciated. Recognition of the universal cellular construction of living organisms came only after another 150 years of observations, which included the discovery of a large body, the *nucleus,* found in the cells of both plants and animals.

Nuclei were first observed in 1831 by the British botanist Robert Brown (1773–1858) in the course of microscopical studies of orchids. Seven years later, M. J. Schleiden (1804–1881) published the notion that cells form by the crystallization of fluid around these nuclei. He was wrong. But at the same time he proposed that all plants, in all their parts, are either communities of cells or derivatives of cells; that is, either they are made of cells or are made by cells. And this important hypothesis was right.

The next year, Theodor Schwann (1810–1882) extended the hypothesis to include both plants and animals, and thereby defined the cell theory: "The cells are organisms, and animals as well as plants are aggregates of these organisms, arranged in accordance with definite laws."

The cell theory of Schleiden and Schwann had a great impact on biology and medicine. Out of the surge of research stimulated by this new idea there emerged over the next 20 years a clear picture of the fundamental nature of cells. The basic architecture of the cell was established: It consists of a nucleus and surrounding cytoplasm. Despite the embryonic state of their science, the chemists correctly concluded that essentially the same substances go into the making of the cells of animals, plants, and protozoans. Sperm and eggs, it was recognized, are also single cells.

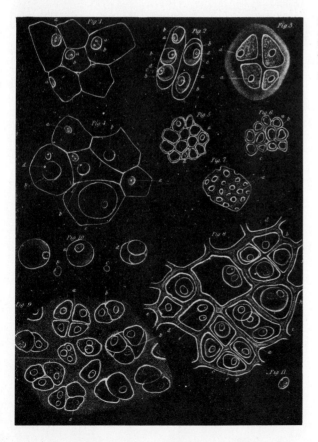

Figure 1-2 Theodor Schwann (1810–1882) drew these pictures to illustrate the fundamental similarity between plant and animal cells. The cell, he concluded, is the basic living subunit of all organisms. *(From T. Schwann, Microsc. Res.,* **1847.)**

4

The greatest advance in the cell theory was a comprehension of the origin of cells—from the division of previously existing cells. In 1858, Rudolf Virchow (1821–1902) published his brilliant theory: "Where a cell exists there must have been a preexisting cell, just as the animal arises only from an animal and the plant only from a plant." The cell had now been identified as the simplest structure capable of life, growth, and multiplication, the building block from which all organisms, plant and animal, are put together. The extraordinary similarity of the diverse forms of life on earth had become evident.

Figure 1-3 In the nineteenth century, swimming sperm with their beating tails, and enormous yolk-filled eggs were recognized as cells. A spermatozoon of the African clawed toad, *Xenopus laevis,* is here seen lying on the surface of an egg; the tail of the sperm wanders off to the left of the corkscrew-shaped head in the foreground (a jelly coat which normally surrounds the egg has been largely removed, though clumps of jelly still adhere to the surface of both egg and sperm). *(Scanning electron micrograph courtesy Robert D. Grey.)*

Figure 1-4 Dividing plant cells from root tip as seen with a modern microscope. *(From McLeish and Snoad, "Looking at Chromosomes," Macmillan, New York, 1958, courtesy B. Snoad.)*

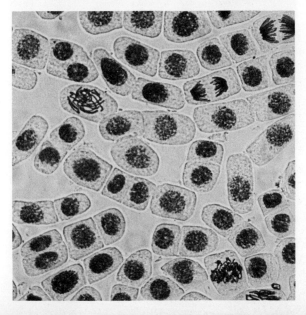

Why is life characterized by both the conspicuous diversity and the profound similarity of its many manifestations? That riddle was solved in 1859 when Charles Darwin (1809–1882) published "On the Origin of Species by Means of Natural Selection, or the Preservation of Favoured Races in the Struggle for Life."

THE EVOLUTIONARY EXPLANATION OF LIFE

Darwin amassed overwhelming arguments to prove his thesis, which he stated in this way: "As many more individuals of each species are born than can possibly survive; and as, consequently, there is a frequently recurring struggle for existence, it follows that any being, if it vary however slightly in any manner profitable to itself . . . will have a better chance of surviving, and thus be *naturally selected.*"* In other words, the struggle for existence will lead to the preferred survival of individuals with a slight advantage over their fellows.

A prerequisite of evolution by natural selection is that individuals of the same species actually differ from each other, that there exist individuals with a slight advantage in a given environment. Darwin pointed out that not only do such variants exist but that it is thanks to them that man has created distinct types of domestic animals; man has continually bred those individuals best suited for his purposes. Darwin then asked, "Why, if man can by patience select variations most useful to himself, should nature fail in selecting variations useful, under changing conditions of life, to her living products?" If such natural selection is admitted, then "From the strong principal of inheritance, any selected variety will tend to propagate its new and modified form."

There in a nutshell is the mechanism of natural selection. Individual variation is the fodder for the natural selection of "superior" individuals, those best suited to survive and reproduce in their particular surroundings; inheritance assures the propagation of the selected improvements. The "accumulation of innumerable slight variations, each good for the individual possessor," as Darwin put it, has thus slowly during the course of several billion years given rise to the present varied inhabitants of the earth.

Immediately upon its publication, Darwin's theory of the evolutionary origin of species by natural selection provoked violent debates among both scientists and the general public. But because it makes possible a rational interpretation of the living world, it has largely supplanted a literal biblical belief in the divine creation of species. Among the multitude of facts and findings which the evolutionary theory explains is the paradoxical endless diversity and simultaneous profound similarity of living organisms.

---

*All quotations in this section are from Darwin's great book.

Figure 1-5 Charles Darwin (1809–1882), author of "On the Origin of Species by Means of Natural Selection, or the Preservation of Favoured Races in the Struggle for Life," as painted by George Richmond in 1840. Although Darwin was not the first to conceive the idea of evolution, he discovered its scientific explanation and supported his hypothesis with overwhelming evidence. Darwin's theory of the evolutionary origin of species forms the conceptual basis of biology. *(Courtesy Down House.)*

Diversity, as Darwin realized, is a logical result of the struggle for life. Very similar creatures find themselves in the most severe competition; variations which result in their divergence will diminish competition and therefore be favored. Ultimately a wide variety of creatures must evolve, exploiting each niche in the economy of nature. "Natural Selection almost inevitably causes much Extinction of the less improved forms of life, and induces what I have called Divergence of Character."

On the other hand, surprising similarities among dissimilar creatures are explained by their descent from a common ancestor. Thus, "The framework of bones being the same in the hand of a man, wing of a bat, fin of the porpoise, and leg of the horse,—the same number of vertebrae forming the neck of the giraffe and of the elephant,—and innumerable other such facts, at once explain themselves on the theory of descent with slow and slight successive modifications."

Darwin postulated the interrelation of all past and present living forms. But he went still further. From the meager facts available to him, he drew the ultimate deduction: "All living things have much in common, in their chemical composition, their germinal vesicles, their cellular structure, and their laws of growth and reproduction. . . . Therefore I should infer from analogy that probably all the organic beings which have ever lived on this earth have descended from some one primordial form, into which life was first breathed."

Figure 1-6 The basic similarity of the skeletons of these three vertebrates is evident: (top) bullfrog skeleton; (lower left) monkey skeleton; (lower right) bat skeleton. Most astonishing is the wing of the bat, fashioned from the bones of the upper arm, forearm, and fingers (the claw at the "wrist" is the thumb bone). *(Monkey and bat skeletons courtesy "Turtox Collection," CCM General Biological, Inc. Bullfrog skeleton courtesy Ward's Natural Science Establishment, Inc., Rochester, New York.)*

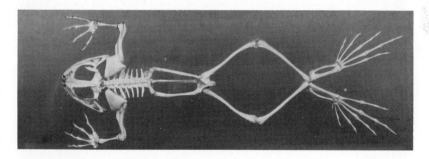

Figure 1-7 This fossil bacterium, *Eobacterium isolatum,* lived 3.2 billion years ago when the earth, now 4.5 billion years old, was still young. It was preserved in a rock formation in South Africa. Although this is the oldest organism yet discovered, it resembles certain modern bacteria both in size and in the apparent structure of its cell wall. *(Courtesy Elso S. Barghoorn.)*

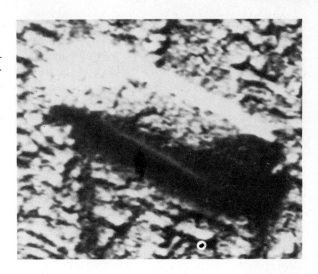

All living organisms descended from a single, original manifestation of life? This was a truly daring hypothesis, yet one which has now been substantiated by over 100 years of research. The common ancestry of every living organism beautifully accounts for similarities which in the twentieth century have become more and more striking.

The nineteenth century established the cell as the common denominator in the construction of living organisms. As described in later chapters, vastly improved microscopes, in particular electron microscopes, have revealed an elaborate internal anatomy shared by all cells. As will be remarked throughout this book, the most fundamental cell processes are common to all cells because at the molecular level the substances which are the chemical basis of life are the same in a bacterium, a human being, or any other organism. Not absolutely identical, to be sure, but then allowance must be made for successive slight chemical changes accumulated during the 2 or 3 billion years since the beginnings of the evolutionary divergence of species.

"Whilst this planet has gone cycling on according to the fixed law of gravity, from so simple a beginning endless forms most beautiful and most wonderful have been, and are being, evolved."

THE DIVERSITY OF CELLS

The diversity of cells is as astonishing as the manifest diversity of the higher plants and animals. The cells of the blue-green algae and bacteria are the least complex, lacking many of the structures found in other cells; for example, they have no nucleus. Nevertheless, the chemical basis on which they function closely resembles that of nucleated cells.

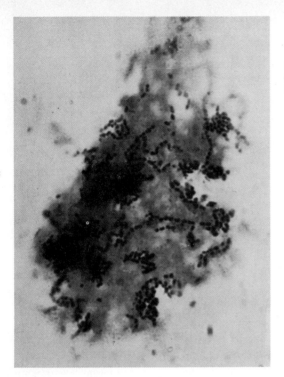

Figure 1-8 Photomicrograph of bacteria (magnification $\times$ 1,500). *(Instant photograph courtesy of Polaroid Corporation.)*

It is for these reasons that molecular biologists so frequently study these lowly creatures; especially the bacteria have been invaluable in illuminating fundamental processes common to all cells.

Even among these simplest cells there is great variety. Some species of blue-green algae live as single cells, but most form filamentous, sometimes branched, chains of cells. Moreover, only about half are blue-green; others are red, blue, green, purple, brown or blue-black.

Bacteria are the smallest unicellular organisms and the most numerous. Fortunately, though some of them are harmful, most are harmless, helpful, or even essential to man. Bacterial cells may be round, rodlike, bent, or twisted. The cells of the round bacteria *(cocci)* tend to stick together, forming pairs, clumps, sheets, or long chains. The cells of the rod-shaped bacteria *(bacilli)* may form pairs or chains, but most live alone as single cells.

There are large numbers of organisms which, like many blue-green algae and bacteria, live as single cells. These unicellular organisms are extraordinarily diverse. Yeasts, which cause bread to rise and beer and wine to ferment, are relatively small, only a few times bigger than a bacterium. Protozoans, single-celled animals, vary greatly in size and appearance: amoebas are about fifteen times bigger than a yeast cell and visible with the naked eye; some protozoans are larger, others much smaller than amoebas.

10

Figure 1-9 Comparative sizes of various cells, unicellular organisms, and a virus. (There is great variability in the dimensions of closely related cells: different species of *Euglena*, for example, range from 15 μ to 500 μm in length.) The metric unit the micrometer (μm) is provided above as the unit of length. The metric system of measurement, used universally by scientists, is simple. The standard measure of length is the meter, m, equal to 39.37 inches. The centimeter, cm. is 1/100 the length of the meter (2.54 cm/inch); the millimeter, mm, is 1/1,000 the length of the meter (25.4 mm/inch); the micrometer, μm, is 1/1,000,000 the length of the meter (25,400 μm/inch).

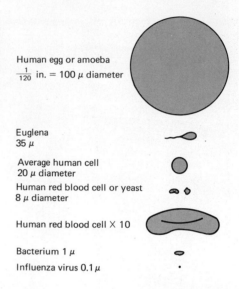

Human egg or amoeba
$\frac{1}{120}$ in. = 100 μ diameter

Euglena
35 μ

Average human cell
20 μ diameter

Human red blood cell or yeast
8 μ diameter

Human red blood cell $\times$ 10

Bacterium 1 μ

Influenza virus 0.1 μ

"And the motion of most of these animalcules in the water was so swift and so various, upwards, downwards, and roundabouts, that it was wonderful to see." Thus Leeuwenhoek, in 1674, described protozoans, with their curious forms and complicated means of feeding and locomotion.

Like the unicellular organisms, the various cells of multicellular plants and animals look quite dissimilar. Multicellular organisms may be composed of many different kinds of cells, each making its particular contribution to the total organization and each depending on the integrity of the organism for its own survival.

A human being, like any other vertebrate, requires nerve cells, muscle cells, liver cells, thyroid gland cells, bone-forming cells, and a host more. Their varying functions necessarily correspond to varying sizes and shapes. Skin cells and the cells lining blood capillaries, for example, are very flat, whereas a liver cell is more or less spherical. A liver cell might be considered an average-sized animal cell, several times bigger than a yeast cell and much smaller than an amoeba or the human egg. On the other hand, a message transmitted from the tip of the toe to the central nervous system passes along a nerve cell several feet in length in a human and several yards in length in a giraffe.

Besides differences in shape and general appearance, the "internal organs" of cells are modified to adapt each for its own particular function in the organism. The cells of every tissue of the higher plants and animals are sufficiently different so that, by means of appropriate techniques, each type can be distinguished with a microscope.

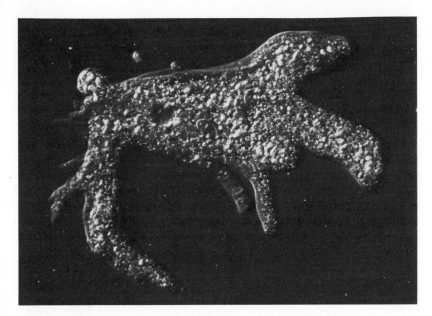

Figure 1-10 An amoeba. *(Courtesy Carolina Biological Supply Company.)*

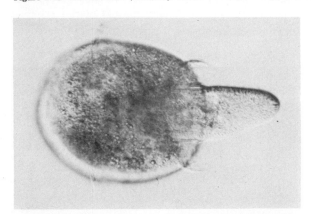

Figure 1-11 Two unicellular organisms: didinium with paramecium prey. *(Courtesy Carolina Biological Supply Company.)*

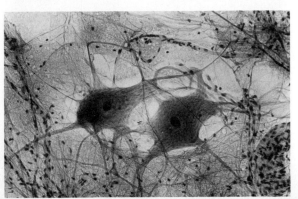

Figure 1-12 Cells with different functions may vary greatly in appearance. The illustration shows two spinal nerve cells and a multitude of interstitial cells (the many black spots are their nuclei). *(Courtesy Carolina Biological Supply Company.)*

WHAT DO CELLS DO? Cells perform the same basic functions as any living creature. What are these *vital functions* indispensable for the maintenance of life in a bacterium or a human being? The intake of food, water, and oxygen, and the excretion of wastes are the most apparent. The ability to react to changes in the environment, which saves human beings from being run over by cars, for example, is another primary attribute of all organisms. Finally, reproduction assures the continuity of the individual, of the species, and, ultimately, of life on earth.

Twenty years after Schleiden and Schwann proposed that cells are tiny organisms, Louis Pasteur (1822–1895) conducted an epoch-making series of experiments which demonstrated that cells, at least bacteria and yeast, eat, breathe, excrete, react, and reproduce.

Metabolism in Microorganisms and Man Like all cells, microorganisms transform nutrients into energy and into the substances of which they are themselves composed, and they excrete waste products. In a word, they metabolize, and this Pasteur demonstrated.

Pasteur showed, for example, that when yeast, now recognized to be a microscopic plant, ferments malt to produce beer, it uses part of the sugar in the malt to synthesize new cell wall. Most of the sugar is utilized to provide energy, in which process it is transformed into alcohol.

Figure 1-13 Louis Pasteur (1822–1895) as painted by Edelfelt. Pasteur proved that microorganisms cause fermentations and disease, thereby inaugurating a revolution in medicine. He also launched immunologic prevention of disease. Pasteur's astonishingly varied accomplishments were of incomparable importance to science and medicine. *(Courtesy Pasteur Institute, Paris.)*

As far as the yeast is concerned, the alcohol is an unwanted and therefore excreted waste product. Similarly, the bacteria which cause the souring of milk excrete lactic acid as a waste product instead of alcohol.

The eating, drinking, breathing, and excreting of wastes by animals such as man, and the corresponding functions in plants satisfy the metabolic needs of the cells of which they are composed. In animals, nutrients, water, and oxygen are transported from the intestines and lungs to every cell by the circulatory system, which also removes cellular waste products.

It has been possible to study the nutritional requirements of the cells of multicellular organisms by means of a technique called *tissue culture* (in which frequently no tissues are grown, or *cultured,* but rather groups of cells). At the beginning of this century, biologists, following in the steps of the bacteriologists who were so successfully growing bacteria in the laboratory, found ways to grow cells taken from multicellular plants and animals. Cultures of plant and animal cells have now been kept alive and growing in the laboratory for decades.

Tissue culture has made it possible to study not only the metabolism of the cells of multicellular organisms. Cells in tissue culture are also the objects of innumerable investigations of cellular function, of cell reactions to substances such as medicines and hormones, of interactions between cells, of virus infection, and of malignancy. As an example, the vaccines against polio were developed in tissue cultures of human and monkey cells. Several experiments involving cells grown in tissue culture will be described in subsequent chapters.

Figure 1-14 Tissue culture is a technique in which cells (or tissues) are kept alive and growing in the laboratory. *(a)* Tissue obtained from a plant or animal is treated to dissolve substances which hold cells together. *(b)* A small number of cells are added to a dish of nutrient solution. *(c)* They fall to the bottom, where they grow until the surface is covered with a layer of cells. Some of these cells are removed and added to a dish of fresh nutrient, where they then continue to grow; this procedure can be repeated indefinitely.

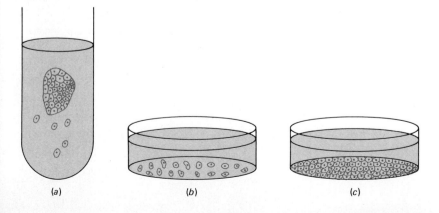

(a)   (b)   (c)

Reaction and Accommodation to Change

Even bacteria, structurally the simplest of cells, react to alterations in their environment. They must, for their survival in a competitive world depends in part on their ability to accommodate to variations in available nutrients.

Pasteur showed, for example, that the brewer or wine maker obtains alcohol only when yeast grows in the absence of oxygen. Similarly, certain bacteria transform sugar into lactic acid, thereby souring milk, only when they grow without oxygen. If oxygen is available, then sugar is utilized in a different and more efficient way, and the waste products are not lactic acid or alcohol, but water and carbon dioxide gas. The alcoholic and lactic acid fermentations are these microorganisms' adaptations to a lack of oxygen.

Muscle cells adapt to an oxygen shortage in the same way as the lactic acid bacteria. During severe muscular exertion, the respiratory and circulatory systems cannot keep up with the muscle cells' requirement for oxygen. So working muscle cells obtain energy not by changing relatively small amounts of sugar to carbon dioxide and water, which requires oxygen, but by changing very large amounts of sugar to lactic acid. The accumulation of lactic acid causes that tired feeling in the muscles. Panting after great exertion furnishes the oxygen with which a small part of the lactic acid is converted to carbon dioxide and water, supplying the energy to change the rest back into sugar.

These transformations of sugar are among the multitude of adaptations which have been demonstrated in bacterial, human, and other cells. Such chemical adaptations to a changing environment may seem very far indeed from the complex behavior of higher organisms, such as a human being. But are they really so different?

Essential to and inseparable from its way of life, each plant and animal

Figure 1-15 Chemical transformations of sugar. In the presence of oxygen, yeast, lactic acid bacteria, and muscle transform sugar into carbon dioxide and water, thereby obtaining a large amount of energy from little sugar. In the absence of oxygen, yeast cells transform sugar to alcohol, while the lactic acid bacteria and muscle tissue transform sugar to lactic acid; a small amount of energy is thereby obtained from a lot of sugar. Both alcohol and lactic acid can be transformed into carbon dioxide and water (providing much energy) if oxygen becomes available.

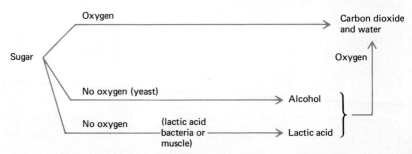

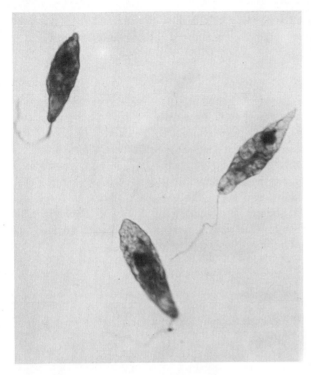

Figure 1-16 *Euglena* is a genus of unicellular algae which with the aid of a whiplike flagellum swim through the fresh or brackish water or mud in which they live. Flagellates of the genus *Euglena* move toward light, which they distinguish by means of an eyespot located at the base of the flagellum. *(Courtesy Carolina Biological Supply Company.)*

has its particular mechanisms for perceiving and reacting to changes in its environment. The unicellular alga *Euglena* is sensitive to light and moves toward it by beating its whiplike flagellum. Its *eyespot* is a light-sensitive pigment which is chemically similar to the yellow pigment in carrots. Higher animals also perceive and react to light stimuli. Their eyes, in conjunction with their nervous and muscular systems, constitute a complex system which receives information from the environment, processes it, and reacts to it. Thus are these animals able to acquire food and avoid danger.

The chemistry which enables a human or other animal to react and act is understood in part. The cells of the retina of the eye contain light-sensitive pigments. One of these is almost identical to the pigment of *Euglena's* eyespot. Once the light pattern is registered on the retina, the information is transmitted along nerve fibers to the brain by a mechanism which has been quite well worked out. How information is processed and stored in the brain is at present a mystery.

The adaptations of bacteria, such as the way they react to changes in their supply of nutrients and oxygen, have already been quite well elucidated. No doubt the more complex behavior of higher animals, the way they perceive and accommodate to their environment, will also one day be thoroughly understood. It will then be reduced to a series of chemical events, the reactions of specialized cells to changes in the outer world and in each other.

Multiplication by Cell Division

Reproduction assures the continuation of life on earth. Yeasts reproduce by budding; bacteria, like most cells, reproduce by dividing in two, giving rise to two daughter cells of approximately equal size.

The growth and reproduction of higher organisms are the result of the growth and division of cells. A human being begins its existence as a fertilized egg. Thus, like most organisms, it starts off as a single cell. This cell divides to form two cells; the two cells divide to form four cells, then eight, then sixteen, and finally the billions of billions of cells which constitute a baby. Only a few more rounds of cell division are needed to change the baby into an adult.

Figure 1-17 Time-lapse sequence of photomicrographs of a budding yeast cell (magnification × 3,600). The white circle toward the lower pole of the mother cell is a vacuole filled with digestive juice. The light gray area between the vacuole and the bud is the nucleus. *(d)* The nucleus is entering the bud. *(e), (f),* and *(g)* It is dividing by elongation and constriction in its middle region. *(h)* There are two nuclei, one in each cell (in the lower cell the nucleus is to the left and a little below the bright circular image of the vacuole). *(From C. F. Robinow, J. Cell Biol.,* **29:** 129 (1966), courtesy C. F. Robinow.)

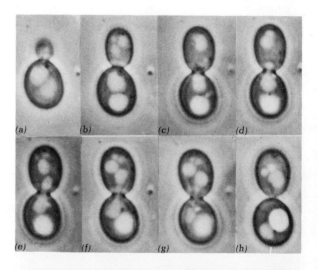

Figure 1-18 Early stages in the development of the frog. *(a)* The fertilized egg has divided once. *(b)* There are eight cells; a first step toward cell specialization is apparent in the different sizes of the cells. *(c)* The differences in cell size in the thirty-two-cell stage give the appearance of a rudimentary structure. *(Courtesy Carolina Biological Supply Company.)*

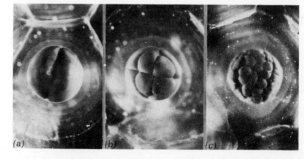

Of course, cell division alone will not make a baby from a fertilized egg. The vital functions of an animal such as a human are carried out by specialized organs, the stomach and intestines, the lungs, the liver, the nervous system, to name a few; specialized cells, such as nerve cells, muscle cells, and liver cells, must evolve. Such cells vary in many respects.

But the vital functions indispensable for the maintenance of life itself are common to all cells and are accomplished by structures called *organelles,* "little organs," which are basically the same in all cells. These organelles, essential to the life of cells and therefore to the life of all creatures, are described in Chap. 3. But before examining the inside of a cell, let us look at the nature of the substances that make up the living and the nonliving worlds.

 SUBSTANCES AND THEIR TRANSFORMATIONS

Human beings are omnivorous—they eat both plants and animals. Are they then made up of a mixture of these ingredients, a bit of tomato here, a smattering of bacon and egg there? If you ate nothing but pork, would you finally become a pig? Of course not! And the difference between a plant and its nutrients is even more striking, for plants take in chiefly water and a gas, carbon dioxide.

Life is sustained by the intake of nutrients, followed by their transformation into the substances needed by cells. Plants absorb simple nutrients, which they transform into the complex substances of which they are composed. Animals such as humans first break down their nutrients: plant starch is degraded to sugar; meat is broken down into its subunits. Within the cells, the bits and pieces are transformed into human-type meat (muscle), into *glycogen* (the animal equivalent of starch), and into all the components of all the tissues; some food is burned to provide energy.

This continual transformation of nutrients is a fundamental characteristic of life. The transformation is the end result of chemical reactions, which in any cell number in the thousands. Thanks to the chemists and biochemists of the nineteenth and twentieth centuries, a large number of these reactions are now understood and can even be made to take place in a test tube.

But what exactly is a chemical reaction? How, for example, can sugar be transformed into water and a gas, or into alcohol, or into cellulose or starch? In order to understand a chemical reaction, it is first necessary to consider the substances which react. What is the sugar called *glucose* (it is not table sugar, which is the sugar called *sucrose*)? What is alcohol? What is starch? What is the pigment in the retina of the eye which is similar to the yellow pigment in carrots? What is vitamin A? What are water and air? What are acids, bases, salts (table salt is one salt, epsom salts another—among thousands)? Until the nineteenth century, the nature of the substances of which the world is made was a mystery.

During 2 millennia it was thought that, as the Greeks had proposed, matter is composed of fire, earth, water, and air. Then in the eighteenth century scientists began experimenting. By combining, heating, and burning substances, they discovered much about the nature of matter.

Armed with this new-found knowledge, Antoine Laurent Lavoisier (1743–1794) toward the end of the century realized that there are only two kinds of pure substances, which he called *compounds* and *elements*. Compounds can be broken down into elements; elements cannot be

THE NATURE OF SUBSTANCES: ELEMENTS AND COMPOUNDS

Figure 2-1   Antoine Laurent Lavoisier (1743–1794), the father of modern chemistry, and his wife, as painted by Jacques David. Whereas burning sustances had been thought to give off phlogiston, a mythical fire principle, Lavoisier demonstrated that they combine with the newly discovered gas oxygen. Lavoisier defined elements, recognizing the true composition of metals and their compounds. His clear concepts enabled him, together with other chemists, to devise the logical system of chemical nomenclature still in use. *(Courtesy the Rockefeller University.)*

broken down into other substances. Water, for example, is a compound made of the elements hydrogen and oxygen.

Lavoisier gave many elements, including hydrogen and oxygen, their modern names and invented the system of chemical nomenclature still in use today. He designated the compounds to indicate their elementary composition; for example, a compound composed of a metal combined with oxygen he called a *metal oxide;* of a metal combined with carbon dioxide he called a *metal carbonate.* Expressions such as "charcoal plus dephlogisticated air gives fixed air" soon gave way to Lavoisier's more descriptive "carbon plus oxygen gives carbon dioxide."

THE ATOMIC THEORY In 1803, John Dalton (1766–1844) proposed that matter cannot be divided up indefinitely into smaller and smaller bits but that ultimately it is composed of indivisible particles, the *atoms.* Lavoisier had given the name "element" to substances which cannot be chemically decomposed into other substances. Dalton now hypothesized that each element corresponds to a particular kind of atom. Chemical compounds, he correctly surmised, are groups of atoms bound in definite proportions into *molecules.* A water molecule, for example, consists of two atoms of the element hydrogen and one of the element oxygen; a carbon dioxide molecule of one atom of carbon and two of oxygen.

And what in this theory are chemical reactions? They are rearrangements, dissociations, and associations of atoms.

Dalton recognized that the atoms of each of the elements must have different weights, but 50 years passed before a way was found to determine the relative weights of the atoms, the *atomic weights.* The lightest atom, that of the element hydrogen, was then given an atomic weight of 1; oxygen atoms, found to be sixteen times heavier than hydrogen

Figure 2-2 Formation of water from hydrogen and oxygen. *(a)* A mixture of hydrogen molecules (H_2), each consisting of two hydrogen atoms, and oxygen molecules (O_2), each consisting of two oxygen atoms; *(b)* water molecules (H_2O) formed by the reaction of hydrogen and oxygen. *(From Linus Pauling, "College Chemistry," 3d ed., Freeman, San Francisco, 1964.)*

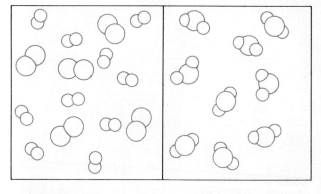

(a)   (b)

atoms, were assigned an atomic weight of 16; and so on for all the elements.*

Once the atoms had been assigned atomic weights, the compounds could be assigned *molecular weights,* which are simply the sum of the weights of their constituent atoms. Water molecules, with two atoms of hydrogen and one of oxygen, have a molecular weight of $1 + 1 + 16 = 18$. What is the molecular weight of carbon dioxide? One carbon, atomic weight 12, plus two oxygens, atomic weight 16, gives $12 + 16 + 16 = 44$.

Dalton's atomic theory made it possible to work out the atomic composition of compounds and the atomic rearrangements which take place in chemical reactions, but during most of the nineteenth century nothing was known about the nature of the atoms themselves. Their existence was even doubted until the beginning of this century when discoveries concerning their structure made it clear that they really do exist.

Atoms are not indivisible particles, as Dalton had supposed; rather, they have a structure of the greatest complexity. Yet even an easily understood, simplified model of their structure suffices to explain some of the properties of matter. Atoms, it has been found, are composed of three kinds of particles: *electrons, protons,* and *neutrons.*

THE STRUCTURE OF THE ATOM

Electrons were the first subatomic particles to be discovered. In the early nineteenth century, there were already clues that atoms and electricity are related. It was known, for example, that the passage of an electric current will decompose some compounds, such as water, into their constitutent elements. Electricity, it was finally deduced, exists as discrete, indivisible particles, the electrons, which are associated with atoms. The actual existence of electrons was proved experimentally by Sir J. J. Thomson (1856–1940) in 1897. Thomson was awarded the Nobel Prize for physics for his brilliant studies of electric conductivity, which enabled him to demonstrate that electrons are particles with a negative electric charge and a very much smaller weight than that of any atom.

The Electrons

The discovery of the negatively charged electron provided the first clue that atoms are not homogeneous, indivisible particles. Atoms are

---

*The atomic weights of the atoms are now calculated in relation to carbon, atomic weight 12, giving hydrogen an atomic weight of 1.008 and oxygen an atomic weight of 15.9994, for example.

electrically neutral, neither negatively nor positively charged, yet they include negative electrons. Therefore they must also have a positively charged part.

The Atomic Nucleus

In 1911, Ernest Rutherford (1871–1937) performed an experiment which enabled him to deduce the nuclear structure of atoms. Rutherford bombarded an extremely thin sheet of gold foil with a stream of *alpha particles,* which are positively charged helium atoms. He found that most of the alpha particles passed right through the gold foil as if nothing were there, while a few, perhaps 1 in 10,000, bounced back as if they had met something impenetrable in their path.

From this epochal experiment Rutherford concluded that most of the atom *is* just space—thus most of the alpha particles pass straight through a piece of thin gold foil. (In this space whirl the negatively charged electrons.) The positively charged part of the atom is concentrated into an extraordinarily small volume, the *atomic nucleus;* only the rare alpha particle which comes upon a gold nucleus in its path is bounced back.

Two years later, in 1913, the great Danish physicist Niels Bohr (1885–1962), then a young man working in Rutherford's laboratory, published a detailed model of the nuclear atom inspired not by the classical laws of physics, which he recognized could not describe atoms, but by the then new quantum theory of Max Planck and Albert Einstein. The Bohr model of the atom, for which Bohr received the Nobel Prize for physics in 1922, has been extended and refined into the present theory of atomic structure.

Figure 2-3 Diagrammatic illustration of the experiment which demonstrated that most of an atom is space, only a very small part of which is occupied by the nucleus. Rutherford had already received the Nobel Prize in chemistry (in 1908) for work on radioactivity when he performed this momentous experiment. *(Adapted from Linus Pauling, "College Chemistry," 3d ed., Freeman, San Francisco, 1964.)*

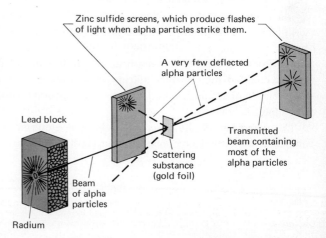

Zinc sulfide screens, which produce flashes of light when alpha particles strike them.

A very few deflected alpha particles

Lead block

Transmitted beam containing most of the alpha particles

Scattering substance (gold foil)

Beam of alpha particles

Radium

Fig. 2-4 The first Solvay Physics Congress, in 1911, was a meeting of great physicists. Standing: Goldschmidt, Planck, Rubens, Sommerfeld, Lindeman, De Broglie, Knudsen, Hasenohrl, Hostelet, Herzen, Jeans, Rutherford, Kamerlinghonnes, Einstein, Langevin. Seated: Nernst, Brillouin, Solvay, Lorentz, Warburg, Perrin, Wien, Curie, Poincaré. *(Courtesy Solvay & Cie.)*

What Does an Atom Look Like?

Of course, it is impossible to say exactly what an atom looks like, for atoms are too small to be seen with any microscope. Moreover, because the electrons are in very rapid motion, this is similar to asking what a moving airplane propeller looks like. The propeller, since it is turning rapidly, looks like a blurred disk. Similarly, the spherical atom is a blur of rapidly moving electrons. They effectively fill up the space around the nucleus, just as the propeller effectively fills up space.

Bohr originally proposed that the electrons move in orbits around the nucleus, like the planets around the sun. It has since been recognized that electron movement is much more complicated and is largely in and out, toward and away from the nucleus. Bohr's orbits have turned out to correspond to the distances from the nucleus where the electrons pass most frequently; they are especially dense spheres in the electron blur.

The atomic nucleus is so extraordinarily small compared with the atom itself that if it were 1 inch in diameter, then the outer edge of the atom would be about 1 mile away. And since, as will be seen in the next section, electrons weigh next to nothing, the atom's weight is concentrated in its nucleus, which has an unbelievable density: 1 cubic inch of solidly packed nuclei would weigh 4 billion tons.

Atoms, Isotopes, and Radioactivity

The atomic nucleus is made up of two kinds of particles: *protons* and *neutrons*. Its positive charge is due to the protons, each of which has a charge of +1. Every element has its own characteristic number of protons; the number of electrons, each with a charge of −1, equals the number of protons, so atoms are electrically neutral.

In 1932, it was discovered that nuclei also contain uncharged, electrically neutral particles called neutrons. Neutrons and protons have almost exactly the same mass—the neutron has a mass 1,839 times and the proton 1,836 times that of an electron. On the atomic-weight scale, the weight of a proton or a neutron is close to 1; this makes the atomic weights of the atoms very close to the sum of the number of neutrons and protons in their nuclei.

The commonplace atom of the lightest element, hydrogen, has no neutrons. It consists of one electron, charge −1, and one proton, charge +1, and so is electrically neutral, like all atoms. Its atomic weight, 1, is due to its lone proton. Like all atoms, its chemical properties result directly from the number of its electrons: one.

The hydrogen bomb does not contain hydrogen of atomic weight 1, designated H^1. It contains two other varieties of hydrogen, that is, two other *isotopes*: H^2, frequently called *deuterium* or *heavy hydrogen,* and H^3, called *tritium.* All three isotopes of hydrogen, H^1, H^2, and H^3, have one proton and therefore one electron, and are, therefore, chemically the element hydrogen; but they differ in the number of neutrons. Whereas the most abundant isotope of hydrogen has no neutrons, and thus an atomic weight of 1, H^2 has one proton and one neutron, and an atomic weight of 2, and H^3 has one proton and two neutrons, and an atomic weight of 3. In nature, most elements are mixtures of isotopes. Tin is the champion, being a mixture of ten.

The number of neutrons in the nucleus of an atom does not affect its chemical properties, but it can greatly affect the stability of the nucleus. H^1 and H^2, for example, are both perfectly stable. H^3 is unstable; its nuclei run a constant risk of exploding, that is, of disintegrating. H^3 is *radioactive*—as are, by definition, all unstable isotopes.

Isotopes, both stable and radioactive, have become tools of primary importance in biochemical research. The metabolism of foods has been studied with their help by administering isotopically labeled substances

Figure 2-5 The isotopes of hydrogen all have one proton in their nucleus but differ in the number of neutrons. The common isotope (H¹) has no neutron. H², present to the extent of about 0.015 percent in hydrogen-containing compounds, has one neutron. The radioactive isotope (H³), or tritium, prepared synthetically, has two neutrons.

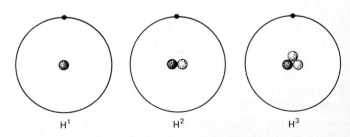

in which one or more atoms have been replaced by a radioactive isotope, whose presence can be detected with a Geiger counter. The first major discovery made with such labeling techniques was the constant turnover of the constituents of living organisms—they are continually being discarded and replaced. Even bones and teeth, seemingly so inert, can exchange a part of their calcium with calcium in the blood. Labeling techniques have also made it possible to work out detailed biochemical pathways. Many experiments using isotopes will be described in this book.

The 100-odd known elements can be arranged consecutively according to the number of protons in their nucleus. The first element is hydrogen, with one proton. The second element, with two protons, two neutrons, and two electrons, atomic weight 4, is the gas helium, used for inflating balloons and dirigibles. Helium is unlike most elements, for it is chemically unreactive, combining with no other element. Five more such chemically inert elements are known, all gases: neon, argon, krypton, xenon, and radon. Together they constitute the group of elements called the *noble gases.*

Why are the noble gases so unreactive? Because these elements have a stable number of electrons, giving them what are called *filled electron shells.* In helium, the so-called *helium shell,* containing two electrons, is filled. In neon, not only is the helium shell of two electrons filled, but

ELECTRONS AND CHEMICAL PROPERTIES

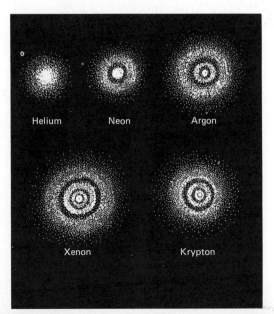

Figure 2-6 Distribution of electrons in the noble-gas atoms showing the successive electron shells. *(From Linus Pauling, "College Chemistry," 3d ed., Freeman, San Francisco, 1964.)*

also the next shell, the *neon shell,* with eight electrons. In radon, there are six filled electron shells:

Helium shell	two electrons
Neon shell	eight electrons
Argon shell	eight electrons
Krypton shell	eighteen electrons
Xenon shell	eighteen electrons
Radon shell	thirty-two electrons (giving radon a total of eighty-six electrons)

The chemical properties of all elements are due to the number of electrons in their atoms, for in one way or another—by giving away, by borrowing, or by sharing electrons—atoms try to arrive at the nearest filled electron shell, that is, at the nearest stable electron configuration.

Table 2-1   Some Biologically Important Elements

ELEMENT	SYMBOL*	ATOMIC NUMBER†	BIOLOGIC FUNCTION
Hydrogen	H	1	Component of water and many biologic substances.
Boron	B	5	Essential in some plants.
Carbon	C	6	Component of many biologic substances.
Nitrogen	N	7	Component of many biologic substances.
Oxygen	O	8	Component of water and many biologic substances.
Sodium	Na	11	Principal extracellular positive ion.
Magnesium	Mg	12	Required in small amounts by animals. In plants, it is an essential component of the green pigment chlorophyll.
Phosphorus	P	15	Component of many biologic substances. Used in energy transfer in biologic reactions.

Table 2-1   (Cont'd)

ELEMENT	SYMBOL*	ATOMIC NUMBER†	BIOLOGIC FUNCTION
Sulfur	S	16	Component of many biologic substances, in particular, proteins.
Chlorine	Cl	17	Principal negative ion in animals.
Potassium	K	19	Principal positive ion inside cells.
Calcium	Ca	20	Major component of bones and teeth.
Iron	Fe	26	Component of many substances, in particular, hemoglobin, the red protein in red blood cells.
Cobalt	Co	27	Component of vitamin B_{12}.
Iodine	I	53	Component of thyroid hormone.

Note: A few other elements, such as manganese, copper, and zinc, are also required in trace quantities.

*Each element is designated by a one- or two-letter symbol.

†The atomic number of an element equals the number of protons in its nucleus.

Metals, Electron Donors

When the elements are arranged in sequence according to the number of protons in their nucleus, then the noble gases are followed by elements with filled electron shells and one additional, unwanted, electron. Helium is followed by lithium. Lithium has three protons and therefore three electrons; so its helium shell of two electrons is filled, and there is just one of the eight electrons which would be required to fill the next shell, the neon shell. Lithium is very eager to get rid of that extra electron, thereby acquiring helium's stable electron configuration.

Like lithium, sodium has one electron to give away. With eleven electrons, sodium has a filled helium shell, a filled neon shell, and one extra electron, the first one of the eight needed to fill the argon shell. Potassium is also in this class, with one electron in the krypton shell, the inner shells being filled. The elements in this group, the *alkali metals,* are lithium, sodium, potassium, rubidium, cesium, and francium.

The most important characteristic of the alkali metals is their extreme chemical reactivity, the result of their readiness to give away that extra electron, thereby acquiring the stable configuration of a noble gas. They will give the electron to any atom that will take it. They thereby acquire a +1 charge because the number of positive protons in the nucleus then exceeds by one the number of electrons. Such electrically charged atoms are called *ions*. The alkali metals are found in nature in the form of very stable positive ions of charge +1.

All metals are substances which acquire a stable electron configuration by giving away electrons, thereby becoming positive ions. The

Figure 2-7 Lithium, sodium, and potassium are among the elements whose atoms have one electron in their outermost electron shell. By giving away this electron, these atoms attain the stable-electron configuration of a noble gas. They also thereby acquire a charge of +1. Atoms which have lost or gained an electron, and are therefore electrically charged, are called ions.

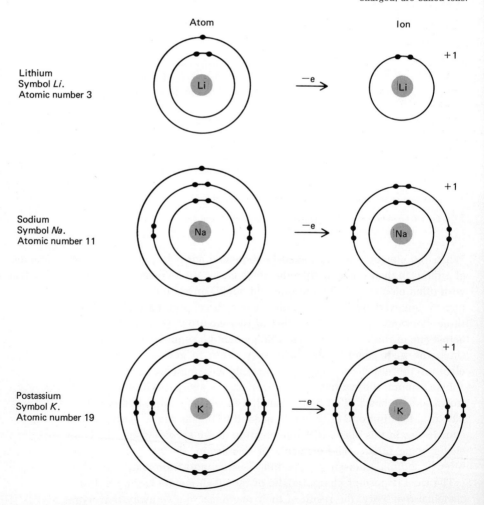

Atom   Ion

Lithium
Symbol *Li*.
Atomic number 3

Sodium
Symbol *Na*.
Atomic number 11

Postassium
Symbol *K*.
Atomic number 19

alkali metals have one electron to give away. Others, called the *alkaline-earth metals,* have two to give away; they are therefore normally found in the form of ions of charge +2. The alkaline-earth metals include magnesium, calcium, strontium, barium, and radium. Aluminum has three electrons to give away.

To whom do the metals give their surplus electrons? One group of elements avid to gain an electron is the *halogens*: fluorine, chlorine, bromine, and iodine. These elements are just one electron short of having a filled electron shell. They are as ready to gain an electron, thereby acquiring the nearest noble-gas configuration and a charge of −1, as the alkali metals are to lose their extra electron. The halogens are usually found in the form of ions of charge −1.

Negative Ions and Ionic Compounds

    Oppositely charged ions are strongly attracted to each other. This attraction is called the *ionic bond.* Ionic compounds consist of negatively and positively charged ions with the total negative and positive charges being equal, providing electrical neutrality.

Figure 2-8   Fluorine and chlorine are among the elements whose atoms have one less electron than a noble gas. By gaining an electron, these atoms therefore attain a stable-electron configuration; they also thereby acquire a charge of −1 and are called negative ions.

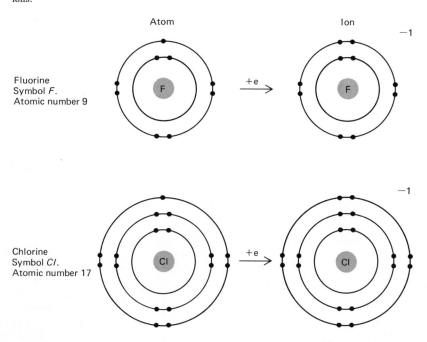

Table salt, sodium chloride (which, using the symbols assigned to sodium and chlorine, is written NaCl), is an example of an ionic compound. Sodium chloride consists of sodium ions (Na^+), charge +1, and chloride ions (Cl^-), charge −1. Like sodium chloride, most ionic compounds are salts.

Many ionic compounds are named, thanks to Lavoisier, in the same way as sodium chloride: The positive ion retains the name of the metal from which it is derived; the negative ion's name ends in "ide." Thus, fluoridated water contains sodium fluoride, and the lackluster appearance of aluminum pots is due to a thin film of aluminum oxide.

Acids: Proton Donors; Bases: Proton Acceptors

Acids, for example hydrochloric acid (HCl), have a hydrogen ion to donate. The positive hydrogen ion (H^+), a hydrogen atom which has given up its lone electron, is simply a proton. Acids are defined as proton donors, that is, substances with a proton to give away.

Acids give their protons to *bases,* defined as proton acceptors. A common base, or *alkali,* is lye, used to unclog drains. Lye is sodium hydroxide (NaOH); it is one of the many bases in which the proton acceptor is a hydroxide ion (OH^-), with a charge of −1. The hydroxide ion is a negatively charged group of two atoms, one each of hydrogen and oxygen, which stick closely together. When a hydroxide ion (OH^-) meets up with a proton (H^+), they unite to form a molecule of water (H_2O). Thus, when sodium hydroxide and hydrochloric acid are mixed, they react to give water and sodium chloride, table salt:

$$NaOH + HCl \rightarrow NaCl + H_2O$$

Figure 2-9 Reaction of sodium hydroxide and hydrochloric acid to form water and salt. *(a)* A solution of sodium hydroxide contains sodium ions (Na^+) and hydroxide ions (OH^-). *(b)* A solution of hydrochloric acid contains hydrogen ions (H^+) and chloride ions (Cl^-). *(c)* After mixing, the H^+ and OH^- ions unite to form water molecules (H_2O). The Na^+ and Cl^- ions are unchanged.

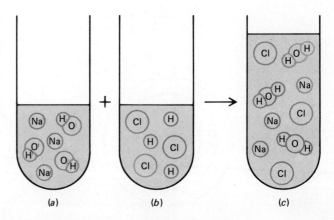

(a)   (b)   (c)

An acid plus a hydroxide-containing base give water and a salt. The hydroxide ion is, of course, a water molecule minus one proton.

The bonds which join the hydrogens and the oxygen of the water molecule are not ionic bonds. They are examples of the most common kind of chemical bond, the *covalent bond*. Covalently bonded atoms do not borrow or give away electrons; they share them. Moreover, they share *pairs* of electrons.

Electron Sharing: The Covalent Bond

In the water molecule, the pair of electrons shared by each hydrogen and the oxygen include one electron donated by the hydrogen and one by the oxygen:

$$\text{H·} + \text{H·} + \text{·}\ddot{\text{O}}\text{·} \,\dagger \rightarrow \text{H:}\ddot{\text{O}}\text{:H}$$

The electrons in the shared electron pairs which constitute the covalent bonds belong to both the hydrogen and oxygen atoms. As a result of this electron sharing, each hydrogen atom effactually has two electrons, the stable helium configuration, and the oxygen effactually has eight electrons, the stable neon configuration.

Atoms with less than a stable number of electrons can achieve the nearest stable configuration either by gaining electrons, thereby becoming negatively charged ions, or by sharing electrons in a covalent bond. Chlorine gas (Cl_2), for example, consists of two chlorine atoms (each with seven electrons in the neon shell) united by a covalent bond: $:\ddot{Cl}:\ddot{Cl}:$. Oxygen gas (O_2) consists of two oxygen atoms, each with six electrons in

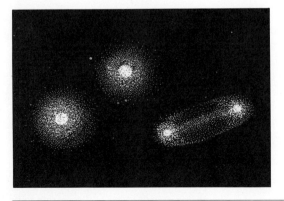

Figure 2-10 Electron distribution in the covalently bonded hydrogen molecule H_2. The two electrons, one donated by each hydrogen atom, move around mainly in the region between the atomic nuclei, as indicated by the denser shading in that region (the electron density is greatest in the regions of the nuclei). These two electrons, held jointly by the two nuclei, constitute the covalent bond uniting the hydrogen atoms. *(From Linus Pauling, "College Chemistry," 3d ed., Freeman, San Francisco, 1964.)*

†*Note:* The Oxygen atom actually has not six but eight electrons, two in the filled helium shell and six in the unfilled neon shell; however, as only those in the unfilled shell are involved in chemical reactions, only these electrons are normally indicated.

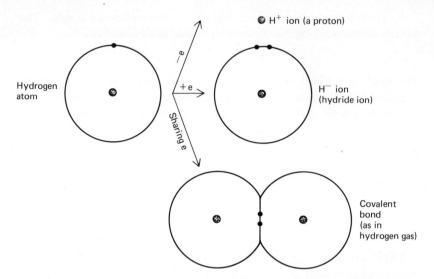

Figure 2-11 Hydrogen atoms can acquire a stable-electron configuration by either gaining or losing an electron. They lose an electron to form H$^+$ ions, that is, protons. They can acquire the stable two-electron helium configuration either by gaining an electron, becoming an H$^-$ or hydride ion, or by sharing electrons in a covalent bond. Hydrogen shares electrons with oxygen to form water; it shares electrons with carbon, oxygen, and nitrogen in a myriad of biologic substances; and two hydrogen atoms share their electrons to form hydrogen gas (H$_2$).

the neon shell, united by a *double covalent bond*, in which *two* pairs of electrons are shared by the atoms: :Ö::Ö:. Since the shared electron pairs effectually belong to both of the covalently bonded atoms, the chlorine atoms and the oxygen atoms have the stable eight-electron neon configuration.

Many compounds have both covalent and ionic bonds. Besides sodium hydroxide, other everyday examples are magnesium sulfate (MgSO$_4$), or epsom salts, silver nitrate (AgNO$_3$), used to disinfect the eyes of newborn babies, and sodium hydrogen carbonate, usually called sodium bicarbonate (NaHCO$_3$), taken for indigestion and used for baking, either alone or mixed, in baking powder, with sodium dihydrogen phosphate (NaH$_2$PO$_4$).

:O:	:O:	:O:	:O:
:Ö:S:Ö:	:Ö:N::Ö	:Ö:C:Ö:	:Ö:P:Ö:
:Ö:			:O:
Sulfate	Nitrate	Carbonate	Phosphate
ion (SO$_4^{--}$)	ion (NO$_3^{-}$)	ion (CO$_3^{--}$)	ion (PO$_4^{-3}$)

The positive metal ions are replaced by protons in the corresponding acids: sulfuric acid (H_2SO_4), nitric acid (HNO_3), carbonic acid (H_2CO_3), and phosphoric acid (H_3PO_4).

What happens when substances burn? In the presence of air, burning substances combine with oxgen. Hydrogen unites with oxygen to form water; carbon unites with oxygen to form carbon dioxide. These are called *oxidation* reactions, and hydrogen and carbon are said to be oxidized:

Oxidation, Reduction, and Electrons

$$2H_2 + O_2 \rightarrow 2H_2O$$
$$C + O_2 \rightarrow CO_2$$

Certain reactions involving a nonmetal other than oxygen so closely resemble the reactions of hydrogen and carbon with oxygen that they too are called oxidations. For example, hydrogen combines with sulfur to form hydrogen sulfide:

$$H_2 + S \rightarrow H_2S$$

and sodium burns in chlorine to form sodium chloride:

$$2Na + Cl_2 \rightarrow 2NaCl$$

In all such reactions, more properly called *oxidation-reduction* reactions, one reactant (the H, C, or Na in the above reactions) is oxidized, while the other (the O, S, or Cl above) is said to be *reduced*. In modern usage, oxidation is defined as the removal of electrons from an atom or group of atoms (for example, the sodium atom), and reduction is defined as the addition of electrons to an atom or group of atoms (the chlorine).

Oxidation-reduction reactions are of prime importance in living cells. Sugars are synthesized in plants by the reduction of carbon dioxide, as described later in this chapter. Sugars and substances derived from them are oxidized to provide the energy to run cells (as described in Chap. 3).

Among all the elements, there is one which is particularly associated with living organisms—apart from rare exceptions, where it is found, life is or once was. This is the element carbon.

ORGANIC, OR CARBON, CHEMISTRY

Carbon, with four electrons in its unfilled neon shell, cannot attain a stable configuration either by giving away its electrons or by borrowing four more—ions with a charge as great as +4 or —4 are unknown. But carbon is the essential ingredient in over a million compounds, for it is truly the master of the covalent bond. In particular, carbon atoms are uniquely proficient at forming covalent bonds with each other, giving rise to long strings, to branched or twiglike molecules, to circles, and to many other more exotic shapes. Such molecules may contain a few, a dozen, a hundred, thousands, or even millions of carbon atoms.

The Hydrocarbons   The simplest carbon compounds are the *hydrocarbons*, made of only carbon and hydrogen. Of these, the simplest is methane, CH_4, with one

carbon and four hydrogen atoms sharing four pairs of electrons: $H\!:\!\overset{\cdot\cdot}{\underset{\cdot\cdot}{C}}\!:\!H$ with H above and H below.

Such shared electron pairs, covalent bonds, are more commonly indicated by a dash.

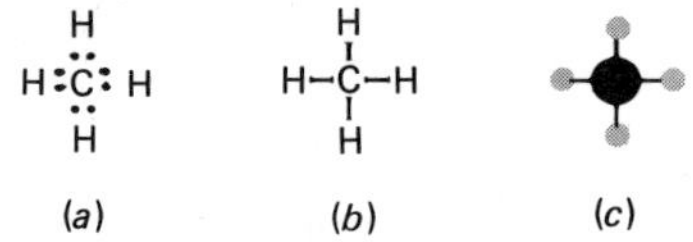

Figure 2-12   Three ways of schematically indicating the structure of methane (CH_4). Each pair of electrons shared by the carbon atom and a hydrogen atom, that is, each double bond, is indicated *(a)* by a pair of dots and *(b)* and *(c)* by a dash. *(c)* The carbon atom is indicated by a large, black circle, and the hydrogen atoms by small, gray circles. This convention will be followed hereafter (atoms other than carbon and hydrogen will be indicated by an open circle enclosing the symbol of the atom, such as Ⓞ for oxygen and Ⓟ for phosphorus).

$H\!:\!\overset{\cdot\cdot}{\underset{\cdot\cdot}{C}}\!:\!H$ with H on top and H on bottom   *(a)*

$H-\overset{\textstyle H}{\underset{\textstyle H}{C}}-H$ *(b)*

(c)

Methane was a component of the primitive atmosphere which surrounded the earth at its birth. Life originated in this atmosphere, and methane is probably the ultimate ancestor of the myriad carbon-containing compounds which have evolved as life has evolved.

Only a few hydrocarbons are found in living organisms. Rubber, obtained from the sap of the rubber tree, consists of endlessly long strings of carbon atoms with recurrent double bonds.

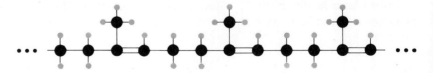

Figure 2-13   A portion of a molecule of rubber.

The substance which gives carrots, butter, egg yolk, and tomatoes their characteristic color is a hydrocarbon called *carotene.*

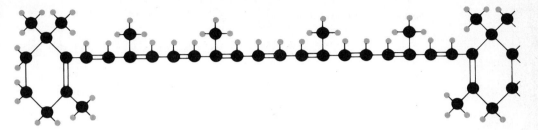

Carotene

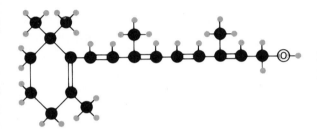

Vitamin A

Figure 2-14 Carotene, an orange pigment found in plants, is converted to vitamin A by being cleaved in two and oxidized. Further oxidation yields retinal, a pigment required for night vision.

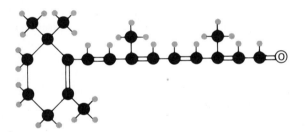

Retinal

Most carbon-containing, that is *organic*, substances contain other elements in addition to carbon and hydrogen. For example, carotene, provitamin A, is transformed into vitamin A by being split in two and having a hydrogen and a hydroxyl attached to the end. Another small change at that end and vitamin A becomes *retinal,* a substance which is found in the retina of the eye and is required for night vision.

The vitamin A and retinal molecules both have an oxygen atom. Retinal, with its double-bonded oxygen, is an example of the class of compounds called *aldehydes.* Vitamin A is an alcohol, as are all organic compounds with a hydroxyl, or –O–H, group. The alcohol in beer, wine, and whiskey is *ethyl* alcohol. Rubbing alcohol is properly called *isopropyl* alcohol.

Some Other Organic Substances

Figure 2-15 Structures of two common alcohols.

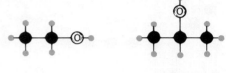

Ethyl alcohol   Isopropyl alcohol

Unlike the basic hydroxyl ion OH^-, which readily combines with a hydrogen ion H^+, the hydroxyl group of alcohols is uncharged and unreactive because it is covalently bonded to carbon.

Organic bases are not hydroxyl compounds but nitrogen-containing compounds. Ammonia, NH_3, is a base; it attracts a hydrogen ion, that is, a proton, becoming NH_4^+:

$$H^+ + \quad \overset{\text{H}}{\underset{\text{H}}{:\!\ddot{\text{N}}\!:\text{H}}} \longrightarrow \overset{\text{H}}{\underset{\text{H}}{\text{H}\!:\!\ddot{\text{N}}\!:\text{H}}} \quad +$$

Ammonia can be covalently bonded to carbon with a nitrogen-carbon bond replacing one, two, or all three nitrogen-hydrogen bonds. In the resulting organic compounds the nitrogen is often still basic, attracting a proton.

The most common organic acids are the *carboxylic acids,* in which the carboxyl group is the proton donor. Vinegar is a weak solution, generally 5 to 7 percent, of the carboxylic acid acetic acid. Many biologically important compounds are organic derivatives of phosphoric acid (H_3PO_4) (for example, see fig. 2–20).

Figure 2-16 Acetic acid is a common carboxylic acid (the carboxyl group is encircled). It dissociates into an acetate ion and a hydrogen ion.

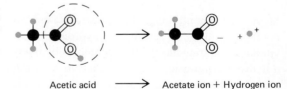

Acetic acid $\longrightarrow$ Acetate ion + Hydrogen ion

Amino Acids and Phenylketonuria

An organic molecule can contain both acidic and basic groups held together by carbon atoms. One example, which will be discussed in more detail in Chap. 5, is the *amino acids,* carboxylic acids which also have an amine. There are many amino acids found in nature. The simplest is *glycine,* in which two hydrogens, an amine, and a carboxyl group are attached to a carbon atom. *Glutamic acid* is another amino acid; it is

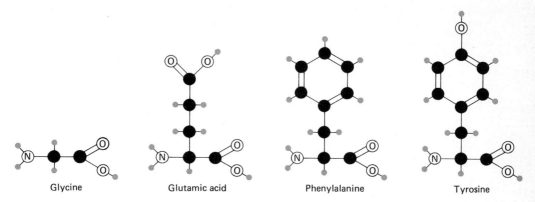

Figure 2-17   Structures of four amino acids.

a double carboxyl, or dicarboxylic, acid. The sodium salt of glutamic acid, monosodium glutamate, or MSG, is a cooking condiment used, especially by the Chinese, to enhance the flavor of food. Two other amino acids are *phenylalanine* and *tyrosine*.

Although amino acids are indispensable to living organisms, excesses must be disposed of. In humans, the first step in getting rid of excess phenylalanine is to change it into tyrosine. Babies suffering from the rare hereditary disease *phenylketonuria* are unable to do this. Until the biochemistry of this disease was understood, such babies suffered widespread metabolic disturbances and ended up feeble-minded. Now they are fine because they are put on a special low-phenylalanine diet.

The differences between various sugars are subtle. The two sugars glucose and galactose, for example, are structurally the same—almost. Both have the same formula, $C_6H_{12}O_6$, for both consist of a string of six carbon atoms, to five of which is attached a hydroxyl group and to the sixth of which is attached a double-bonded oxygen (an aldehyde).

Sugars and Asymmetric Carbon Atoms

Yet glucose and galactose are different, with a difference that can mean normalcy or feeblemindedness to the rare infant with galactosemia. Milk is rich in galactose, which this baby cannot metabolize. If he is put on a diet in which galactose is replaced by another sugar, such as glucose, he is fine; if not, he is feeble-minded.

The difference between glucose and galactose lies in the arrangement in space of an *asymmetric* carbon atom: If a carbon atom has four *different* groups bonded to it, then these groups can be arranged in two different ways in space. These are mirror images of each other and are different, just as a right and left hand are different.

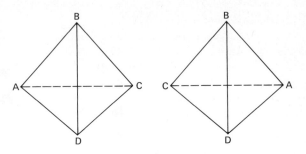

Figure 2-18 Two asymmetric carbon atoms represented as pyramids with a different group bonded to each apex. No amount of turning or rotating of these pyramids will make them identical, for they are mirror images of each other.

Figure 2-19 Structures of sugars. In water, only a small fraction of sugar molecules have the open-chain structure. Most molecules have a cyclic configuration, depicted as hexagonal or pentagonal structures in which the plane of the ring is perpendicular to the plane of the paper, as indicated by the shaded bonds nearer the reader.

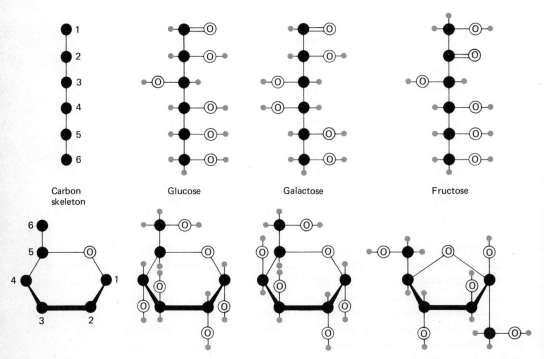

In both galactose and glucose, carbon atoms 2, 3, 4, and 5 are asymmetric. These two sugars differ in the spatial arrangement at carbon 4. Changing the spatial arrangement at any of the asymmetric carbons gives a different sugar—mannose, talose, sixteen sugars in all.

Sugars may also differ in other aspects of their structure. In general, sugars have a hydroxyl group attached to every carbon but one, to which is attached a double-bonded oxygen. Glucose and galactose have an oxygen atom double-bonded to carbon 1. The double-bonded oxygen in fructose, fruit sugar, is at carbon 2 instead of carbon 1. Sugars do not all have six carbon atoms like glucose, galactose, and fructose. Some biologically important ones have five carbons, or four, three, or seven.

Sugars can also be linked together head to tail. Sucrose, table sugar, is a double sugar, composed of glucose and fructose. Lactose, milk sugar, is another double sugar, consisting of a galactose joined to a glucose. Sugars may also be linked together into long, sometimes branched, chains; starch, cellulose, and glycogen are examples. *Carbohydrate* is the name given to sugars and the substances, such as starch, which are made from them.

HOW ARE SUBSTANCES SYNTHESIZED?

In any chemical reaction, new substances are synthesized. Sodium hydroxide and hydrochloric acid react, and water is synthesized. Carbon and oxygen react, and carbon dioxide is synthesized. Within cells, chemical reactions result in the synthesis of amino acids, sugars, vitamins, and the other complex substances needed by the living organism.

Fundamentally, these biochemical reactions are no different from any other chemical reactions, but they have special features and refinements. When sodium hydroxide and hydrochloric acid are mixed, nothing more need be done or added in order for the reaction to take place; salt and water are synthesized spontaneously, and the solution gets very hot because there is a concomitant spontaneous release of energy. When carbon or any organic matter such as wood is burned in oxygen, the formation of carbon dioxide is spontaneous, and so is the release of energy in the forms of heat and light. The loss of energy is an accompaniment of all *spontaneous reactions,* reactions which take place by themselves, the way a stone all by itself rolls downhill.

Sunshine and Energy-requiring Reactions

Unlike the reaction of sodium hydroxide and hydrochloric acid or the burning of carbon, life depends on many chemical reactions which are not spontaneous. They are *uphill* processes, requiring an input of energy to make them go. The ultimate source of the energy needed by living organisms is sunlight.

Light energy is transformed into chemical energy in the chloroplasts of green plants (organelles described in Chap. 3). There, in a complex series of reactions known collectively as *photosynthesis,* carbon dioxide, water, and light energy $h\nu$ are converted to oxygen and a sugar:

$$6CO_2 + 6H_2O + h\nu \rightarrow C_6H_{12}O_6 + 6O_2$$

Photosynthesis starts with the absorption of light, principally by the green pigment chlorophyll. This light energy is used to regenerate molecules needed in the synthesis of glucose. One such molecule is NADPH (nicotinamide adenine dinucleotide phosphate), which supplies the electrons to reduce carbon dioxide to glucose. NADPH is regenerated from light and $NADP^+$, used-up NADPH.

Light energy is also used for the regeneration of a substance ATP (adenosine triphosphate), which can well be called the cell's energy "money," for it pays the energy "debt" of virtually all the cell's uphill reactions.

ATP Pushes Reactions Uphill

In the chloroplasts, light energy is trapped in the phosphate bonds of ATP: In a complicated series of chemical steps, light energy is used to covalently bond the third and last phosphate to ADP, adenosine diphosphate, used-up ATP molecules which have given away their terminal phosphate. (See fig. 2-20.)

A lot of energy is consumed in coupling the third phosphate of ATP. How can this energy be used to push energy-requiring reactions uphill? Let us take as an example a carboxylic acid which must be reduced to an aldehyde. This is an energy-requiring, uphill reaction, for the low-energy carboxyl group is transformed into a high-energy aldehyde group. The necessary energy is supplied by the transfer of ATP's third phosphate to the carboxyl group. This is a downhill reaction, for the products, the phosphorylated carboxylic acid and ADP, have less energy than the reactants, the carboxylic acid and ATP.

The phosphorylated carboxyl group is now reduced to the aldehyde, hydrogen (that is, an electron transferred as a hydrogen atom) being supplied by NADPH. This is again a downhill reaction. (See fig. 2-21.)

Thus, at the expenditure of the energy invested in the phosphate bond of ATP, the uphill reaction *carboxylic acid → aldehyde* is transformed into the downhill reactions *carboxylic acid + ATP → phosphorylated carboxylic acid + ADP* and *phosphorylated carboxylic acid + NADPH → aldehyde + phosphate + NADP*. These reactions are among the most important in the photosynthesis of glucose from carbon dioxide and water.

The Photosynthesis of Glucose

About 25 years ago, Melvin Calvin (1911–   ) of the University of California at Berkeley began a series of experiments to discover the steps by which carbon dioxide and water are transformed into glucose. He provided photosynthesizing algae with radioactive carbon dioxide in which the normal isotope of carbon C^{12} had been replaced by the radio-

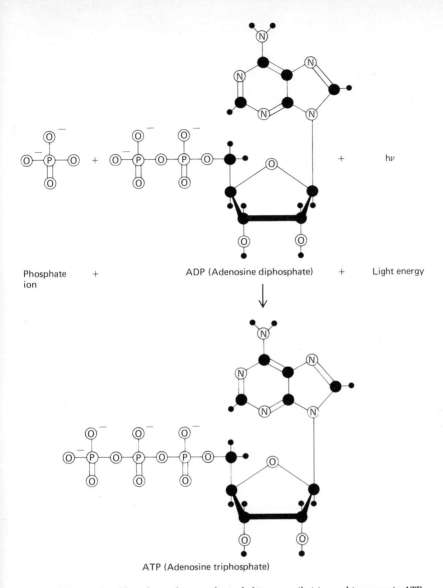

Phosphate ion   +   ADP (Adenosine diphosphate)   +   Light energy

ATP (Adenosine triphosphate)

Figure 2-20 In the chloroplasts of green plants, light energy *(hν)* is used to generate ATP from ADP and phosphate. The ATP molecule consists of a string of three phosphate groups attached to a sugar, ribose (drawn in the cyclic configuration), which is in turn attached to a weak nitrogen-containing base, adenine. Adenine-ribose is called adenosine, hence ATP's name, adenosine triphosphate.

active isotope C^{14} (containing two more than the normal number of neutrons). He let the algae grow for a few seconds in the radioactive carbon dioxide. He then killed them and determined which substance had already become radioactive. He discovered that the very first compound to become radioactive was the three-carbon compound phosphoglyceric acid. (See fig. 2-22.)

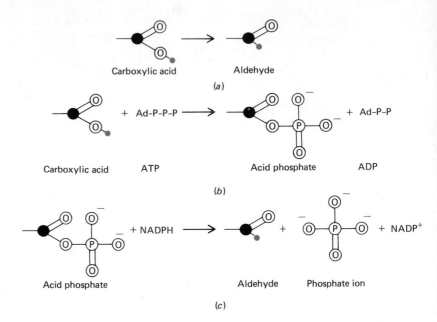

Figure 2-21 The reduction of a carboxyl group to an aldehyde *(a)* is an uphill, energy-requiring reaction. *(b)* and *(c)* It can nevertheless be accomplished by being coupled to the hydrolysis of ATP to ADP, for this hydrolysis yields even more energy than the reduction requires. In the chloroplasts, phosphoglyceric acid is transformed into diphosphoglyceric acid and then reduced to phosphoglyceraldehyde by steps *(b)* and *(c)* above; these are essential reactions in the reduction of carbon dioxide to glucose.

Figure 2-22 In order to unravel the steps leading to the photosynthesis of glucose from carbon dioxide and water, Melvin Calvin furnished growing algae with radioactive carbon dioxide labeled with C^{14} and then analyzed the compounds which subsequently became radioactive. The first substance to become labeled was phosphoglyceric acid. In 1961, Calvin was awarded the Nobel Prize in chemistry for his elucidation of the biochemical pathway of photosynthesis.

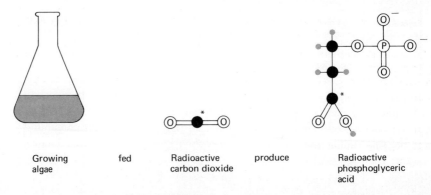

Further experiments showed that the phosphoglyceric acid is not made from three molecules of carbon dioxide: only one of the three carbons was radioactive, the carbon of the carboxyl group. Had the radioactive carbon dioxide been attached to a two-carbon substance? This would seem logical, but actually the carbon dioxide, it was found, attaches to a five-carbon sugar phosphate, ribulose diphosphate, to give a six-carbon compound which then splits to give two molecules of phosphoglyceric acid.

The series of chemical steps which transforms ribulose diphosphate, carbon dioxide, and water into glucose is outlined in fig. 2–23. Each new glucose molecule with its six carbons is the end product of the addition not of one molecule of carbon dioxide to one of ribulose diphosphate but of six molecules of carbon dioxide to six of ribulose diphosphate. Most of the phosphoglyceraldehyde produced at the third step never goes on to become glucose. Instead, it follows the arrows on around the circle and back to the starting point. In a half-dozen steps, in which there are formed four, six, and seven-carbon sugars, the three-carbon glyceraldehyde molecules are added together and broken apart to regenerate the five-carbon ribulose diphosphate molecules needed to start again.

Glucose Oxidation and the Recovery of Energy

In plants as well as animals, glucose is oxidized to carbon dioxide and water, thereby recovering in the form of ATP a large part of the energy used in the synthesis of this molecule. The first part of the breakdown of glucose resembles the last part of its synthesis, but in reverse: Glucose is degraded step by step to phosphoglyceric acid. A few more steps change the phosphoglyceric acid to pyruvic acid. Pyruvic acid is oxidized the rest of the way to carbon dioxide and water in organelles called *mitochondria*, described in the next chapter.

Why does the oxidation of glucose require so many steps? The complete oxidation of glucose furnishes a large amount of energy. The stepwise oxidation releases this energy not in one big burst but in relatively small bits, the right size to regenerate ATP molecules with a minimum of waste. As a result, about two-thirds of the energy derived from the complete oxidation of each glucose molecule is recovered in the form of regenerated ATP. An automobile engine, which burns gasoline instead of glucose, is less than half as efficient in turning the energy of oxidation into useful work.

Other Biochemical Syntheses

The ATP obtained by oxidizing glucose provides the energy for chemical reactions, for muscle contraction, for transmitting nerve impulses. It is truly the cells' energy "money," by means of which the cells' energy

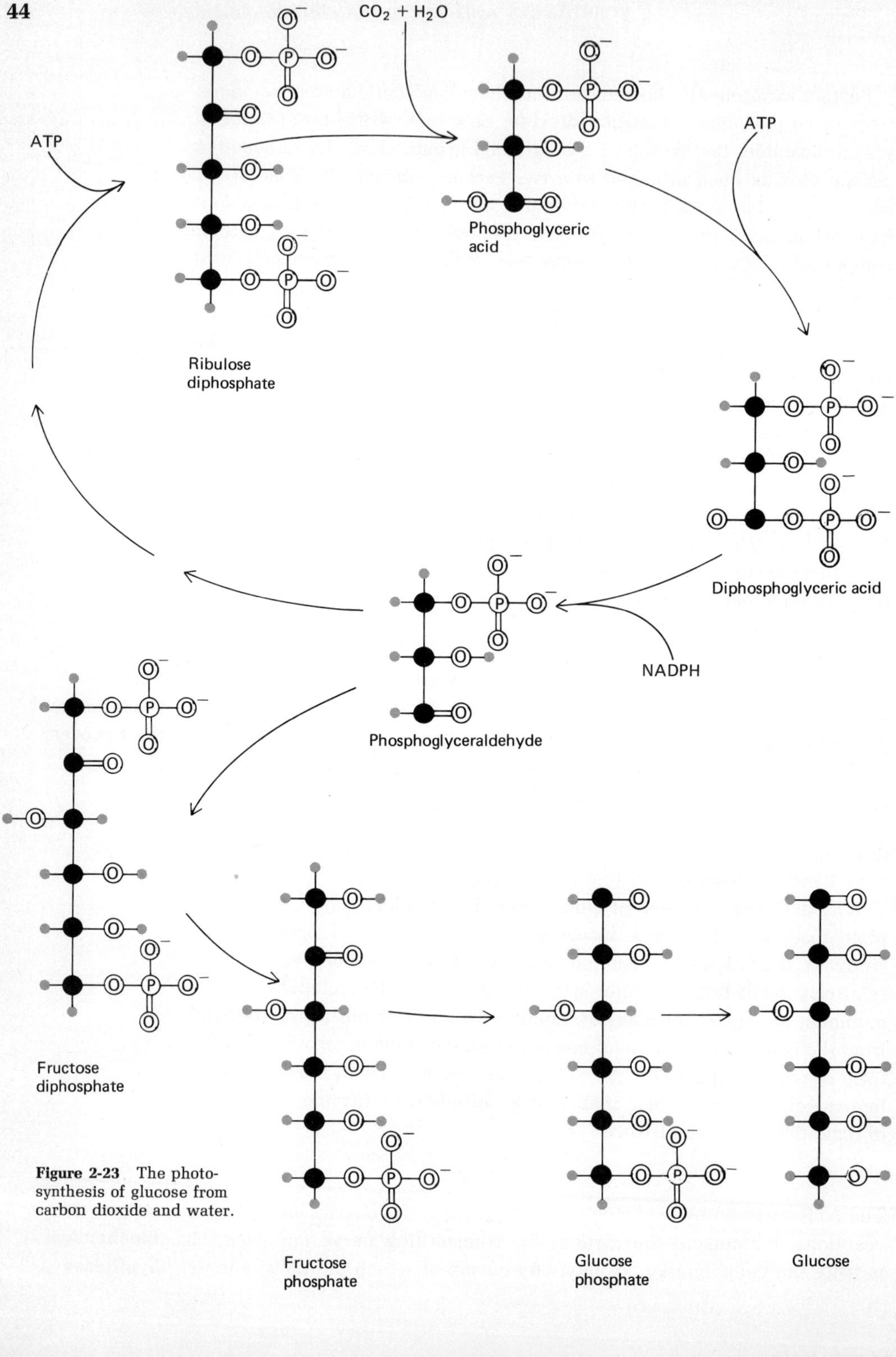

Figure 2-23 The photosynthesis of glucose from carbon dioxide and water.

$CO_2 + H_2O$

ATP

Phosphoglyceric acid

ATP

Ribulose diphosphate

Diphosphoglyceric acid

NADPH

Phosphoglyceraldehyde

Fructose diphosphate

Fructose phosphate

Glucose phosphate

Glucose

requirements are "paid for" with sunlight. Moreover, compounds formed as a step in the synthesis or breakdown of glucose may be used as starting materials to synthesize still other substances. Starch, cellulose, and other carbohydrates are made from glucose. Fats are the end products of a long series of chemical reactions which begins with phosphoglyceric acid and phosphoglyceraldehyde. Phosphoglyceric acid starts the pathway which leads to the amino acids and other carboxylic acid.

Thus, through complex series of chemical reactions, the materials of life are created—in plants from carbon dioxide, water, and sunlight; in some bacteria from sugar and salts; and in humans from the breakdown products of breakfast, lunch, and dinner. A description of all that is now known of such biochemical pathways would fill volumes. Only a few will be described in subsequent chapters, those which best illustrate the unique features of the chemistry of life.

THE ANATOMY OF CELLS

The microscope has come a very long way since its invention at the end of the sixteenth century, and the impact of this development on biology has been enormous. With a seventeenth-century microscope, Robert Hooke distinguished the cells of plants, or rather the cellulose walls which surround them. Van Leeuwenhoek even saw the much tinier bacteria. In the early nineteenth century, the cell nucleus was discovered and soon recognized as a general feature of cells. The nucleus and the surrounding cytoplasm both appeared at that time to be made of an amorphous, gelatinlike substance.

By the end of the century, thanks to improved microscopes and techniques of tissue preparation and staining, the gelatin was clearly not uniform. A few organized structures had become visible in the cytoplasm, and within the nucleus could be seen oddly shaped rods, the chromosomes. The development of the microscope indispensable for these observations had been achieved over a period of 200 years.

The development of the electron microscope was more rapid. In 1924, the physicist Louis de Broglie (1892–   ) hypothesized that electrons behave in certain respects like light (a discovery for which he was honored with the Nobel Prize in physics in 1929). Within 8 years, an embryonic form of the electron microscope had been invented. Within 20 years, it had been perfected almost to the theoretical limit. Replacement of a beam of light by a beam of electrons makes it possible to see objects

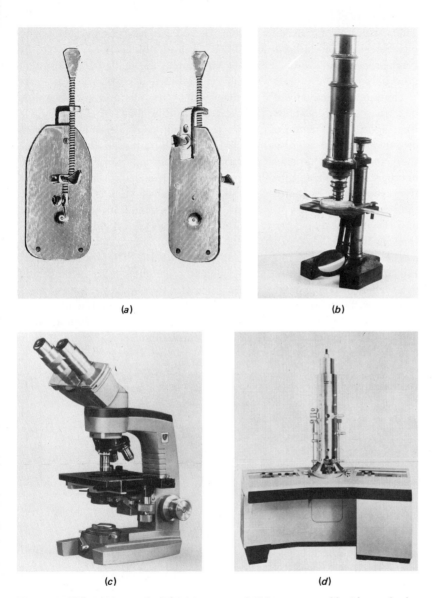

Figure 3-1 Biology owes much to the microscope. *(a)* Microscope used by Leeuwenhoek, seventeenth century. *(Courtesy Bettmann Archive.)* *(b)* Microscope used by Pasteur, nineteenth century. *(Courtesy Pasteur Institute, Paris.)* *(c)* Modern light microscope. *(Courtesy American Optical Company.)* *(d)* Modern electron microscope. *(Courtesy Perkin-Elmer Corporation.)*

several thousand times too small to be seen with a light microscope.

The methods of preparing and staining cells for examination with the light microscope are useless with the electron microscope. Since the

1950s, electron microscopists have worked out new techniques which have revealed the hitherto invisible structures filling the cell. Even the complex architecture of these tiny structures, the cell's organelles, can now be seen.

The internal anatomy of cells disclosed by the electron microscope is described in this chapter. Only extremely thin slices of cells, about a thousandth the diameter of a typical living cell, can be examined with an ordinary electron microscope. Not only cells but even the organelles they contain must be sliced up like a loaf of bread. From the electron micrographs of these ultrathin sections, electron microscopists deduce the three-dimensional structures of the organelles—this is like trying to figure out the structure of a lemon, with its segments, its seeds, its rind, and its overall shape, by examining thin slices cut at different angles through it.

The electron microscope has supplied a wealth of information about the structure and organization of cells and organelles. The 1970s should see further striking advances in this domain, for two new types of electron microscope, the scanning electron microscope and the ultrahigh-voltage electron microscope, are emerging from the experimental stage and are beginning to provide dramatic three-dimensional views of cells and their components.

Figure 3-2 Ultrahigh-voltage electron microscopes such as this Hitachi 1-million-volt electron microscope are only beginning to be exploited for the study of biologic materials. The penetrating power of their electron beam makes possible the study of much thicker specimens than with conventional electron microscopes. This depth can be visualized by stereoscopic photography (see fig. 3-25, for example). *(Courtesy Perkin-Elmer Corporation.)*

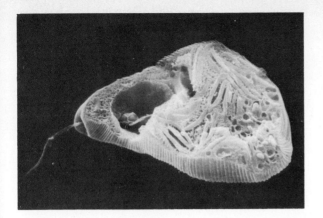

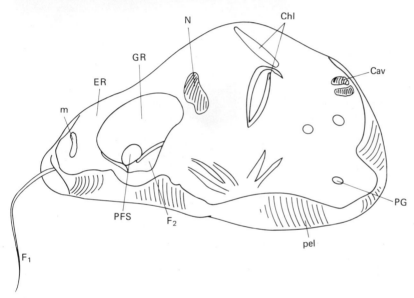

Figure 3-3 Interior of a single-celled organism *Euglena* as seen with the scanning electron microscope. This microscopically tiny alga was frozen and then fractured to reveal its internal anatomy. The cytoplasm consists of a seemingly spongy matrix, the endoplasmic reticulum (ER), in which are embedded chloroplasts (Chl), mitochondria (m), and paramylum granules (PG) (paramylum is the *Euglena's* storage form of sugar), as well as cavities (Cav) which had held paramylum granules. Part of the nucleus (N) is visible. The flagellum (F_1), paraflagellar swelling (PFS), a small, second, useless flagellum (F_2), and the gullet reservoir (GR) are organelles not seen in most other cells. The *Euglena* is surrounded by a flexible pellicle (pel), which lies outside the cell wall. *(Courtesy Helene N. Guttmann.)*

Just as in a complex organism such as a human being the various basic functions are carried out by specialized structures and organs such as the skin, the digestive system, and the liver, so within cells the functions are carried out by specialized structures and organelles. As can be seen in the accompanying electron micrographs (figs. 3–3 to 3–8), these organelles are revealed by the electron microscope (though they are gener-

A BIRD'S-EYE LOOK AT THE CELL

50

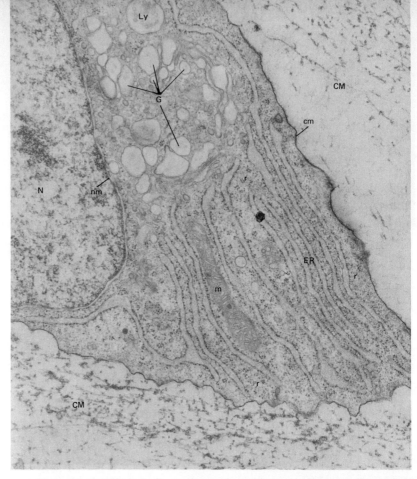

Figure 3-4 Part of a typically angular cartilage cell. Such cells secrete the cartilage substance (CM, cartilage matrix) which surrounds them. Note the prominent Golgi apparatus and endoplasmic reticulum; the tiny dots which fill the cytoplasm are ribosomes. *(Courtesy Jean-Paul Revel.)*

ally not all visible in a particular electron micrograph for the same reason that seeds are not present in every slice of a lemon). As is also apparent, the internal anatomy of each type of cell is somewhat modified to adapt it for its specialized role. Let us take a bird's-eye look at the internal anatomy of cells before examining each organelle in detail.

The cell is separated from the rest of the world by an enclosing skin, the *cell membrane* (designated *cm* on the adjoining electron micrographs). Within cells are synthesized a multitude of substances, commonly in association with a labyrinthine, membranous structure, the *endoplasmic reticulum (ER)*, which may pervade the cytoplasm of the cell. Small particles required for the synthesis of protein, *ribosomes (r)*, may be associated with the endoplasmic reticulum or may float free in the cytoplasm. The *Golgi apparatus (G)* is an extension of the endoplasmic reticulum concerned with the packaging into granules of substances such as those

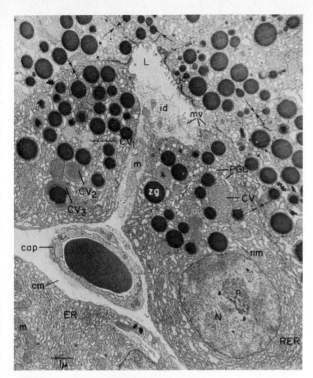

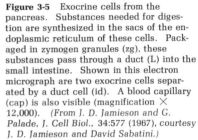

Figure 3-5 Exocrine cells from the pancreas. Substances needed for digestion are synthesized in the sacs of the endoplasmic reticulum of these cells. Packaged in zymogen granules (zg), these substances pass through a duct (L) into the small intestine. Shown in this electron micrograph are two exocrine cells separated by a duct cell (id). A blood capillary (cap) is also visible (magnification × 12,000). *(From J. D. Jamieson and G. Palade, J. Cell Biol., 34:577 (1967), courtesy J. D. Jamieson and David Sabatini.)*

Figure 3-6 Parts of two rat liver cells. Liver cells contain granules of glycogen (gly), a substance consisting of long branching chains of linked glucose molecules. Glycogen, the storage form of glucose in animals, is found principally in liver and muscle cells (magnification × 19,000). *(Courtesy David Sabatini.)*

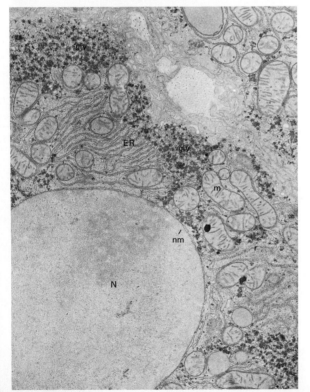

which are to be exported from the cell. The Golgi apparatus also packages digestive juices into sacs called *lysosomes (ly)*, which participate in the digestion of ingested particles and unwanted matter.

The many chemical syntheses taking place in cells require energy. The ultimate source of energy is sunlight, which is transformed into chemical energy and thence into carbohydrates and other substances in the *chloroplasts (chl)* of green plants. In all cells, plant or animal, energy is obtained from the oxidation of substances; this oxidation is harnessed to the regeneration of ATP, mainly in organelles called *mitochondria (m)*.

The many chemical activities of the cell are coordinated and controlled by orders sent out from the *nucleus (N)*, where the blueprints of the cell are stored. The nucleus is surrounded by the *nuclear membrane (nm)*. Within it is a prominent organelle concerned with the synthesis of ribosomes, the *nucleolus (n)*.

In the following sections, the structure and functions of the organelles will be described in greater detail.

Figure 3-7 Cell of a plant *(Nicotiana tabacum)*, showing chloroplasts (chl). The chloroplasts contain starch granules (s). Starch, a mixture of straight and branched chains of linked glucose molecules, is the storage form of glucose in plants. In mature plant cells such as this one, a large vacuole (V) containing cell sap occupies most of the cell (magnification × 3,000). *(Courtesy R. W. Horne.)*

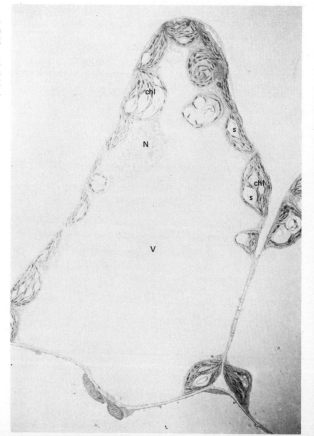

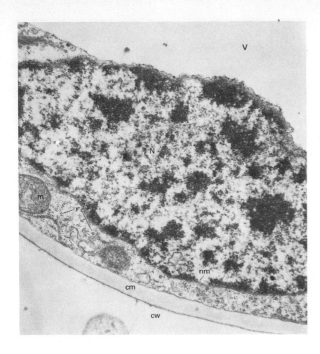

Figure 3-8 Plant cell at higher magnification, showing the nucleus (N), nuclear membrane (nm), mitochondria (m), ribosomes (r), and the cell membrane (cm) lying just within the thick cellulose wall (cw). Like the large vacuole (V), the cellulose wall is typical of mature plant cells. *(Courtesy R. W. Horne.)*

Plant cells are surrounded by a readily visible cellulose wall, but all cells, plant or animal, are surrounded by a *cell membrane,* which in plant cells lies just within the cellulose wall.

THE CELL MEMBRANE

The cell membrane keeps the cell intact; if damaged, the membrane can often be repaired, but in the meantime some of the cell's contents

Figure 3-9 In many cells, cell membrane is folded into numerous fingerlike projections called *microvilli.* These enormously increase the surface area of the cell, thereby facilitating transport of materials across the membrane. *(a)* Overall view of the inner surface of the duodenum, the first part of the small intestine, of a chick embryo. The intestinal wall is deeply convoluted, which increases the surface area; the rough-surfaced knobs are individual cells (magnification × 1,200). *(b)* The duodenal surface at higher magnification (× 10,000). The rough appearance of the cells evident in *(a)* is here seen to be due to a multitude of white protuberances, the microvilli, which in these immature embryonic cells partially cover the cell surface (in mature cells the surface is thickly studded with microvilli). These electron micrographs were taken with a scanning electron microscope. *(From Robert D. Grey, J. Morphol. 137:193 (1972), courtesy of the author.)*

(a)   *(b)*

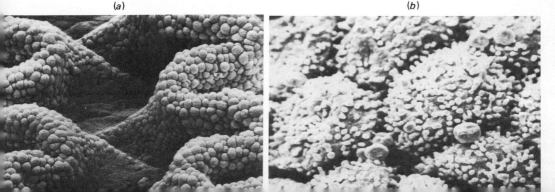

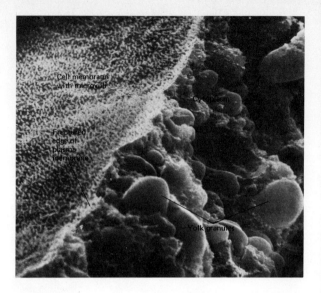

Figure 3-10 The cell membrane of egg cells is commonly covered with microvilli, as seen in this scanning electron micrograph of an egg of the African clawed toad, *Xenopus laevis.* To the right of this fractured egg is the cytoplasm filled with yolk granules. *(Scanning electron micrograph courtesy Robert D. Grey.)*

leak out. But the cell membrane is much more than a skin holding the cell together. Everything entering or leaving the cell must pass through it. As will be described below, some substances pass through freely, others are actively pumped through, and some things get from the outside to the inside without passing through the membrane at all.

Some Substances Diffuse across the Cell Membrane

Nonliving membranes generally either will or will not allow a substance to pass freely from one side to the other; that is, they are either *permeable* or *impermeable* to any particular substance. A cellophane membrane, for example, is permeable to small molecules such as water, salts, and sugars (unless it has been specially treated to make it impermeable, as is usually done to wrapping cellophane). It behaves more or less like a sieve, allowing small molecules to pass through its microscopic pores. Bacteria, on the other hand, are much too big to pass through these holes; cellophane is impermeable to bacteria.

If a container is divided into two parts by a cellophane membrane and if pure water is put on one side and sugar water on the other, then the sugar will pass through the cellophane membrane, moving into the pure water. Finally, the sugar concentration on both sides will be the same. The tendency to spread out into areas of lower concentration is called *diffusion.*

The membrane surrounding cells is permeable to certain substances such as some *lipides,* which are substances such as oils and fats that are insoluble in water. These diffuse freely into or out of the cell, so the concentrations inside and outside are more or less the same. But the behavior of the cell membrane is infinitely more complex than that of a piece of cellophane. For example, substances to which it is impermeable may be actively pumped from one side to the other.

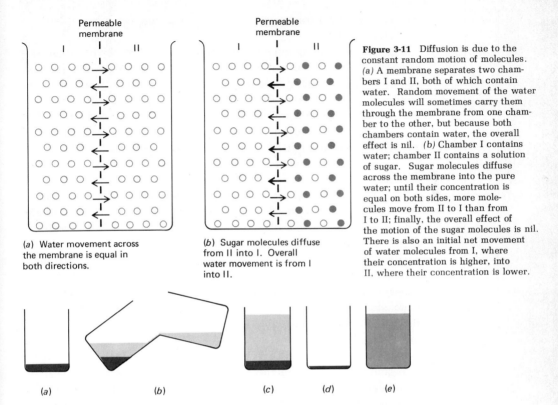

Permeable membrane

I   II

(a) Water movement across the membrane is equal in both directions.

Permeable membrane

I   II

(b) Sugar molecules diffuse from II into I. Overall water movement is from I into II.

Figure 3-11 Diffusion is due to the constant random motion of molecules. (a) A membrane separates two chambers I and II, both of which contain water. Random movement of the water molecules will sometimes carry them through the membrane from one chamber to the other, but because both chambers contain water, the overall effect is nil. (b) Chamber I contains water; chamber II contains a solution of sugar. Sugar molecules diffuse across the membrane into the pure water; until their concentration is equal on both sides, more molecules move from II to I than from I to II; finally, the overall effect of the motion of the sugar molecules is nil. There is also an initial net movement of water molecules from I, where their concentration is higher, into II, where their concentration is lower.

(a)   (b)   (c)   (d)   (e)

Figure 3-12 The process of diffusion is extremely slow, as can easily be demonstrated by allowing ink to diffuse into water. (a) Some concentrated sugar solution strongly colored with ink is put in a test tube or drinking glass. (b) and (c) Water is carefully layered over it; this can be done without mixing because of the concentrated sugar. (d) and (e) If the container is not jarred, it will take many weeks for the ink to diffuse throughout (naturally, the sugar also diffuses, but only the ink is visible).

The concentrations of many salts are strikingly different inside and outside of the cell. In animals, sodium is the most abundant positive ion outside cells, that is, in extracellular fluids such as blood, lymph, and the fluid which bathes most cells; yet inside cells sodium is almost absent. Potassium ion, on the other hand, is nearly forty times, magnesium ion fifteen times, more concentrated inside cells than out. In extracellular fluids, positive ions are neutralized for the most part by chloride ions, whereas inside cells the principal negative ion is phosphate.

The maintenance of these concentration differences is a function of the cell membrane. Lodged in the membrane are protein *pumps* (discussed in the next chapter), which pump unwanted ions such as sodium ion back out when they enter and pump wanted ions such as potassium ion

Some Substances Are Pumped across the Cell Membrane

in. The continual transport of ions by the pumps consumes energy in the form of ATP.

Plants play two essential roles in the economy of life. Living organisms require not only carbon but also minerals—sodium, potassium, magnesium, calcium, iron, sulfur, chlorine, phosphorus, fifteen or twenty minerals in all. Photosynthesis in plants transforms the carbon dioxide in the air into a form utilizable by animals. Concentration of the salts present in extremely low concentrations in the water of the soil makes essential ions accessible to animals. The ion pumps in the cell membranes of root cells are thus as vital to all life on earth as the chloroplasts of the leaves.

The maintenance of differential salt concentrations is common to all cells. In nerve cells, the differential salt concentrations inside and outside of the fibers have a unique importance, for they underlie the transmission of nerve impulses. Very briefly, when the end of a nerve fiber is excited, sodium ions progressively enter the fiber, thereby creating a negative charge which moves rapidly along the outside of the fiber and is almost as rapidly neutralized by the exit of potassium ion. The normal ionic state—sodium outside, potassium inside—is restored within a thousandth of a second, and the nerve is again ready to transmit an impulse.

Many substances besides salts are pumped into cells. A specific pump is required for each. In the case of certain nutrient substances, the particular pumps are only present when the cell needs the nutrient. The membrane's pumps are thus a part of the mechanism whereby cells accommodate to changes in their environment, the extracellular fluid in which they bathe.

Some Substances Enter the Cell Enclosed in Cell Membrane

Most salts and nutrients enter most cells either by diffusing freely across the cell membrane or by being pumped across, but single-celled organisms such as protozoans eat particles of food which are too large to pass through the cell membrane.

Phagocytosis, ingestion by engulfing, permits amoebas and other unicellular animals to eat smaller plants and animals without the prey actually passing through the cell membrane. The amoeba, a rather jellylike blob, moves by flowing forward and retracting itself from behind. It eats in about the same way. Part of the amoeba pushes out until it has engulfed the prey. When the amoeba has completely surrounded the prey, the cell membrane pinches off a sac which contains the prey, now *inside* the amoeba. This sac, the food *vacuole,* fuses with small sacs of digestive juices, and digestion of the prey proceeds within the vacuole. Nutrients pass into the amoeba's cytoplasm through the membrane surrounding the vacuole. Indigestible leftovers are excreted from the amoeba by a re-

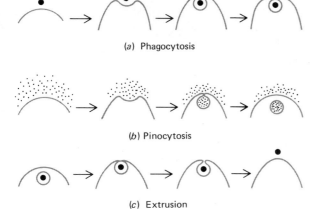

(a) Phagocytosis

(b) Pinocytosis

(c) Extrusion

Figure 3-13 *(a)* Particles and prey are taken into cells by phagocytosis: the particle is surrounded by cell membrane, which pinches off to make a vacuole that is within the cell. *(b)* Liquid droplets are ingested by an exactly analogous mechanism called pinocytosis. *(c)* Vacuoles containing wastes or substances to be exported from the cell are extruded by a process which is simply the reverse of these processes.

versal of the process of phagocytosis: the food vacuole fuses with the cell membrane and then opens to the exterior, dumping out its contents.

Phagocytosis is not unique to unicellular organisms. In higher animals, specialized phagocytic cells such as blood cells called *leukocytes* scavenge dust particles, bacteria, the remains of dead cells, and other refuse by phagocytosis. The cell membrane of a leukocyte folds inward around the undesirable material, the edges fuse, and the material is enclosed in a vacuole. This process does not serve to nourish the leukocyte—it often results in its death—but rather to protect the entire animal from noxious material. The cells of higher animals do not feed by phagocytosis. Food is digested in the gut, and cells receive their predigested nutrients from the circulatory system.

Pinocytosis, or cell "drinking," is very similar to phagocytosis, and much more widespread: Droplets of liquid are taken into the cell by the mechanism used in phagocytosis, in a vacuole pinched off from the cell membrane. Pinocytosis is not a means of "drinking" water but rather of obtaining substances which are dissolved in the extracellular fluid.

Pinocytosis has been observed in unicellular organisms and in many specialized cells, such as those of muscle and intestine. The walls of the blood capillaries are lined with cells which transport material from the blood to the surrounding tissues by pinocytosis followed by extrusion: pinocytotic vacuoles containing blood fluid form on the cell surface toward the inside of the capillary; the vacuoles then traverse the cell; at the opposite side they fuse with the cell membrane, pouring their contents into the extracellular fluid bathing the tissue cells near the capillary.

58

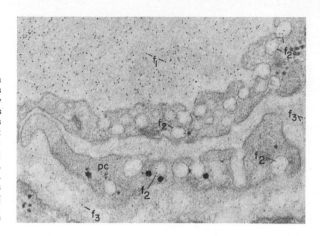

Figure 3-14 Pinocytosis as seen in cells lining a blood capillary in the diaphragm of a rat 24 hours after an intravenous injection of ferritin (a very big iron-containing protein). The ferritin appears in the blood plasma (f_1), in pinocytotic vesicles (f_2) of a cell lining the capillary and of an adjacent cell (pc), and the spaces around these cells (f_3). Pinocytotic vesicles labeled with ferritin open to the blood, are surrounded by cytoplasm, or open into the spaces surrounding the cells. Pinocytosis here serves to transport blood plasma across the capillary wall into the fluid surrounding the cells outside the capillary (magnification $\times$ 87,000). *(Courtesy George E. Palade.)*

The Structure of the Cell Membrane

What is the structure of the cell membrane, and how does this structure explain the membrane's properties? Much research has been aimed at answering these questions. The electron microscope discloses a three-layered structure, and it was long ago proposed that the membrane consists of a layer of lipides (fatty substances) sandwiched between two layers of protein, substances described in the next chapter. In the 1970s, evidence is converging on a modified sandwich structure for the cell membrane.

The membrane has an inner bimolecular layer of lipides, long molecules with a water-soluble *head* (water-soluble because it includes a phosphate and other water-soluble groups), attached to two water-insoluble, hydrocarbon *tails*. The lipides form two sheets, each one molecule thick. In both sheets, the water-soluble heads are toward the outside, and the water-repellent tails are toward the inside. The inner and outer surfaces of the bimolecular lipide layer are thus water-soluble, whereas the inside is water-insoluble.

The lipide layer of the cell membrane effectively separates the inside of the cell from the rest of the world. Both inside and outside of the cell is water with substances dissolved and suspended in it. Neither water nor water-soluble substances such as sugars and salts can cross the water-repellent interior of the lipide layer at an appreciable rate.

How, then, do these substances get into and out of the cell? The lipide layer is thickly studded on both sides with proteins. The proteins do not form uniform inner and outer layers between which is sandwiched the lipide layer. Rather, although much of the protein lies outside the lipide layer, many proteins intrude into the lipide layer or even traverse it completely; about 10 to 20 percent of the so-called *lipide layer* is probably protein. At least some of these proteins must be the cell's pumps, which get water-soluble substances across the cell membrane. Do they ferry

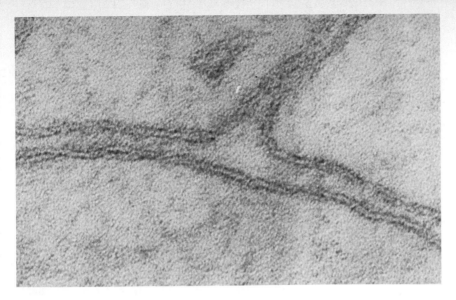

Figure 3-15 Cell membranes of three adjacent cells, showing the sandwich structure of the membrane. *(Courtesy J. D. Robertson.)*

Figure 3-16 *(a)* Structure of a phospholipide typical of the complex lipides found in the cell membrane. One end of the molecule, the *head*, includes two charged groups, the negative phosphate and the positive aminonitrogen, and is therefore water-soluble. The other end, the *tail*, is a hydrocarbon, with only hydrogen and carbon atoms, and is therefore water-insoluble. *(b)* In the cell membrane, the lipides are arranged with their heads toward the outside and their tails toward the inside. This gives the membrane a water-soluble exterior and a water-insoluble interior.

(a)

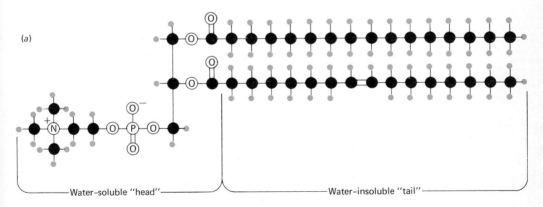

Water-soluble "head"   Water-insoluble "tail"

(b)

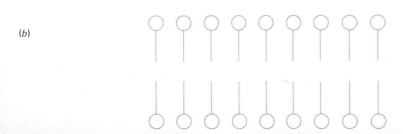

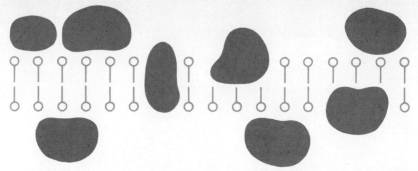

Figure 3-17 Schematic illustration of the structure of the cell membrane. In the 1970s, evidence is converging on the model shown here in which some protein molecules completely traverse the bimolecular lipide layer, some intrude into it partially, and most lay upon it. Probably about 10 to 20 percent of the lipide layer is protein.

them across? Do they bind a substance on one side of the membrane, then turn around and release the substance on the other side? This is not yet known. Nor is it known how the membrane pinches off pinocytotic and phagocytic vacuoles.

This recently discovered arrangement of proteins in the cell membrane provides a beautiful flexibility in membrane function. Thus, it would appear relatively easy to introduce new proteins into the membrane structure, for example when new pumps must be added to adapt the cell to a change in nutrients. Moreover, as will be seen throughout this chapter, membranes are an important part of the various cellular organelles. The electron microscope shows that cellular and organelle membranes have the same general structure, yet their functions, though more or less similar, are not identical. Probably the overall organization of cell membrane and organelle membrane is the same—unchanged by alterations in the composition of the lipides and proteins, alterations which doubtlessly modify the functioning of the membranes.

LYSOSOMES, SACS OF DIGESTIVE JUICES

Electron microscopy has revealed many different organelles inside cells. Food vacuoles and pinocytotic vacuoles are among these organelles. So are the sacs, discovered by C. de Duve of the University of Louvain, which contain the cell's digestive juices. These are called *lysosomes,* meaning "dissolving bodies." Lysosomes vary in size and shape, but they are always surrounded by a membrane which resembles the cell membrane.

Lysosomes are involved in many processes besides digestion of foods. If a cell is irreparably injured or diseased, it may be digested by its own lysosomes. Cell destruction can play a role in animal development—the loss of the tadpole's tail is one example among many. In starvation, lysosomes digest some of the cell's organelles without going so far as to kill it. This partial autodigestion provides the cell with an emergency supply of food.

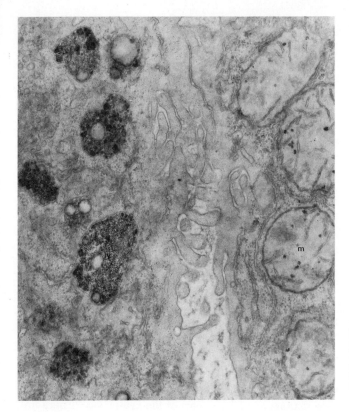

Figure 3-18 Electron micrograph of a cell from rat liver, showing dense bodies, the lysosomes (ly), lined up along the edge of a bile canaliculus (on the other side of which can be seen four mitochondria). *(Courtesy P. Baudhuin and C. de Duve.)*

A number of rare inherited diseases of man are now recognized as due to the absence of one or another component of the lysosome's digestive juice. In Tay-Sachs' disease, for example, failure of the lysosomes to digest certain substances results in their accumulation, particularly in the brain; infantile idiocy is the catastrophic result.

ENDOPLASMIC RETICULUM, SITE OF CHEMICAL SYNTHESES

The life of every cell depends on the continual transformation of nutrients into a myriad of substances. Even in mature animals, some cells, such as the blood-forming cells in the bone marrow, are continually growing and dividing. Such cells must fabricate additional cell membrane, multiply all the organelles, and, in general, increase all the constituents of the cell. Cells which are not growing are constantly renewing themselves, discarding and replacing worn-out parts. Specialized cells manufacture hormones, saliva, mucus, milk.

The site of many of these chemical syntheses is an organelle called the *endoplasmic reticulum*, meaning the "intracellular network." The endoplasmic reticulum differs somewhat in appearance from one cell type to

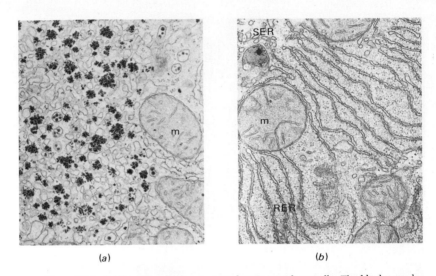

(a) (b)

Figure 3-19 (a) Smooth endoplasmic reticulum in a rat liver cell. The black granules are glycogen; mitochondria (m) are also visible (magnification × 50,000). (Courtesy George E. Palade.) (b) Rough endoplasmic reticulum (RER) in a rat liver cell. The grains in the rough endoplasmic reticulum are ribosomes. Smooth endoplasmic reticulum (SER) begins in the upper left corner of the picture (magnification × 82,000). (Courtesy David Sabatini.)

another, but it is always made of membrane. It seems to be a labyrinthine infolding of the cell membrane which gives rise to more or less parallel layers or tiny tubes that occupy a large part of the cytoplasm. There are two types of endoplasmic reticula, called *smooth* and *rough,* each associated with a different type of chemical synthesis.

Lipides such as the fatty substances found in the membranes, hormones such as the sex hormones, and carbohydrates such as starch, glycogen, and cellulose are synthesized on the *smooth* endoplasmic reticulum. Why does the synthesis of these substances take place on a membrane? Each is the end product of a series of chemical steps which must take place in the correct sequence. It seems likely that the endoplasmic reticulum provides a surface on which all the steps take place one after the other in space as well as in time. The smooth endoplasmic reticulum thus makes possible the organization of chemical assembly lines. Moreover, substances which are to be exported from the cell get channeled out through the endoplasmic reticulum.

The *rough* endoplasmic reticulum is the site of the synthesis of proteins. Proteins serve such a host of functions that altogether they constitute the bulk of the solid material of almost all cells (the rare exceptions being special cells such as those which store fat). The elucidation of the mechanism of protein synthesis has been one of the great biochemical

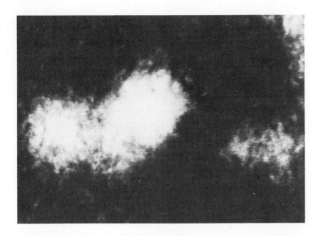

Figure 3-20 Bacterial ribosome (partially dissociated into the smaller and larger subunits of which it is composed). This ribosome, seen here at a magnification greater than 2 million, was photographed with a high-voltage scanning electron microscope. *(Courtesy A. V. Crewe.)*

achievements. It is recounted in Chap. 9. This synthesis requires a special piece of cellular machinery, a small spherical organelle called a *ribosome.* Sometimes ribosomes float free in the cytoplasm. Otherwise they are attached to endoplasmic reticulum, giving it the knobby appearance of the rough endoplasmic reticulum.

Most proteins which are to be used within the cell are synthesized by free ribosomes. Proteins which, like the digestive-juice proteins of lysosomes, must be enclosed in a membrane, and proteins which are destined for export from the cell, are synthesized on the rough endoplasmic reticulum.

Some cell products require packaging. Digestive juices get packaged inside lysosomes, thereby protecting the cell from autodigestion. Other substances, destined for use outside the cell, are packaged as granules before being extruded from the cell by a process which is the reverse of phagocytosis and pinocytosis. These export substances include hormones, milk, cell-coating secretions such as the mucus which protects the exterior of cells of the gut, and even tooth enamel, bone, and cartilage.

THE GOLGI APPARATUS DOES THE PACKAGING

The chemical finishing touches are put on these substances, and they are then packaged, in the *Golgi apparatus,* an organelle discovered in 1898 with the light microscope by Camillo Golgi (1843–1926), recipient of the 1906 Nobel Prize in medicine-physiology for his microscopical studies of the nervous system. The role of the Golgi apparatus and the way it functions are still being clarified.

The electron microscope has demonstrated that the Golgi apparatus is an extension of the endoplasmic reticulum. It consists of stacks of flattened sacs which, like the endoplasmic reticulum itself, are made of membrane. Substances synthesized in the endoplasmic reticulum collect

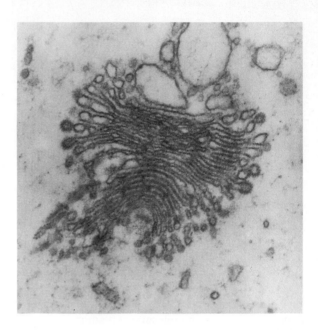

Figure 3-21 Electron micrograph of the Golgi apparatus. *(Courtesy A. V. Grimstone.)*

in the sac at the bottom of the stack, where carbohydrates are attached to them. The now swollen sac rises to the top of the stack, perhaps pushed up by new sacs forming beneath it. Once on top, bits of its membrane pinch off, transforming the sac into a multitude of globules, the finished lysosomes or secretion granules.

CHLORO-PLASTS, SITE OF PHOTO-SYNTHESIS

Energy is used up at every step and stage of cellular growth and division, for cell maintenance, and for the performance of specialized functions. As described in Chap. 2, the ultimate source of this energy is sunlight. Photosynthesis, the process by which light energy is used to synthesize glucose and other carbohydrates, the process on which life on this planet depends, takes place in green plants in organelles called *chloroplasts*.

Chloroplasts typically contain *grana*, stacks of flattened membranous sacs; parallel sheets of membrane interconnect the grana. The membrane of the grana consists of protein and lipide; the molecular arrangement of these components is not certain but, like other cell membranes, may consist of a bimolecular layer of lipide which is partially covered and to some extent penetrated by protein. Located in the grana, probably in association with protein, is the chlorophyll; the grana are thus the sites where light energy is captured.

The membranous organization of the grana is of the greatest importance, for it makes possible the harnessing of the sun's energy. In a test

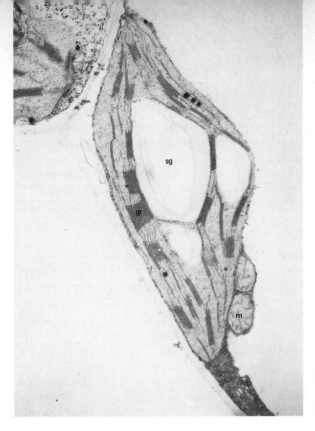

Figure 3-22 Electron micrograph of a chloroplast. Chlorophyll-containing grana (gr) and large starch granules (sg) are visible within the chloroplast, on which lie two mitochondria (m). *(Courtesy R. W. Horne.)*

tube, pure chlorophyll absorbs light, but the light is immediately re-emitted—the chlorophyll merely fluoresces, and the light energy is dissipated. But in the complex structure of the grana the light energy absorbed by chlorophyll is passed to a series of molecules which use it to regenerate NADPH from $NADP^+$ and ATP from ADP.

The material between the grana is called the *stroma*. The synthesis in the stroma of glucose and other carbohydrates from carbon dioxide and water consumes the NADPH and ATP regenerated in the grana with light energy.

The chloroplast described above is typical of the cells of higher plants, for example, those of the leaves of spinach and trees. Such cells may contain a large number of chloroplasts, fifty or more. Some single-celled photosynthetic organisms contain only one chloroplast, which almost fills the cell. The structure of all chloroplasts is basically the same; all contain chlorophyll, and all carry out the same photochemical reactions.

Plant cells may contain *plastids* other than chloroplasts; these organelles, unlike chloroplasts, contain no chlorophyll. *Leucoplasts* are colorless; they may function in the storage of starch, as in the potato. Carrots, tomatoes, and flower petals owe their color to *chromoplasts*, which contain pigments other than chlorophyll. Chloroplasts, leucoplasts, and chromoplasts are similar in structure; all develop from small, colorless, immature *proplastids*.

**MITOCHON-
DRIA, POWER-
HOUSE OF
THE CELL**

In chloroplasts are synthesized glucose and other carbohydrates which are transformed in their turn in both plants and animals into all other carbon-containing substances. These myriad substances can be oxidized to provide vital energy in the form of ATP.

The oxidation of glucose to pyruvic acid (see Chap. 2) takes place in association with no organelle or other structure; the same is true of the first steps in the oxidation of other substances, for example, fats. During these steps, only a small fraction of the total energy invested in these molecules is retrieved in the form of regenerated ATP.

Oxidations are completed, with the liberation of carbon dioxide and water and the concomitant regeneration of most of the cell's ATP, inside organelles called *mitochondria*. It is within the mitochondria that most of the oxygen we breathe is utilized; it combines with the hydrogen obtained in the series of oxidations to form water.

The cells of both plants and animals contain mitochondria. There may be only one large mitochondrion, as in the parasitic protozoans, trypanosomas, or there may be a few hundred or many thousands in a cell; they are most abundant in cells with the greatest energy expenditure, such as those of muscle. Mitochondria are somewhat different in appearance in different types of cells, but they are usually more or less sausage-shaped. With the most modern light microscopes, they can be observed within living cells, where they appear to swell, shorten, contract, fragment, and, in some cells, move around.

What is this organelle, the powerhouse where the bulk of the ATP needed to meet the cell's energy requirements is generated? The mitochondrion is enclosed in an outer membrane which resembles cell membrane. Within this membrane, and separated from it by a small space, is another, inner, membrane which is pleated and folded, forming deep ridges within the mitochondrion; this inner membrane is covered with knobs attached to it by slender stalks. The importance of the mitochondrial membranes is emphasized by the fact that in bacteria, which themselves are about the size of a mitochondrion and therefore contain none, oxidation reactions are associated with the cell membrane itself.

Within the cavity of the mitochondrion takes place a cyclic sequence of reactions which is the hub of metabolism in most cells. This sequence is variously called the *tricarboxylic acid cycle*, the *citric acid cycle*, or frequently the *Krebs cycle* in honor of the great English biochemist Sir Hans Krebs (1900–   ), who proposed the cycle in 1937 and recognized that it accomplishes the complete oxidation of pyruvic acid to three molecules of carbon dioxide.

Pyruvic acid enters the Krebs cycle after a preliminary reaction in which it is oxidized to carbon dioxide and acetate (the negative ion of acetic acid); the acetate is attached to a substance called *coenzyme A*.

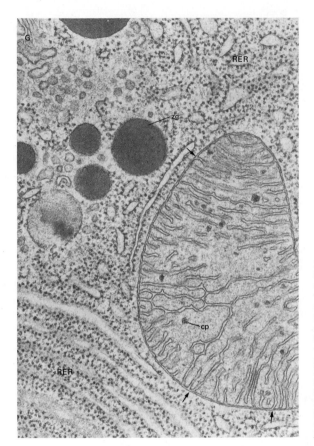

Figure 3-23 Electron micrograph of a mitochondrion. The double-membrane structure of the mitochondrion is clearly visible. The inner membrane is folded and pleated (note in particular the infoldings indicated by an arrow). The folding enormously increases the surface area of the interior of the mitochondrion (within which is calcium phosphate (cp), seen as dark spots). The mitochondrion shown here, from a bat pancreas cell, is surrounded by rough endoplasmic reticulum (RER) thickly studded with ribosomes. Zymogen granules (zg), such as those in fig. 3-5, and part of the Golgi apparatus (G) are also visible. *(Courtesy Keith Porter.)*

Many other substances, such as fats, also enter the Krebs cycle after being converted to *acetyl CoA,* as coenzyme A with an attached acetate is called. (The discoverer of coenzyme A, Fritz Lipmann, and Hans Krebs shared the Nobel Prize in medicine-physiology in 1953.)

In the first reaction of the Krebs cycle, acetyl CoA combines with oxalacetic acid to form citric acid. The citric acid is oxidized step by step, with the loss of two molecules of carbon dioxide, finally being transformed back into oxalacetic acid. The cycle then recommences with the introduction of another molecule of acetyl CoA.

In the course of the Krebs cycle, the oxidation reactions result not only in the liberation of carbon dioxide but also in the transfer of electrons (as hydrogen atoms) to an acceptor molecule. As the last step in a series of reactions which take place on the pleated inner membrane of the mitochondrion, this hydrogen combines with oxygen to form water.

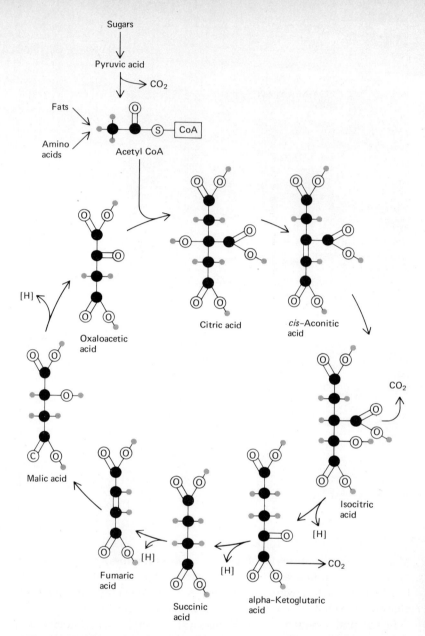

Sugars

Pyruvic acid

CO_2

Fats

Amino acids

Acetyl CoA

Citric acid

cis-Aconitic acid

Oxaloacetic acid

[H]

Malic acid

CO_2

Isocitric acid

[H]

Fumaric acid

[H]

Succinic acid

[H]

CO_2

alpha-Ketoglutaric acid

Figure 3-24   The citric acid, or Krebs, cycle.   Substances enter the Krebs cycle in the form of acetyl CoA, an acetate attached by a sulfur to the complex molecule called coenzyme A, CoA.   This acetate is then transferred to the four-carbon acid oxaloacetic acid, transforming it into the six-carbon acid citric acid.   The citric acid is transformed back again into oxaloacetic acid in a sequence of seven steps.   During these steps two carbons are removed as carbon dioxide.   Four hydrogen atoms are also removed and passed from one substance to another in a series of reactions (not shown), which are not yet fully understood; in the course of these reactions the energy invested in the hydrogens is utilized to regenerate ATP from ADP.   The hydrogens ultimately combine with oxygen to form water.

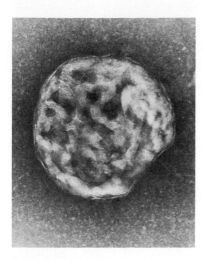 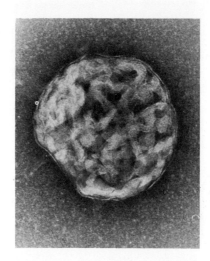

Figure 3-25 Stereo pair of electron micrographs of a mitochondrion showing the elaborate infolding of the inner membrane. These pictures were taken with the 800,000-volt beam of an ultrahigh-voltage electron microscope. *(Courtesy K. Hama.)* (The pairs of stereo photographs in this book can be viewed with the aid of a pocket mirror. Place the mirror between the photographs, facing left; with the nose against the top edge of the mirror, close the right eye; look at the image in the mirror with the left eye, tilting the mirror so that the image appears to lie flat; then open the right eye. It is important that the two images be illuminated equally and, therefore, that the mirror not cast a shadow on one or the other.)

If hydrogen gas and oxygen gas are mixed and ignited, there results an explosion—water is formed, and a great deal of energy is violently liberated. On the inner membrane of the mitochondrion, the energy in the hydrogen atoms is drawn off step by step, so finally hydrogen of low energy combines gently with oxygen. The energy obtained in this process is used to regenerate ATP from ADP and phosphate.

The pleating and folding of the inner mitochondrial membrane serves an important function: It enormously increases the surface available for these membrane-associated reactions. The knobs attached to the membrane are probably the sites where ATP is regenerated.

A great deal has already been learned about the much-studied mitochondrion. Biochemists in the 1970s are carefully taking apart the mitochondrial membrane, studying the pieces, and successfully putting them back together into functional pieces of membrane. Such experiments, it is hoped, will eventually furnish a complete picture of the organization and functioning of mitochondria.

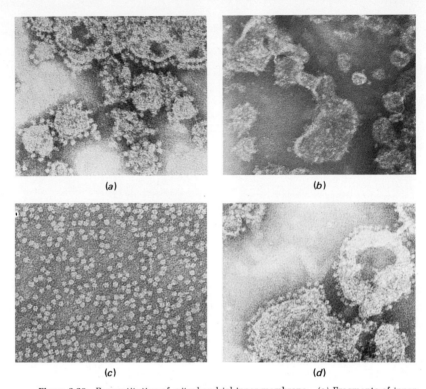

(a)   (b)

(c)   (d)

Figure 3-26 Reconstitution of mitochondrial inner membrane. *(a)* Fragments of inner membrane, with attached knobs; these fragments, like the intact membrane, are capable of the sequence of reactions which regenerate ATP from ADP. *(b)* Inactive membrane fragments with spheres removed. *(c)* Inactive purified spheres (the spheres degrade ATP to ADP, probably the reverse of their role in the intact mitochondrion). *(d)* Sphere-less membrane fragments and spheres are recombined into active membrane with the characteristic appearance and ATP-generating capacity of intact mitochondrial inner membrane. Other experiments, in which the inner membrane is taken apart into more and more of its many components and then reassembled, are yielding information about the structure and functioning of mitochondria. *(Courtesy Efraim Racker.)*

THE NUCLEUS, CELLULAR CONTROL CENTER

Growth, maintenance, division, and the performance of specialized functions are the end result of the continual transformation of nutrients into the substances of which cells are made or which cells synthesize to fill the needs of the organism of which they are a part. In any living cell, thousands of chemical reactions are constantly and harmoniously taking place. They give rise to thousands of substances, the needed end products or intermediates in the synthesis of these end products.

Neither an excess nor a deficiency of these multifarious substances can be tolerated by the cell, for an excess would soon inundate it while a deficiency would slow down the entire cellular metabolism. How are all the processes taking place within a cell so accurately balanced, so beautifully coordinated and controlled?

The control center of the cell is the nucleus, the largest cellular organelle and the first to be discovered. From the nucleus, orders and directions are sent out to the working part of the cell, the cytoplasm; these orders determine, directly or indirectly, what is synthesized, how much is synthesized, and how it is synthesized.

How does the nucleus know which orders to send out, directing which particular substances to be synthesized? This is determined by the cytoplasmic concentrations of the substances themselves. If there is too little of a substance, then its scarcity acts as a signal in the nucleus; if there is too much of a substance, then its abundance is the signal. The coordination of cellular activities is thus achieved by a delicate interaction between nucleus and cytoplasm.

How is it known that the nucleus plays the controlling role in the cell? There are many experiments which have demonstrated this. For example, if an amoeba is cut in two, the half containing the nucleus heals, eats, grows, and ultimately divides—it is a small but normal amoeba. The half without a nucleus dies within 1 or 2 weeks unless another nucleus is injected into it.

By determining what substances a cell makes, the nucleus determines what kind of a cell it is, as has been demonstrated in experiments with the green algae *Acetabularia*. These plants have a small rootlike base from which extends a slender stalk terminating in a cap. The entire 1-inch-tall tropical algae are but a single cell with its nucleus located in the base. Two species, *Acetabularia mediterranea* and *A. crenulata*, differ in the shape of their cap. If to the base of *A. mediterranea*, for example, is grafted a capless stalk of *A. crenulata*, this hybrid plant will grow a cap like that of a normal *A. mediterranea*. The type of cap, and thus the type of *Acetabularia*, is determined by the small nucleus-containing base and not by the large cytoplasm-containing stalk.

Figure 3-27 The green alga *Acetabularia mediterranea*, showing its stem and cap. (Courtesy "Turtox Collection," CCM General Biological, Inc.)

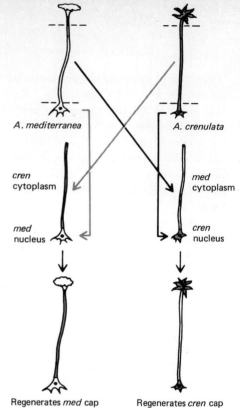

Figure 3-28 Two species of *Acetabularia*, *A. mediterranea (med)* and *A. crenulata (cren)*. Both have a rootlike base which contains the nucleus, and a stem, at the end of which is a cap; the two species differ in the shape of the cap. Experiments in which the stem of one species was grafted onto the nucleus-containing base of the other species have demonstrated that the type of cap which regenerates is determined by the fragment containing the nucleus.

To a limited extent the nucleus shares its responsibilities. Some organelles are fabricated following directions which come in part from the nucleus but which in part are stored within the organelles themselves. Chloroplasts and mitochondria are such organelles. A cell cannot make functional new mitochondria or chloroplasts without the necessary nuclear information. Neither can it construct these organelles if there are none already in the cell. A mitochondrion or chloroplast, like the cell itself, arises only from a preexisting mitochondrion or chloroplast—given a big helping hand from the nucleus.

What is the structure of the nucleus? It is surrounded by a double membrane which in the electron microscope can be seen to be full of holes or pores and which is continuous with the endoplasmic reticulum, where so many chemical syntheses take place.

The nucleus contains several smaller organelles. Of these, the chromosomes play such a key role in the cell that they are described separately below. Ribosomes, the cellular machinery for synthesizing proteins, are in part synthesized in a prominent organelle called the *nucleolus,* or "little nucleus," of which there may be one or several in a nucleus. Yet another organelle, the self-duplicating *centriole,* is located just outside the nucleus; it is concerned with the intricate events (described in Chap. 6) which take place in the nucleus just before a cell divides.

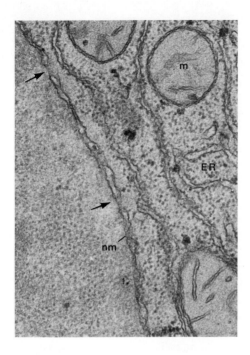

Figure 3-29 Electron micrograph of a segment of nuclear membrane (nm). Two pores are indicated by arrows. In the cytoplasm are seen endoplasmic reticulum (ER) covered with ribosomes, and mitochondria (m). *(Courtesy David Sabatini.)*

The master plan, the information needed to make and run the cell, is stored in the nucleus in organelles called *chromosomes*. Chromosomes are readily seen with a light microscope during cell division, for at that time they become condensed and thickened; in this state, each chromosome can be identified by its distinctive rodlike shape. At other times the chromosomes relax to form fine, almost invisible filaments.

Every plant and animal has a characteristic number of chromosomes. Human cells contain twenty-three different pairs of chromosomes, forty-six in all. The honor of having the fewest chromosomes, two, goes to a threadworm; that of having the most, five hundred, to a fern.

An enormous amount of experimental data accumulated since the beginning of this century, and partially described in Chap. 6, has proved beyond doubt that the chromosomes contain the blueprints of the cell. Very recently, a promising new way has been found to assign detailed roles to the chromosomes of mice and men. The cells of animal tissues can be separated from each other and, given the right conditions and the right nutrients, will grow and divide on the bottom of a laboratory dish. This is the technique called tissue culture, described in Chap. 1 (see fig. 1-14). In the 1960s it was discovered that if different kinds of cells are grown together in the same dish, then very occasionally two different cells fuse to form a hybrid cell.

CHROMO-SOMES, INFORMATION STOREHOUSES

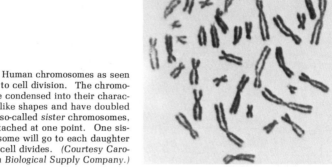

Figure 3-30 Human chromosomes as seen just prior to cell division. The chromosomes have condensed into their characteristic rodlike shapes and have doubled to give two so-called *sister* chromosomes, which are attached at one point. One sister chromosome will go to each daughter cell when the cell divides. *(Courtesy Carolina Biological Supply Company.)*

In 1967, Mary Weiss and Howard Green at the New York University School of Medicine succeeded in crossing mouse cells with human cells. Human chromosomes have a tendency to be discarded or lost when the hybrid cells multiply, so most of the chromosomes in the hybrids are mouse chromosomes. In their appearance, the hybrid cells therefore more closely resemble the mouse parent cells than the human parent cells; in their detailed chemistry, the hybrid cells are also largely mouse-like, but they do synthesize some human-type substances. Moreover, which human-type substances are synthesized, it has been demonstrated, depends on which particular human chromosomes the hybrid cells have retained. For example, it has been found that a protein called thymidine kinase is synthesized only if the human chromosome designated E-17 is present in the hybrid cells.

Experiments on hybrid cells continue. It is hoped that, thanks to them, it will eventually be known exactly how the job of directing the cell is divided up among the twenty-three different kinds of human chromosomes.

CELL AND ORGANELLE

Broadly speaking, the functions of a cell can be related to its structure and to the organelles which carry out particular jobs. Enormous progress is currently being made in the study of the structure and function of the cellular organelles. Electron microscopists are working out their intriguing, detailed architecture. Biochemists are learning more and more about their functions and about the precise nature of the substances of which they are made. But the ultimate goal has not yet been achieved—a clear picture of their molecular structure, which explains in detail how they function.

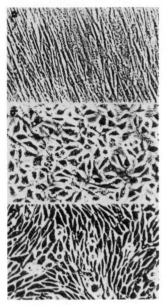

(a)
Human

(b)
Mouse

(c)
Hybrid

Figure 3-31 Light micrographs of cells grown in tissue culture. *(a)* Human cells; *(b)* mouse cells; *(c)* human-mouse hybrid cells. The hybrid cells contain almost all the mouse chromosomes but only about one-third of the human chromosomes. They also resemble the mouse parent cells much more than the human parent cells. *(From M. C. Weiss and H. Green, Proc. Natl. Acad. Sci. U.S., 58:1104 (1967), courtesy H. Green.)*

There remain great gaps in this area, as well as in other areas, of biologic knowledge, but there have also been tremendous successes in unraveling the mysteries of the cell, and thus the mysteries of life itself. A great deal is now known about the multitude of chemical reactions which take place in cells; about the mechanisms for regulating and controlling these reactions; about the structure, function, and synthesis of proteins, substances which are unique to living matter and which confer on each cell and each organism its particular character; and about the substance in the chromosomes in which is encoded the master plan of the cell and the organism. These spectacular advances in molecular biology will be described in the succeeding chapters.

WHAT DO PROTEINS DO?

Proteins are the stuff of life, the principal solid component of living creatures. There are thousands of proteins, each with a unique function.
A few of the jobs performed by proteins have been mentioned: the pumps
in cell membranes, in large part the cell membranes themselves, and the
digestive juices of the gut and of lysosomes are proteins. So are hair,
feathers, and fish scales. So is hemoglobin, the oxygen transporter,
which gives blood its red color. So are some hormones. Muscle is largely protein. Immunity to measles and mumps depends on proteins. And
every one of the thousands of chemical reactions that take place in cells
requires the help of a protein. The vital role of these complex substances
was already surmised in the early nineteenth century when they were
given their name, from the Greek word *prōteios,* "holding first place."

SOME
FAMILIAR
SUBSTANCES
ARE
PROTEINS

What are proteins? What do they look and feel like? Some proteins, for
example, hair, egg white, and gelatin, are familiar substances.

Hair is a hard and elastic substance that is insoluble in water. These
are the characteristics of *keratin,* the protein of which hair is made. The
keratin of curly hair is a slightly different protein from that of straight
hair. The various colors of hair are due not to keratin, which like most
proteins is colorless, but to pigments in the hair. Animals protect themselves from the knocks of life with feathers, fingernails, fish scales, skin,
silk, horn, and wool, all made of keratin.

Egg white, rich in protein, is an indispensable food for the unhatched chick. But before being consumed, egg white serves another purpose—it surrounds the yolk and later the developing chicken embryo with a cushion. The cushioning property of egg white depends on its thickness, which in turn depends on its composition: Egg white has a consistency typical of a concentrated solution of protein. Most is the protein called *egg-white albumin,* which is soluble in water, as are many proteins.

Egg white is white only after it has been cooked. Albumin and most other proteins as well are damaged by heat, becoming insoluble in water and therefore white instead of transparent. This is called *denaturation,* meaning a change from the natural state. Denaturation can be brought about by means other than heat. Acid, for instance, will denature egg white, transforming the dissolved albumin into a white, insoluble, coagulated curd.

Gelatin is another colorless and water-soluble protein. It causes the gelling of gelatin desserts and the water in which fish, chicken, or pigs' feet have been cooked. The shiny, almost white, powdery or flaky substance sold in stores is so typical in appearance that it could be any one of a large number of dried proteins.

Gelatin is not denatured by heat; in fact, it dissolves in boiling water. This is exceptional, but gelatin is a special case, for it does not exist in nature. It is an altered protein, derived by prolonged boiling from the protein *collagen,* which constitutes about one-third of a mammal's protein. Tough fibers of collagen are found in bone, cartilage, tendon, and other connective tissues; the ropelike strength of tendon, in particular, is due to bundles of collagen fibers.

Keratin and collagen are among the structural proteins; so is egg-white albumin before it is consumed. These proteins fulfill their roles because of their physical characteristics—the hardness of keratin, the toughness

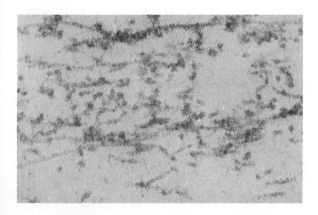

Figure 4-1 Electron micrograph of cartilage, showing long fibrils of collagen embedded in a uniform matrix. *(Courtesy Jean-Paul Revel.)*

of fibers of collagen, and the great solubility of albumin, which makes possible a thick, concentrated solution.

Other proteins serve vital functions which are not structural. Some proteins make muscle contract; others confer immunity to disease; still others are essential agents in biochemical reactions. These proteins will now be described.

SLIDING MUSCLE PROTEINS

When you flex your arm to show off your biceps or when you lift a heavy object by bending your arm, you can easily see the typical bunching up, or shortening, of the biceps. When they are not relaxed, muscles do only one thing: shorten, or contract. That one thing, contraction, is enough, for it is the basis of all movement in animals.

Voluntary muscles move the various appendages—arms, legs, heads, and tails—found among vertebrates. The stringiness of tough meat attests to the organization of muscle tissue as long fibers; these run the length of a muscle from one tendon to the next. The muscle fibers are

(a)   (b)

Figure 4-2 Single muscle cells isolated from the stomach muscle of the toad *Bufo marinus.* *(a)* Relaxed; *(b)* contracted. *(From R. M. Bagby et al., Nature, 234:351 (1971), courtesy Roland M. Bagby.)*

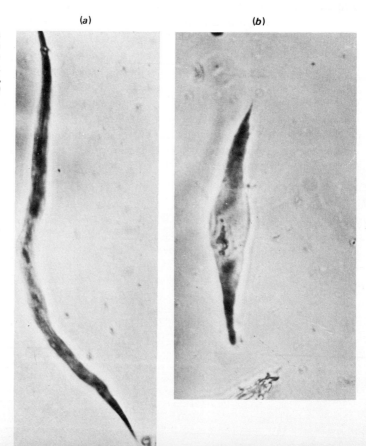

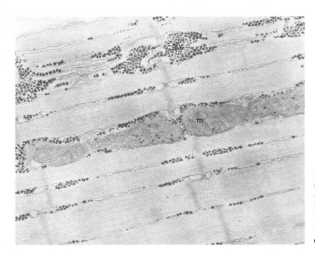

Figure 4-3 Electron micrograph of voluntary muscle from frog. The banded appearance of the muscle tissue is typical. Mitochondria (m) and glycogen granules (gly) attest to the great energy requirement of muscle. *(Courtesy Bruno Ceccarelli and David Sabatini.)*

composed of microscopic *myofibrils*. It is these myofibrils which contract. How? Do they coil up? Do they become pleated, like a jack-in-the-box? High-powered microscopes gave H. E. Huxley and A. F. Huxley* detailed pictures which enabled them in 1957 to solve the mystery of muscle contraction.

Myofibrils, they found, are composed of two types of filaments, *thick* and *thin*; thick filaments have twice the diameter of thin ones. There are rows of segments, or pieces, of thin filament, each separated by a space. These alternate with rows of segments of thick filament located between the segments of thin filament. Perpendicular bands hold the thin filaments in place. (See Fig. 4-4.)

When a muscle contracts, the spaces between the thin filaments disappear; further contraction even causes the thin filaments to bunch up where their ends meet. In muscle contraction, then, the thick and thin filaments slide past each other, filling up the spaces and thereby shortening the muscle.

Precisely how this sliding takes place is not certain. The thick and thin filaments are not in direct contact, but the electron microscope shows that they are connected by slender bridges. Probably the bridges attach to the thin filaments, pull them along a little distance, then detach, move back, and, reattaching, pull the thin filaments again. Bit by bit, the thin

---

*These Huxleys are not related, although several famous Huxleys are. A. F. Huxley, who shared the Nobel Prize in medicine-physiology in 1963 for work on nerve conduction, is half brother of the writer Aldous Huxley and of the biologist and philosopher Sir Julian Huxley; all are grandsons of the biologist T. H. Huxley, Darwin's champion.

filaments are pulled past the thick ones. The energy required for this sliding, and thus the energy to contract muscle, comes from ATP, the cells' energy "money." The bit-by-bit advance of the thin filaments uses up one ATP after the next—when a myofibril contracts, each one of the multitude of bridges consumes 50 to 100 ATP molecules per second.

Figure 4-4 Electron micrographs of stretched and relaxed muscle myofibrils. *(a)* The muscle has been stretched, so the thick and thin filaments overlap only at their ends, as illustrated in the drawing. *(b)* In resting muscle, the thick and thin filaments overlap over much of their length. *(Courtesy H. E. Huxley.)*

(a)

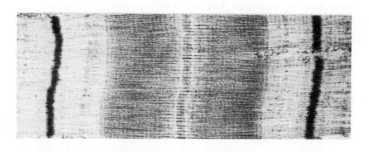

(b)

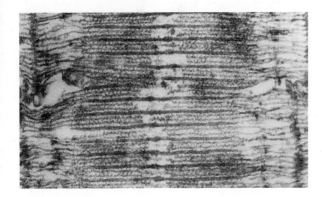

Figure 4-5 Cross bridges between the thick and thin filaments are visible in this electron micrograph. Between each pair of thick filaments are two thin filaments; in the three-dimensional myofibril each thick filament is surrounded by six thin filaments in a hexagonal array. *(Courtesy H. E. Huxley.)*

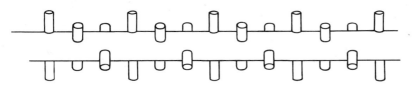

Figure 4-6 Model of the cross bridges about the thick filament. These bridges extend to the surrounding thin filaments. *(From H. E. Huxley and W. Brown, J. Mol. Biol., 30:383 (1967), courtesy H. E. Huxley.)*

Myofibrils are composed almost entirely of two proteins, *myosin* and *actin*. When muscle is washed with salt water, the thick filaments disappear. So does the myosin—it has dissolved in the salt water. Thick filaments, it is concluded, are made of the protein myosin. Similar methods have shown that the thin filaments are composed for the most part of actin. **Actin and Myosin, the Muscle Proteins**

Myosin and actin dissolved in concentrated salt water and then mixed combine to form a complex called *actomyosin*. If this solution is diluted with water, the actomyosin, insoluble in the less concentrated salt, precipitates out in the form of long fibers. The biochemist and Nobel laureate Albert Szent-Györgi discovered that adding ATP causes these artificial muscle fibers to contract.

The cells of animals must have oxygen—it is required in mitochondria to complete the oxidation of foodstuffs to carbon dioxide and water. Blood travels through the circulatory system to the far corners of the body delivering food and oxygen. In large animals, because most cells are not directly exposed to air and food, this circulatory system is essential. **HEMOGLOBIN, THE OXYGEN-TRANSPORTING PROTEIN**

The transport of oxygen from lungs to tissues poses a problem because oxygen, like most gases, is only slightly soluble in water and therefore only slightly soluble in blood. Human beings and other mammals overcome this difficulty by means of an oxygen-transporting protein, *hemoglobin*. But if all the hemoglobin needed for oxygen transport were dissolved directly in the blood serum, our blood would be thick like raw egg white, too thick to circulate. So hemoglobin is compacted into the red blood cells, something like packing a room full of feathers into a pillow.

In mammals, red blood cells are simply sacs of protein, 90 percent of which is hemoglobin. They do not even contain a nucleus when they leave the blood-forming tissues and enter the bloodstream. The red blood cells of other vertebrates contain a nucleus. Some annelids, mollusks, and crustaceans have no red blood cells at all. They do have hemoglobin, a relatively small amount, dissolved directly in the serum. The octopus, squid, and some snails are truly "blue-blooded"; instead of hemoglobin, they make use of a blue, copper-containing protein called *hemocyanin*. This protein and a green iron-containing protein found in some annelids are less efficient oxygen transporters than hemoglobin.

Hemoglobin Is Perfectly Tailored to Do Its Job

Hemoglobin must pick up oxygen in the lungs, where the concentration is high, and unload it in the tissues, where the concentration is almost as high. This is like taking a pillow which has become damp in a humid room and trying to dry it out in another room which is almost as humid. The pillow will not get very dry. Neither will hemoglobin give up all its oxygen to the tissues. But it is amazingly efficient, being so sensitive to variations in oxygen concentration that it even gives up more to tissues which require more, like working muscle.

Myoglobin is another red, iron-containing protein and is very similar to its cousin hemoglobin. Myoglobin combines with and stores oxygen in muscle tissue.

More is known about myoglobin and hemoglobin than about almost any other proteins. Hemoglobin is of especial interest, for there are many diseases, in particular various anemias, which are related to it in one way or another. The most common type of anemia, in which the number of red blood cells is insufficient, is due to a shortage of the iron needed to make hemoglobin. Very much less commonly, anemia is an inherited disease in which the anemic person has a normal number of red blood cells. It has recently been discovered that these hereditary anemias are due to abnormal hemoglobin, which differs ever so slightly from the normal protein. Hemoglobin is so perfectly designed to fulfill its vital function as oxygen transporter that almost any tiny change is a change for the worse.

Most people who have once had an attack of measles do not catch this disease again. A single infection of mumps, chicken pox, or polio also almost always confers lifelong immunity. Important in the body's fight against disease and all-important in immunity are proteins called *antibodies,* which circulate in the blood.

ANTIBODIES, DISEASE-FIGHTING PROTEINS

Antibodies are produced in response to the presence of a foreign material, or *antigen,* in the body. The antigen may be a virus, a bacterium, transfused red blood cells of the wrong blood type, or a foreign protein such as a bacterial toxin (diphtheria toxin, for example) or a snake venom toxin.

An attack of measles confers immunity against no disease except measles. This is typical, for a characteristic of antibodies is their specificity: an antibody will react only with the particular antigen which provoked its synthesis. If, for example, a rabbit is injected with chicken egg-white albumin, new antibodies will appear in the blood in about a week. The blood serum of such an immunized rabbit will precipitate egg albumin in a test tube. The antibodies are so specific that they react poorly even with the very similar albumin of turkey egg white.

Human beings are injected with antigens when they are vaccinated. The word "vaccine" (derived from *vacca,* Latin for cow) was invented by Pasteur to honor Edward Jenner (1749–1823), who at the end of the eighteenth century discovered that immunization against smallpox can be achieved by inoculating the harmless cow version of the disease (antibodies formed against the cowpox virus react sufficiently with the very similar antigens of smallpox virus).

Pasteur, almost 100 years after Jenner's discovery, developed vaccines against a number of diseases. The vaccines were prepared from bacteria or viruses which had been killed by heat or chemicals or from which a noninfectious variant had been obtained. Best known is his antirabies vaccine. Nowadays, rabies vaccination may be supplemented with serum from an animal previously immunized against the disease. The patient thus receives ready-made antibodies.

Nature uses the same technique. Calves are provided with ready-made antibodies in the first milk they receive from their mother. During the calf's life, these are the only proteins which pass intact from its intestines into its bloodstream.

Human babies receive ready-made antibodies from their mother just before birth; they are normally the only proteins which pass between mother and baby. These antibodies can cause a serious problem if the mother is of the blood type known as Rh negative and her unborn baby is her second child of the blood type Rh positive. If at its birth red blood cells from the first Rh-positive baby leaked into the mother's circulatory system, they

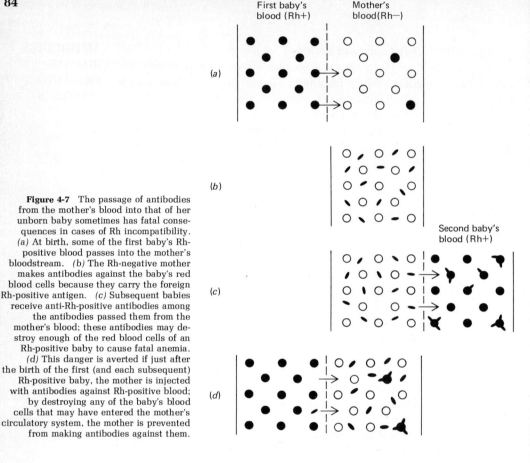

First baby's blood (Rh+)

Mother's blood (Rh−)

(a)

(b)

Second baby's blood (Rh+)

(c)

(d)

Figure 4-7 The passage of antibodies from the mother's blood into that of her unborn baby sometimes has fatal consequences in cases of Rh incompatibility. (a) At birth, some of the first baby's Rh-positive blood passes into the mother's bloodstream. (b) The Rh-negative mother makes antibodies against the baby's red blood cells because they carry the foreign Rh-positive antigen. (c) Subsequent babies receive anti-Rh-positive antibodies among the antibodies passed them from the mother's blood; these antibodies may destroy enough of the red blood cells of an Rh-positive baby to cause fatal anemia. (d) This danger is averted if just after the birth of the first (and each subsequent) Rh-positive baby, the mother is injected with antibodies against Rh-positive blood; by destroying any of the baby's blood cells that may have entered the mother's circulatory system, the mother is prevented from making antibodies against them.

may have elicited the formation of anti-Rh-positive antibodies (whether or not this happens depends on a number of factors). These, passing into the blood of a second Rh-positive baby just prior to its birth, can break down the baby's red blood cells, causing severe anemia and even death.

In the late 1960s a method was devised to avoid this problem. Rh-negative mothers who have given birth to an Rh-positive baby are promptly injected with anti-Rh-positive antibodies. Any of the baby's Rh-positive blood cells that may have entered the mother's circulatory system are thereby destroyed before the mother can make antibodies against them, antibodies which could prove fatal to a subsequent baby.

The Antigen-Antibody Complex   Antibodies combine with the antigen which elicited their synthesis, forming a stable antigen-antibody complex. How does the antibody-antigen combination help fight disease? Poisonous proteins, toxins, are harmless when combined with antibodies. Antibodies may clump bacteria or

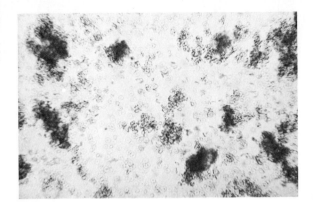

Figure 4-8 Red blood cells agglutinated by antibody. *(Courtesy Ortho Diagnostics, Raritan, N.J.)*

viruses together or render them susceptible to destruction by other blood proteins or by phagocytic cells, which can then engulf them more easily.

How does an antibody combine with its antigen? What makes the complex so specific? Nobody knows exactly, but it is hoped that these questions will be answered in the next few years. It is known that each antibody has two *sites*, places which combine with the antigen. Presumably these combining sites have the right shape to fit one particular antigen and the right chemical properties to make that antigen stick. Since each antibody has two combining sites, huge aggregates of alternating antibody and antigen can form. In a test tube these aggregates precipitate, as can be seen in the case of egg-white albumin or red blood cells. In a living animal, aggregation may inactivate the antigen—bacteria, viruses, or foreign substances.

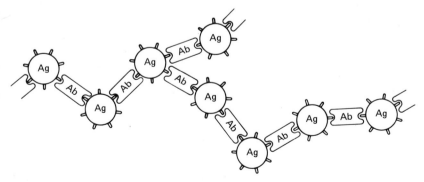

Figure 4-9 Antibody molecules (Ab) have two sites that can combine with the antigen (Ag). If the antigen has two antigenic sites, then huge aggregates of alternating antibody and antigen can form. If the antigen has more than two antigenic sites (as is true of blood cells and bacteria, for example), then the aggregates can be branched, as illustrated in this drawing. It should be noted that a blood cell or bacterium is in reality incomparably bigger than an antibody molecule.

ENZYMES, BIOLOGIC CATALYSTS

Cells are made of complex substances which must be synthesized from relatively simple chemicals. Sugars, starch, fats, vitamins, pigments, hormones, proteins, all are the end products of numerous, in some cases hundreds, of chemical reactions. The degradation of substances, which may facilitate their excretion or furnish energy, necessitates many more reactions. A few have been described in preceding chapters. In most cells, thousands are constantly taking place.

The physical conditions inside cells do not encourage chemical reactions to take place quickly. Cells are essentially neutral, neither acidic nor basic; they are lukewarm, 98.6°F (37°C) in warm-blooded animals such as humans, usually considerably cooler in cold-blooded animals and plants. Under such conditions, most chemical reactions take place slowly.

The chemist in his laboratory knows this well. He speeds up reactions by heating the reaction mixture, by adding a metal such as iron or platinum, or, more commonly, by adding an acid or alkali. But living cells cannot tolerate heat, acid, or alkali because these additives denature proteins. Despite this, chemical reactions take place in cells at extraordinarily rapid rates. This is because all biologic reactions are *catalyzed*.

Catalysts Speed Up Reactions

What is a *catalyst?* It is a substance which speeds up a chemical reaction. The catalyst combines with the *reactant,* the molecule which is about to take part in the chemical reaction. Sometimes a covalent or ionic bond forms temporarily between catalyst and reactant. But when the chemical reaction is over and the reactant has been transformed into the product of the reaction, *the catalyst is again intact* and ready to combine with another molecule of reactant. An understanding of precisely how a

Figure 4-10 A classical example of catalysis. The oxidation by oxygen gas of sulfur dioxide to sulfur trioxide is greatly accelerated by the addition of nitrogen oxide. The nitrogen oxide is first oxidized by the oxygen gas to nitrogen dioxide; the nitrogen dioxide then oxidizes the sulfur dioxide to sulfur trioxide, itself being reduced to nitrogen oxide, the starting material. Thus the nitrogen oxide, like all catalysts, enters into the reaction, but when the reaction is terminated, it has been reconstituted. Again like all catalysts, the nitrogen oxide speeds up the reaction because the two reactions in which it participates are much faster than the single reaction, the direct oxidation of sulfur dioxide by oxygen gas.

$$2\,NO + O_2 \longrightarrow 2\,NO_2$$

$$2\,NO_2 + 2\,SO_2 \longrightarrow 2\,NO + 2\,SO_3$$

$$O_2 + 2\,SO_2\ (+\ 2\,NO) \longrightarrow 2\,SO_3\ (+\ 2\,NO)$$

particular catalyst speeds up a particular reaction requires detailed knowledge of the mechanism by which the reaction takes place.

Biologic catalysts are called *enzymes*. Let us consider, as an example, the enzyme-catalyzed degradation of hydrogen peroxide (H_2O_2). Those who use peroxide as a bleach or disinfectant know that it is unstable: the bottle must be replaced from time to time because it has become a bottle of water, for hydrogen peroxide decomposes slowly but surely into water (H_2O) and oxygen (O_2):

$$H_2O_2 \rightarrow H_2O + \tfrac{1}{2}O_2$$

This reaction is speeded up enormously by the enzyme called *catalase*, which is widespread in plant and animal cells. The catalase enters into the reaction, forming a peroxide-catalase complex. But whereas the hydrogen peroxide decomposes, the catalase remains intact:

$$H_2O_2 + catalase \rightarrow H_2O_2 - catalase \rightarrow H_2O + \tfrac{1}{2}O_2 + catalase$$

A single molecule of catalase, one of the most efficient enzymes known, can perform this reaction 18 million times per minute.

Catalase is just one of the thousands of enzymes in cells. The dozen reactions required for the synthesis of glucose demand as many different enzymes. In fact, every chemical reaction which takes place in a living organism is catalyzed by its specific enzyme.

The pumps which are located in the cell membrane and which maintain concentration differences of salts and other substances inside and out of the cell are also enzymes. Little or nothing is known about most of the enzymes which act as pumps. However, an enzyme which seems to be responsible for the low concentration of sodium ions inside cells despite a high concentration outside and for the high concentration of potassium ions inside despite a low concentration outside has been found in blood cells, nerve cells, and many other tissues. This enzyme degrades ATP to ADP in a test tube provided that both sodium and potassium ions are present. When the enzyme is part of the cell membrane, it is affected only by sodium ions inside and potassium ions outside the cell; for each ATP molecule spent, three sodium ions are ejected from the cell, and two potassium ions are accumulated. How this is accomplished is still a matter for speculation.

Some enzymes are found outside of cells, although they are synthesized within the cells that secrete them. The digestion of food in the stomach and intestines, for example, depends on enzymes. Starch is broken down to sugar by amylase. Other enzymes, such as trypsin, chymotrypsin, and pepsin, break down proteins. Papain, another *proteolytic*, or protein-dissolving, enzyme, is obtained from the papaya tree. It is the active ingredient in commercial meat tenderizers.

Enzymes Are Proteins The meaning of the word "enzyme," coined in 1878, has nothing to do with catalysis—it means "in yeast." The use of yeast to leaven bread and ferment beer and wine dates back to antiquity—the Mesopotamians were drinking beer 8,000 years ago. But it was only in the nineteenth century that chemists began studying the chemical reactions, called *fermentations,* brought about by yeast.

For a long time it was thought that fermentations, such as the transformation of sugar into alcohol, require live yeast. In 1897, Eduard Büchner (1860–1917) prepared a yeast juice, or *extract,* containing no live cells but still capable of causing fermentation. He thereby laid to rest the *vitalist theory,* which held that living organisms are animated by a vital force which puts them beyond the laws governing other physical and chemical phenomena and therefore beyond human understanding. His discovery was also the impetus for a burst of research on the enzymatic activity of cell extracts and of extracellular fluids such as stomach juice, which had long been known to dissolve meat.

Figure 4-11 James Batcheller Sumner (1887–1955) crystallized an enzyme for the first time in 1926. For this remarkable achievement, which demonstrated that enzymes can be purified, he was awarded the Nobel Prize in chemistry in 1946. *(Courtesy New York State College of Agriculture at Cornell University.)*

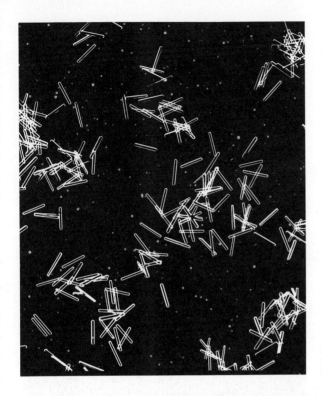

Figure 4-12 Crystals of the enzyme trypsin. *(Courtesy M. Kunitz and the Rockefeller University Archives.)*

In 1926, it was demonstrated that enzymes are proteins. In order to
find out what they are, enzymes had to be purified. This posed great
difficulties, partly because each enzyme constitutes only a minute part
of the solid matter of a cell. Finally, J. B. Sumner (1887–1955) prepared
pure crystals of an enzyme called *urease*. Sumner found that urease is
a protein. One piece of evidence was its destruction by proteolytic
enzymes.

Sumner's success was followed 4 years later by J. H. Northrop's crystallization of the proteolytic enzyme pepsin. Soon many other enzymes,
including most of those mentioned above, had been crystallized. When
they also had been shown to be proteins, it could finally be concluded
that all enzymes are proteins, specialized in the job of speeding up chemical reactions.

**How Do Enzymes
Catalyze
Reactions?**

Catalysts were known long before enzymes were discovered. The name
was invented to describe the degradation of peroxide catalyzed not by
catalase but by metals such as platinum. The acids and bases so frequently used by chemists to speed up reactions act as catalysts. Enzy-

J. H. Northrop

W. M. Stanley

Figure 4-13 John Howard Northrop (1891–   ) crystallized the proteolytic enzyme trypsin in 1931 and subsequently crystallized several other digestive enzymes. Wendell Meredith Stanley (1904–   ) studied the chemical nature of tobacco mosaic virus. Northrop and Stanley shared half the Nobel Prize in chemistry in 1946 for their work on enzyme and viral proteins. *(Northrop photo courtesy the Rockefeller University Graphic Services.) (Stanley photo courtesy the Nobel Foundation.)*

matic catalysis in many ways resembles catalysis by metals, acids, and bases. Some enzymes, including catalase, actually contain an atom of a metal, just as hemoglobin contains iron atoms.

But enzymatic catalysis is unique in two respects. The catalytic power of enzymes is phenomenal; the chemist doing his best to hurry a chemical reaction may achieve less than a millionth of the speed attained by an enzyme. Moreover, each enzyme is specific and will combine with only one particular reactant, its *substrate.*

The specificity of the combination of an enzyme with its substrate parallels that of an antibody with its antigen. The mechanism is thought to be the same. Each antibody's combining sites are presumed to have precisely the shape and chemical properties needed to bind its particular antigen. In 1967, it was proved that an enzyme, *lysozyme,* actually has just such a site, the *active site,* to which its substrate is bound. Knowledge about antibodies has lagged partly because of the difficulty, only very recently surmounted, in obtaining a single species of antibody, such as pure antimeasles antibody. But detailed knowledge about antibodies and, to a much greater extent, about enzymes is rapidly accumulating, thanks to recent successes in answering the question, "What exactly are proteins?"

WHAT ARE PROTEINS? 5

Proteins differ in their physical characteristics: Most are colorless, but hemoglobin and myoglobin are red; egg albumin and gelatin are soluble in water, myosin and actomyosin only in salt water, and keratin in almost nothing. They perform numerous and varied jobs: Collagen is a fibrous structural element in connective tissue; hemoglobin transports oxygen, which in muscle is stored by myoglobin; tens of thousands of antibody proteins recognize and combine with their specific antigen; and perhaps another 10,000 enzymes catalyze as many chemical reactions. How can proteins have such diverse properties and multifarious functions? What kind of chemical substances are they?

Proteins are very large molecules, and, like most other large molecules, they are *polymers*. A polymeric molecule is made of many small molecules attached to each other end to end. Starch, for example, is a polymer, a long string of glucose molecules. Nylon is a man-made polymer consisting of two different, alternating molecules. Proteins are chains of amino acids; twenty kinds of amino acids are commonly found in proteins. But whereas in nylon the order of small molecules is regular A—B—A—B—A—B—. . . , in proteins the order is irregular.

Proteins are thus like long trains made up of twenty different kinds of cars. In a train, the cars are all joined by a single kind of coupling; this

PROTEINS ARE POLYMERS OF AMINO ACIDS

92

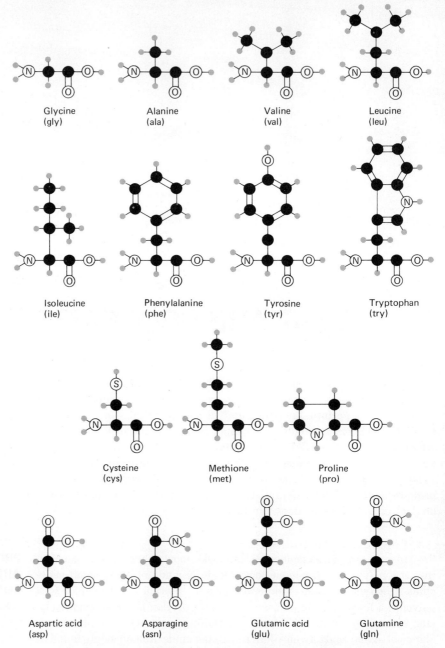

Glycine
(gly)

Alanine
(ala)

Valine
(val)

Leucine
(leu)

Isoleucine
(ile)

Phenylalanine
(phe)

Tyrosine
(tyr)

Tryptophan
(try)

Cysteine
(cys)

Methione
(met)

Proline
(pro)

Aspartic acid
(asp)

Asparagine
(asn)

Glutamic acid
(glu)

Glutamine
(gln)

Figure 5-1 Some naturally occurring amino acids. The twenty amino acids commonly found in proteins are shown in the first five rows. Five uncommon amino acids are shown in the last row (p. 93): Hydroxylysine and hydroxyproline are found only in the protein collagen; thyroxine occurs only in the protein thyroglobulin, the hormone secreted by the thyroid gland; β-alanine is a component of coenzyme A; penicillamine is a component of the antibiotic penicillin.

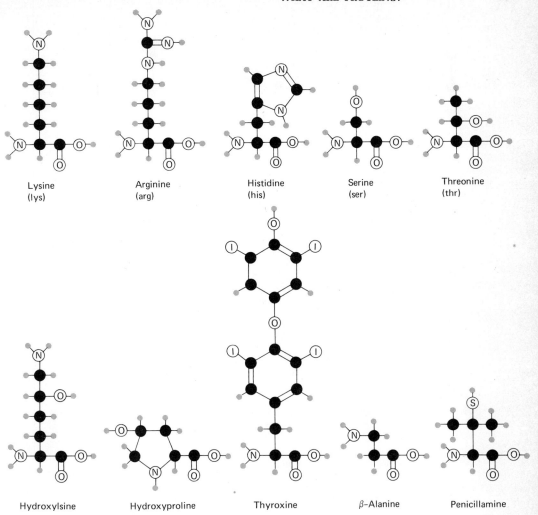

Lysine
(lys)

Arginine
(arg)

Histidine
(his)

Serine
(ser)

Threonine
(thr)

Hydroxylsine

Hydroxyproline

Thyroxine

β-Alanine

Penicillamine

allows them to be hooked together in any order. Similarly, in a protein the amino acids are attached to each other by the same kind of chemical linkage, called a *peptide bond*. Each of the twenty kinds of amino acids is different, just as every type of car making up a train is different, but the parts by which each amino acid—or each car—attaches to its two neighbors are always the same.

Proteins are fabulously large molecules. Let us compare their molecular weights with those of the molecules with which they react. Oxygen gas O_2, molecular weight 32, is stored by myoglobin, molecular weight 17,000, and transported by hemoglobin, molecular weight 68,000. Catalase, molecular weight 225,000, catalyzes the degradation of hydrogen

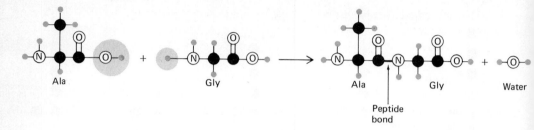

Figure 5-2 Peptide bonds join together the amino acids in proteins. The carboxyl group of each amino acid (alanine in the drawing) is joined to the amino group of the next amino acid (glycine in the drawing) with the loss of the elements of a molecule of water, H^+ and OH^-, to form the peptide bond.

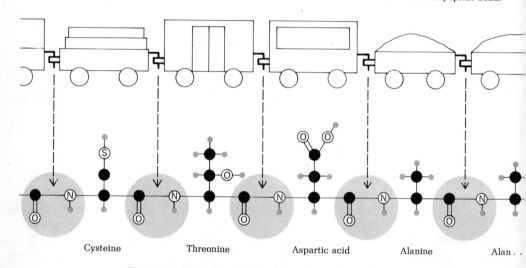

Figure 5-3 Identical peptide bonds join the amino acids of a protein just as identical couplings join the different cars of a train. Thus, the twenty different amino acids can be joined together in any order.

peroxide, molcular weight 19. The degradation of urea, molecular weight 60, is catalyzed by the first enzyme to be crystallized, urease, molecular weight 480,000. Finally myosin, the muscle protein, molecular weight 620,000, removes the terminal phosphate from ATP, which is 1,200 times smaller.

A small protein, such as myoglobin, is made of about 150 amino acids strung together. A rather average-sized protein, such as hemoglobin, consists of about 600, and myosin of about 6,000. Proteins are incredibly long molecules, and must be compared to colossal trains—a train with 6,000 cars would be almost 70 miles long. Yet proteins react with molecules which are comparable in size to a single car of the train. Why are proteins so big? How is their size related to their function?

Proteins are indeed extremely long molecules, but the protein chain does not flop around like a giant piece of wet spaghetti. Rather, it winds and coils and folds in a way which is unique for each protein. The overall shape of most proteins, instead of being long and thin, ends up more or less round, or globular (hence the names hemoglobin and myoglobin). The globular proteins, which include the enzymes, look rather like a lumpy ball. Somewhere on the surface or within an enzyme the winding chain shapes the active site, into which the substrate (or, in the case of an antibody, the antigen) fits.

PROTEINS HAVE COMPLICATED FORMS

The way in which the amino acid chain folds up to give a protein its form depends entirely on the sequence of amino acids in the chain. Each protein has its own unique amino acid sequence; each therefore has its own unique shape. In addition, some proteins consist of two or more associated chains. An example is hemoglobin; it consists of four folded amino acid chains stuck together in a precise way.

The biologic activity of a protein depends on all these features of its structure—the sequence of amino acids, the way the chain folds up to give the protein its three-dimensional form, and in some cases the association of two or more folded chains. Unraveling the structure of such intricate molecules poses gigantic problems, but advances in protein chemistry in the past few years have been gigantic, and the complete structures of several proteins are now known. It is even possible to see precisely how a few enzymes function. The first step in getting to know a protein, inside and out, is to determine its amino acid composition and sequence.

Proteins differ not only in the total number of amino acids in the chain and in the amino acid sequence. They also differ in their composition, that is, in the relative amounts of each amino acid. Myoglobin, for example, lacks the amino acid called cysteine, so its amino acid chain includes only nineteen of the twenty common amino acids. Collagen has a particularly bizarre amino acid composition: it lacks cysteine and another amino acid, tyrosine, and it is much richer than other proteins in the amino acids glycine (almost every third amino acid is glycine) and proline; moreover, it includes in its chain two amino acid variants, hydroxyproline and hydroxylysine, not found at all in other proteins.

AMINO ACID COMPOSITION OF PROTEINS

To determine the amino acid composition of a purified protein, the peptide bonds linking the amino acids must first be ruptured, and the amino acids then separated from each other and assayed (that is, the amount of each determined). The first step, breaking the peptide bonds, is easy. They are *hydrolyzed* (broken with the addition of the elements of water, H^+ and OH^-) by prolonged boiling of the protein in concentrated acid.

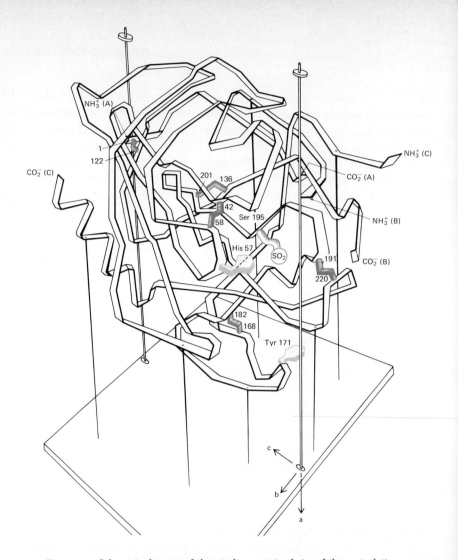

Figure 5-4 Schematic drawing of the winding protein chains of the proteolytic enzyme alpha chymotrypsin. This protein consists of three intertwined protein chains A, B, and C; the two ends of chain A are labeled NH_3^+ (A) and CO_2^- (A); the two ends of chain B are labeled NH_3^+ (B) and CO_2^- (B); and the two ends of chain C are labeled NH_3^+ (C) and CO_2^- (C). Tracing the protein chains with your finger from one end to the other makes their tortuous windings strikingly clear. *(From Nature,* **214:** 652 (1967), *courtesy D. M. Blow.)*

The second step, the separation of the amino acids, was enormously simplified in the early 1940s by improvements in a technique called *chromatography.* In paper chromatography, a mixture of substances, for example a mixture of amino acids, is placed in a spot near the bottom of a strip of paper. The bottom edge of the paper is then dipped into a solvent, which creeps up the paper, carrying along the substances in the mixture. The rate at which each substance moves up the paper depends on its solubility in the solvent.

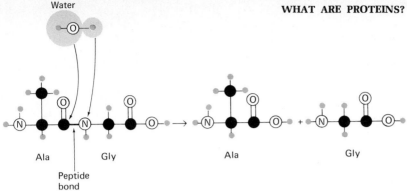

Figure 5-5   The amino acids linked together in a protein chain by peptide bonds may be separated by *hydrolysis,* meaning to break with the addition of the elements of water, H^+ and OH^-. The hydrolysis of a peptide bond is exactly the reverse of its formation (fig. 5-2). Hydrolysis can be accomplished by boiling in acid or by the action of proteolytic enzymes.

By using the appropriate solvent and a long enough piece of paper, complex mixtures can be separated. (Why does the length of the paper matter? Consider two cars which start off from the same place at slightly different speeds, say 20 and 25 miles/hour. After 1 hour, they are already 5 miles apart, but after 10 hours they are 50 miles apart. Like the cars, two substances can be separated better if they travel longer and therefore farther.)

It is easy to do paper chromatography; a strip of newspaper works very well for the separation of black ink into its component dyes. Since amino acids are colorless, they can be located only after spraying the paper with a chemical which combines with them to give a color. The intensity of the color at each spot provides a measure of the amount of the particular amino acid at that spot.

Chromatographic techniques greatly simplified the determination of the amino acid composition of proteins. In addition, they made possible what previously had seemed hopeless, the determination of the amino acid sequence of a protein. Frederick Sanger, an English biochemist, undertook this incredibly difficult task. He chose for study a tiny protein, insulin, molecular weight 5,733. Insulin is a hormone secreted by the pancreas; it regulates sugar metabolism in vertebrates, and is lacking in persons suffering from diabetes.

AMINO ACID SEQUENCE OF PROTEINS

How was the order of the fifty-one amino acids in insulin determined? A start was made by finding out which amino acids are at the ends of the protein chain. The terminal amino acid at one end has a free amino group, whereas the one at the other end has a free carboxylic acid group; they are therefore called the *N-terminal* and the *C-terminal* amino acids.

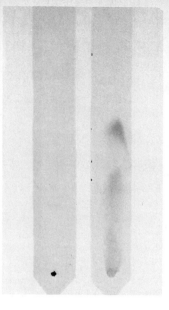

Figure 5-6 The paper chromatography of ink. A spot of black ink (Parker's Quink permanent black ink was used for this illustration) is dried on a strip of filter paper (or newspaper). The strip is hung in a tall covered jar containing a little water. As the water creeps up the paper, it separates the ink into its differently colored components.

Sanger found a chemical called DNP (for dinitrophenyl group) which attaches only to the N-terminal amino acid, to which it imparts a yellow color. It thereby enables the N-terminal amino acid to be distinguished from the others. Sanger ultimately worked out the sequence of insulin's fifty-one amino acids by a combination of paper chromatography, DNP, ingenuity, and perseverance.

To illustrate how the problem was attacked, let us determine the sequence of a little protein fragment consisting of six amino acids. The fragment is first treated with DNP and then hydrolyzed in boiling acid solution; the amino acids are now separated by paper chromatography. On the paper chromatogram there is one yellow spot, whose position indicates that it is the DNP derivative of the amino acid called serine. Thus, the N-terminal amino acid of the fragment is serine. Analysis of

Figure 5-7 A protein chain has, of course, two ends. The amino group of the last amino acid at one end is not engaged in a peptide bond; this end is called the N-terminal end. The carboxyl group of the last amino acid at the other end is also not engaged in a peptide bond; this end is called the C-terminal end.

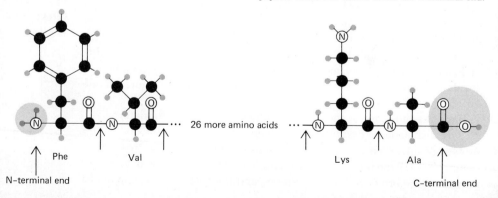

Phe   Val   26 more amino acids   Lys   Ala

N–terminal end   C-terminal end

the remaining spots on the paper reveals that the other amino acids in the fragment are alanine, glutamic acid, histidine, leucine, and valine. Making use of the abbreviations for the names of the amino acids, the fragment can now be designated

ser(ala,glu,his,leu,val)

Serine is written first because it is the N-terminal amino acid. The other amino acids, here written in alphabetic order, are placed between parentheses and separated by commas to indicate that their sequence is unknown. (Periods separating amino acids indicates that they are written in the known sequence.)

To find out the sequence of the remaining five amino acids, we start again. This time we hydrolyze the fragment incompletely by milder acid hydrolysis. Mild acid hydrolysis leaves some peptide bonds intact, thereby producing *all possible* little pieces of one, two, up to five amino acids. (Remember that there are vast numbers of molecules being hydrolyzed; in some, one bond is hydrolyzed, in some another. For example, incomplete hydrolysis of the three-amino-acid fragment ser.his.leu could hydrolyze the bond joining serine and histidine in one molecule, giving ser and his.leu, and hydrolyze the bond joining histidine and leucine in another molecule, giving ser.his and leu.)

Incomplete hydrolysis thus gives many little pieces, which are then treated with DNP and separated by paper chromatography. The N-terminal amino acid and the amino acid composition are determined for those pieces which can be purified in sufficiently large quantity—fortunately, it is not necessary to examine every one of the many possible pieces in order to determine the sequence. The complete method then is:

1. Determination of the N-terminal amino acid and the total amino acid composition gives

ser(ala,glu,his,leu,val)

2. Four pieces obtained by incomplete hydrolysis are

ser.his
his(leu,val,glu)
val.glu
val(glu,ala)

3. The deduced sequence is

ser.his.leu.val.glu.ala

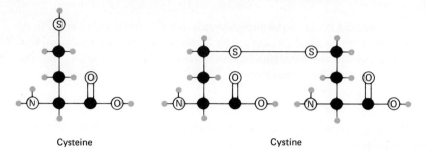

Cysteine   Cystine

Figure 5-8 The amino acid cysteine has a sulhydryl group —S—H. Oxidation of cysteine results in the loss of hydrogen atoms and the joining of two cysteine molecules by their sulfur atoms; the resulting double amino acid, called cystine, has a disulfide bond.

Amino Acid Sequence of Insulin

Determining the amino acid sequence of a little fragment of a protein is difficult. Establishing the amino acid sequence of an entire protein is clearly a tremendous job, even if the protein is small, like insulin. The first step in determining the sequence of insulin was to determine the overall amino acid composition and N-terminal amino acid. Two N-terminal amino acids were found. Thus it was discovered that insulin is made of two chains. They are attached together by *disulfide bonds*: the amino acid cysteine contains a sulfur atom which can bond to the sulfur atom of another cysteine, forming a two-sulfur, or disulfide, bond.

In many proteins, disulfide bonds between cysteines in two different amino acid chains link these chains together. They can also link together distant parts of a single chain, forming a loop. In insulin, the two chains are held together by two disulfide bonds. A third disulfide bond makes a loop in the shorter chain.

After breaking the disulfide bonds, the two chains were separated. Each was then incompletely hydrolyzed with acid, and fragments were analyzed using the method described above. (The fragment used as an example is part of the insulin molecule.)

The sequences of a number of long stretches of amino acids could now be pieced together, but there were still some gaps. A new trick had to be used. Instead of acid, the chains were hydrolyzed with the proteolytic enzymes trypsin, chymotrypsin, and pepsin. Proteolytic enzymes, like acid, break the peptide bonds which link amino acids together, but, unlike acid, they will not break all such bonds. Chymotrypsin, for example, breaks the protein chain only when it comes upon either of the amino acids tryptophan or tyrosine. The chain is therefore broken by enzymes into only a few large fragments. Determination of their N-terminal amino acid and amino acid composition provided sufficient information to fill in gaps and complete the sequence. All the little pieces obtained with acid and enzymes are shown in fig. 5-10.

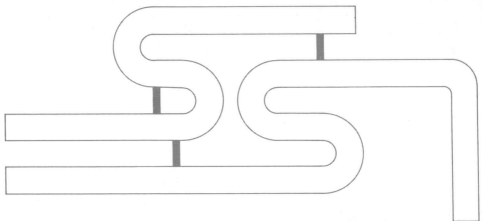

Figure 5-9 Insulin consists of a short and a long chain attached by two disulfide bonds. A third disulfide bond makes a loop in the short chain. In this schematic drawing, the disulfide bonds are indicated by bars.

But the structure was still incomplete! It remained to locate the disulfide bonds which attach the two insulin chains together and form the loop. Insulin contains six cysteine residues; they form three disulfide bonds. Is cysteine 1 attached to cysteine 2, 3, 4, 5, or 6?

When Sanger tried to find out, by acid hydrolysis of insulin whose disulfide bonds had not been broken beforehand, he found that cysteine 1 was attached in all possible ways, to cysteines 2, 3, 4, 5, *and* 6, as if the chains were attached together in all possible ways. He then discovered that, in acid, rearrangements were taking place between the disulfide bonds of different fragments. Finding a way to chemically inhibit these rearrangements and then determining the true arrangements turned out to be another big job.

Finally the task was done. For the first time a protein's amino acid sequence was known, its disulfide bonds located. This epochal achievement was the culmination of 10 years of work.

Amino Acid Sequences of Other Proteins

Six years after Sanger's success, the amino acid sequence of a second protein had been worked out. In 1960, insulin with 51 amino acids was joined by an enzyme called *ribonuclease* with 124 amino acids. W. H. Stein and S. Moore, who determined the order of the amino acids in ribonuclease, also invented a modification of the chromatographic techniques used to separate amino acids. As a result, the separation is now done automatically. Continued improvements in techniques have so simplified the job that the amino acid sequences of many proteins are now known. Comparing them has produced some surprises.

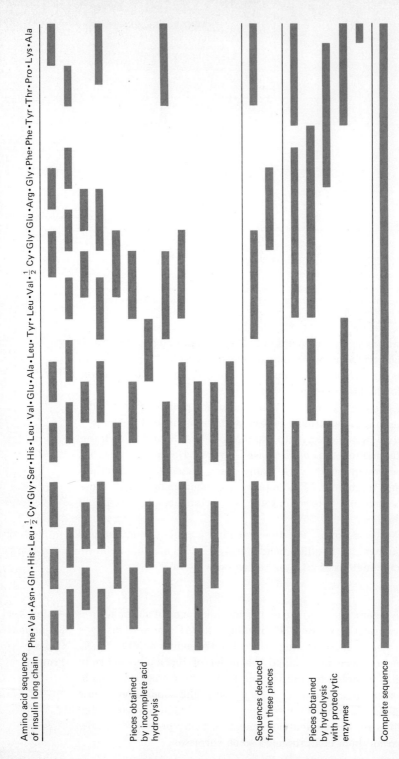

Figure 5-10 Determination of the amino acid sequence of the long chain of insulin. A host of small pieces obtained by acid hydrolysis of the long chain were analyzed. The amino acid sequences of five long segments could thereby be deduced; however, the order of these segments was unknown, and there were some gaps between them. Hydrolysis with various proteolytic enzymes yielded large pieces, whose analysis indicated the order of the segments and filled in the gaps.

Amino acid sequence of insulin long chain

Phe·Val·Asn·Gln·His·Leu·$\frac{1}{2}$Cy·Gly·Ser·His·Leu·Val·Glu·Ala·Leu·Tyr·Leu·Val·$\frac{1}{2}$Cy·Gly·Glu·Arg·Gly·Phe·Phe·Tyr·Thr·Pro·Lys·Ala

Pieces obtained by incomplete acid hydrolysis

Sequences deduced from these pieces

Pieces obtained by hydrolysis with proteolytic enzymes

Complete sequence

Figure 5-11 Frederick Sanger (1918–   ) was awarded the Nobel Prize in chemistry in 1958 for his outstanding achievement, the unraveling of the amino acid sequence of the protein insulin. *(Courtesy Central Office of Information.)*

Sanger had studied insulin from cows. Are all insulins the same? Sanger undertook a comparison of insulins obtained from cows, dogs, horses, humans, pigs, rabbits, sheep, and whales. He found that they are almost identical. All have fifty-one amino acids; of these, forty-seven are always the same. Would a change in any of these forty-seven amino acids lead to an insulin with impaired hormonal control of sugar metabolism? This is not known.

Different Insulins Are Not So Different

Figure 5-12 The complete amino acid sequence of insulin.

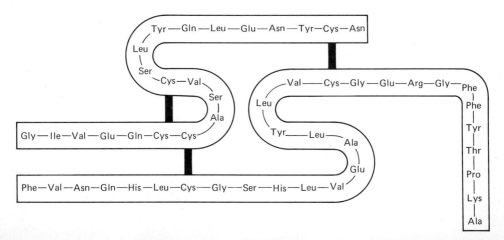

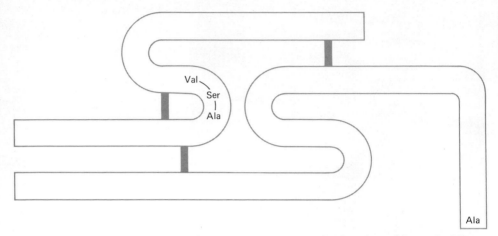

Figure 5-13 Sites of amino acid substitutions in insulins obtained from eight different animals: cows, dogs, horses, humans, pigs, rabbits, sheep, and whales. Of the fifty-one amino acids in insulin, only the four shown vary.

Sanger did find replacements of four of the fifty-one amino acids. The final, C-terminal, amino acid of insulin's long chain is almost always the amino acid alanine, but in man it is threonine, and in the rabbit it is serine. The other three variable amino acids are adjacent to each other within the loop made by a disulfide bond. In cows, the three amino acids in the loop are ala.ser.val. In other animals alanine is sometimes replaced by threonine, but by no other amino acid; serine may be replaced by glycine; and valine by either isoleucine or threonine. These are very limited changes indeed.

Species Differences between Proteins A comparison of the amino acid sequences of proteins from different species has shown that, in general, proteins which serve the same function are very much the same, no matter from what creature they come; more closely related species tend to have more similar proteins. Proteins are most similar if their biologic role is of great importance. (This is not surprising, for natural selection acts most powerfully on proteins with vital functions. The protein, that is, the amino acid sequence, which best fulfills such a function is strongly selected and maintained by the elimination of the disadvantaged individuals with a less efficient protein.)

A protein which has been found to be extraordinarily similar in many different species is the enzyme called *cytochrome c*. This enzyme plays a key role in mitochondria, trapping energy derived from the oxidation of acetate. Whether cytochrome c comes from a man or a mouse, from a chicken, a snake, a fly, a frog, or a fish, from cauliflower or wheat germ,

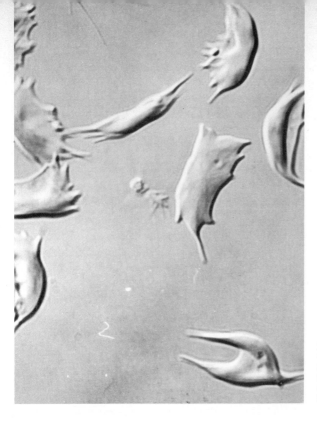

Figure 5-14 At low oxygen concentrations the red blood cells of persons with sickle-cell anemia assume the bizarre *sickled* shapes seen in this photograph. Normal red blood cells are round and more or less flat. *(Courtesy M. Bessis.)*

from bread mold or yeast, its structure is similar. Could this be fortuitous? In fact, it is considered one of the strongest pieces of evidence that all life on earth has a single common ancestor.

Normal red blood cells are round. The red blood cells of persons suffering from the inherited disease called *sickle-cell anemia** can assume a characteristic sickle shape. They sickle because they contain an abnormal hemoglobin which when it is not carrying oxygen tends to clump.

In 1949, the great American chemist Linus Pauling found a chemical difference between normal and sickle-cell hemoglobin: The normal hemoglobin is slightly more acidic. This seemed to mean that the normal hemoglobin contains more acidic amino acids than the sickle-cell hemoglobin. But Pauling could find no difference in their amino acid compositions—the techniques then available were not good enough to detect a change in one or two amino acids in a protein consisting of six hundred.

Finding the Differences between Hemoglobins

---

*In the United States, close to 10 percent of the black population are carriers of sickle-cell anemia; in parts of Africa, as much as 60 percent of the population carry the trait. Carriers, persons who inherit the sickle-cell trait from only one parent, do not suffer from the sickle-cell disease, as do the much rarer individuals who inherit the trait from both parents (these individuals usually die in childhood). The prevalence of this trait in Africa is explained by the relative immunity to malaria enjoyed by carriers.

In 1959, Vernon Ingram invented a special paper chromatographic technique for detecting small amino acid differences between proteins, a shortcut to determining the entire amino acid sequence. It is called *fingerprinting*. First Ingram prepared a *tryptic hydrolysate* by hydrolyzing hemoglobin with the proteolytic enzyme trypsin. Trypsin only breaks the protein chain next to either of two amino acids, lysine or arginine.

Since there are thirty lysine and arginines in hemoglobin, the protein is broken by trypsin into thirty-one fragments. But that is too many to be separated by ordinary paper chromatography because many of the thirty-one spots would overlap. So Ingram first applied an electric field to a wet square of paper in a corner of which his tryptic hydrolysate had been spotted. The distance that each fragment moves along the edge of the paper then depends on its electric charge, that is, how acidic or basic it is. Ingram then turned the paper by 90° and further separated the fragments by ordinary chromatography, which depends on differences in solubility.

When Ingram prepared fingerprints from both normal and sickle-cell hemoglobin, he found that almost all the spots were the same. But one spot on the normal-hemoglobin fingerprint was missing from the sickle-cell-hemoglobin fingerprint, where it was replaced by a new spot. The difference in their positions indicated that the normal spot was more acidic than the spot from sickle-cell hemoglobin, just as Pauling had predicted.

Following Sanger's techniques, Ingram then determined the amino acid sequences of the fragments of hemoglobin in the normal and aberrant spots. They differed in one amino acid. An acidic amino acid, glutamic acid, is replaced by a neutral amino acid, valine, in sickle-cell hemoglobin.

Figure 5-15 Fingerprinting is a technique for separating complex mixtures of protein fragments. *(a)* The solution of partially hydrolyzed protein is spotted in a corner of a large square of filter paper; an electric field is then applied to the paper. *(b)* The dissolved protein fragments move along the paper at a rate which is proportional to their charge, that is, to their acidity or alkalinity. *(c)* The paper is then turned by 90°, and the fragments are further separated by ordinary paper chromatography according to their solubility in the solvent used.

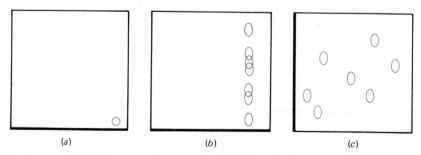

(a)　　　　　　　(b)　　　　　　　(c)

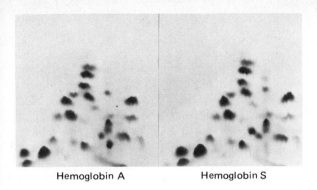

Hemoglobin A   Hemoglobin S

Hemoglobin A   Hemoglobin S

Figure 5-16 Fingerprints of protein fragments obtained by tryptic hydrolysis of normal hemoglobin, hemoglobin A, and hemoglobin obtained from a person suffering from sickle-cell anemia, hemoglobin S. Almost all the spots, each of which corresponds to a fragment of protein, are the same in the two fingerprints. However, one spot in the hemoglobin A fingerprint is missing from the hemoglobin S fingerprint, where it is replaced by a new spot. *(Courtesy Vernon Ingram.)*

Persons who inherit the fatal disease sickle-cell anemia inherit a hemoglobin containing one wrong amino acid:

Hemoglobin A (Normal)	val.his.leu.thr.pro.*glu*.glu.lys
Hemoglobin S (Sickle-cell)	val.his.leu.thr.pro.*val*.glu.lys

Ingram then examined the hemoglobin of patients with another inherited anemia. He found that the same glutamic acid was replaced by lysine. This, however, has not turned out to be the only possible place in the hemoglobin molecule for amino acid replacements. In the 100 abnormal hemoglobins which have now been studied there are many.

Amino Acid Replacements

The amino acid replacements which have been found in abnormal hemoglobins are restricted. Let us take a closer look at the various amino acids. All have a carboxylic acid group and an amine. These two reactive groups join to form the peptide bonds which link each amino acid to its neighbors. A protein is a chain of peptide bonds from which project the different amino acid *residues,* the part of each amino acid which is not involved in a peptide bond.

Two of the amino acids, glutamic acid and aspartic acid, have acidic residues, for they have a second carboxylic acid group; these amino acids make a protein acidic. Several amino acids have basic residues; most are neutral. Of the twenty amino acids commonly found in proteins, nine have water-soluble residues which tend to make proteins water-soluble. These include the acidic and basic amino acids, as well as some others. These nine amino acids are shown on lines 4 and 5 of fig. 5-1. Eleven amino acids have water-insoluble residues, usually hydrocarbons with only hydrogen and carbon atoms. These amino acids, whose structures are shown on the first three lines in fig. 5-1, tend to make proteins insoluble in water.

Nearly all the 100 amino acid replacements which have now been discovered in abnormal hemoglobins involve water-soluble amino acids. Why are abnormal hemoglobins with replacements of water-insoluble amino acids so rare? Such hemoglobin molecules, it has been discovered, function so badly that they are unable to transport oxygen.

Until very recently it was impossible to appreciate the role of the water-insoluble residues in proteins. Today, however, the complete three-dimensional structures of some proteins, including hemoglobin, are known. Their folded protein chains are held in place in large part by interactions of water-insoluble residues. Exchanging these residues leads to molecular catastrophe.

THE THREE-DIMENSIONAL STRUCTURE OF PROTEINS

No microscope is good enough to reveal the winding chains of a protein. So how is a protein's three-dimensional structure determined?

At the beginning of this century, the physicist Max von Laue (1879–1960) discovered that a beam of x-rays is *diffracted*, that is, broken into parts, when it passes through a crystal. This finding, for which Laue was honored with the Nobel Prize in physics in 1914, was extremely important for an understanding of the nature of x-rays: It proved that they are similar to light. Sir Lawrence Bragg (1890–1971) and his father, Sir William Bragg (1862–1942), realized that x-ray diffraction not only reveals the nature of x-rays but also provides a powerful tool for studying the structure of the crystals themselves. Out of their work has developed the technique called *x-ray crystallography,* by means of which the three-dimensional structures of molecules are determined.

Structure Determination by X-ray Crystallography

A requirement for determining the structure of a substance by x-ray crystallography is that the substance be crystalline. In a crystal, atoms are arranged in a regularly repeating pattern in three dimensions. In the very simple arrangement found in a crystal of table salt, for example, each sodi-

Figure 5-17 Sir Lawrence Bragg received the Nobel Prize in physics in 1915, at the age of 25, jointly with his father, Sir William Bragg, for the x-ray analysis of crystal structure. Sir Lawrence Bragg died in 1971, at the age of 81, having lived to see x-ray crystallography, the science he had created when a young man, revolutionize mineralogy, metallurgy, chemistry, and, perhaps more than all others, molecular biology. *(Courtesy the Nobel Foundation.)*

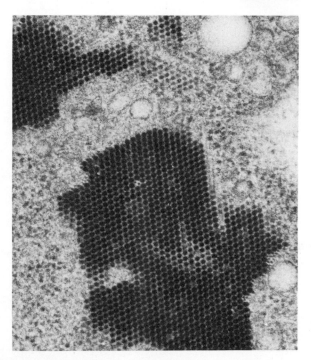

Figure 5-18 In a crystal, atoms are arranged in a regularly repeating pattern. The figure shows a crystal of polio virus in an infected cell. *(From S. Dales et al., Virology,* **26:**379 (1965), *courtesy Samuel Dales.)*

um ion is surrounded by six chloride ions: one above, one below, one to the right, one to the left, one in front, and one in back. This also describes each chloride ion: it is surrounded in the same way by six sodium ions.

If you look at this crystalline arrangement in certain directions, up, down, diagonally, or toward the front or back, you see sodium ions at regularly repeating distances. In any crystal, no matter how complicated the molecule and the arrangement of molecules, this is true for every atom: In certain directions each is found again and again at regularly repeating intervals. The repeating atoms in a crystal can be arranged on parallel planes, and this can be done in various ways. Three possible arrangements, that is, three *sets of parallel planes,* in a crystal of sodium chloride are illustrated in fig. 5-19.

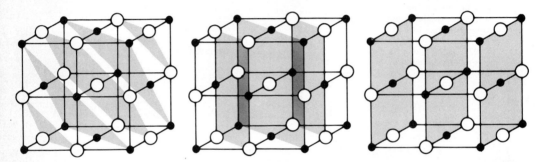

Figure 5-19 Illustration of the arrangement of atoms in a crystal of sodium chloride. The repeating atoms can be arranged in various ways on parallel planes. Three such arrangements, that is, three sets of parallel planes, are shown.

Figure 5-20 Pattern of spots produced by x-rays which have passed through a crystal of the protein myoglobin. *(Courtesy John Kendrew.)*

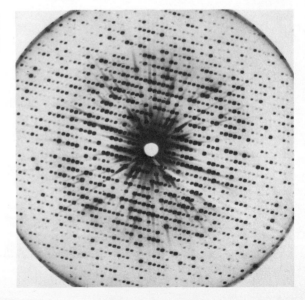

Figure 5-21 Linus Pauling (1901–   )
has not only made many brilliant
contributions to chemistry. He has also
been outspoken on scientific issues of
public concern. That the dangers of
radioactive fallout are widely recognized,
for example, is due in large part to his
efforts. Pauling was honored with the
Nobel Prize for chemistry in 1954 for his
work on the chemical bond and with the
Nobel Prize for peace in 1962. *(Courtesy
the Nobel Foundation.)*

Figure 5-22 A hydrogen bond can bind a hydrogen which has a slight positive charge,
such as a hydrogen bonded to a nitrogen atom, to an atom with a slight negative charge,
such as an oxygen atom. The hydrogen bond is relatively weak; it can be broken by
about one-tenth the energy required to break an average covalent bond.

When a beam of x-rays passes through a crystal, the sets of parallel
planes act like sets of mirrors placed at different angles; they reflect
some of the beam's rays in different directions. If a photographic film is
mounted behind the crystal, a very intense central spot caused by the
direct beam is surrounded by many small spots, the reflections from the
sets of parallel planes of atoms. By measuring the position and the intensity, or darkness, of each spot, and by a combination of complicated calculations and intelligent guesses, the pattern of repeating atoms in the
crystal and thus the structure of the molecules in the crystal can be
figured out—if the molecule is a simple one. Protein molecules are
not.

Nevertheless, in 1951 Linus Pauling was able to make some predictions
about protein structure after he and a group of coworkers at Caltech had
spent 15 years making x-ray crystallographic studies of simple molecules,
such as amino acids and pairs of amino acids united by a peptide bond.
Pauling's proposed structures depend on the attraction between the oxygen atom of one peptide bond and the amino hydrogen of another.

**The Alpha Helix
and the
Antiparallel
Pleated Sheet**

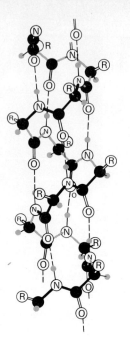

Figure 5-24 The super-coiled coil is made of protein molecules coiled into the alpha-helix configuration. A central alpha helix is surrounded by six coiled coils, each consisting of two alpha helices wound round each other.

This attraction, called a *hydrogen bond,* is very weak, much weaker than an ionic or covalent bond. However, Pauling calculated that certain structures would be stable because many hydrogen bonds would reinforce each other. One such structure is a coil called the *alpha helix.*

It was soon demonstrated by x-ray crystallography that the keratin of hair is coiled into the alpha helix predicted by Pauling. Hair, as proposed both by Pauling and by Francis Crick of Cambridge, England, is a super-coiled coil; it is made up of protein cables, each a central alpha helix surrounded by six coiled coils consisting of two alpha helices coiled around each other. The flagellum, or long tail, which moves certain bacteria through water makes use of an even superer coil, a seven-strand cable of seven-strand cables.

The amino acid chains of the round, or globular, proteins, such as the enzymes, are only coiled in some parts of the chain. The enzyme alpha chymotrypsin, for example, has only one alpha-helical region, at the C-terminal end of the so-called *C chain* [designated $CO_2(C)$ in fig. 5-4].

Pauling also proposed that, besides stabilizing the alpha helix, hydrogen bonds hold together different chains and distant parts of single chains. This type of structure, in which protein chains are held parallel, is called the *antiparallel pleated sheet.* The antiparallel pleated sheet had been rather neglected by protein chemists because it was thought to exist in only a few fibrous proteins and not in the more interesting globular proteins.

But the protein chemists were mistaken. Every wind and turn of the protein chain of a number of globular proteins is now known, and in some there is almost as much antiparallel pleated sheet as alpha helix. The

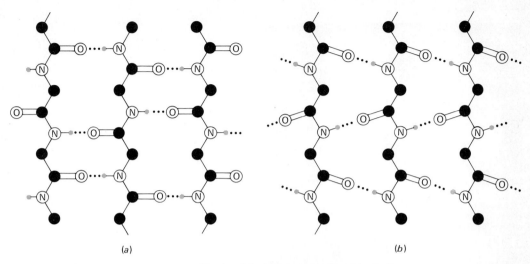

(a)   (b)

Figure 5-25 These two protein structures, like the alpha helix, were proposed by Pauling and are maintained by hydrogen bonds between the amine hydrogens and the oxygens of peptide bonds; they bind parallel protein chains together. Structure (a) is called the antiparallel pleated sheet, structure (b) the parallel pleated sheet.

two structures serve different functions. The alpha helix gives rigidity to sections of the protein chain. The antiparallel pleated sheet binds portions of a chain together. Moreover, previously unsuspected modifications of these parallel and helical structures have been found. They also help to maintain the three-dimensional conformation of proteins.

With his proposals of the alpha helix and the antiparallel pleated sheet, Pauling took the first giant step toward solving the mystery of the three-dimensional structures of proteins. But the x-ray crystallographic methods available to Pauling were hopelessly inadequate for unraveling the structures of the globular proteins. New techniques in protein chemistry had to be developed, as well as new techniques in x-ray crystallography. Credit for these goes to Max Perutz and John Kendrew of Cambridge, England, who solved the first structures, those of hemoglobin and myoglobin.

In 1957, the fuzzy outlines of a protein's form were first glimpsed. The protein was myoglobin, the oxygen storer of muscle. The investigator was John Kendrew, who saw for the first time the way a protein chain twists, goes off in a straight line, then turns and changes direction, and on and on to form a sort of ball. He could not yet see which segments were coiled into an alpha helix, for his x-ray crystallographic data were still inadequate; but he could see, cradled in that complicated structure, the small iron-containing molecule called *heme,* to which the oxygen is bound.

The Structure of Globular Proteins

Figure 5-26 John Kendrew (1917–   ), English x-ray crystallographer, was the first to work out the three-dimensional structure of a protein, myoglobin. This success was achieved by analyzing the spots produced by x-rays passing through crystals of myoglobin (fig. 5-20) and of chemically modified myoglobin. Analysis of many tens of thousands of spots and the use of the fastest computers has produced a detailed model in which the position in space of almost every one of myoglobin's 2,600 atoms is known. *(Courtesy Medical Research Council, Cambridge, England.)*

Figure 5-27 Max Perutz (1914–   ), pioneer in the field of the x-ray crystallographic determination of protein structure, completed the three-dimensional structure of hemoglobin in 1968. In 1962, Perutz and Kendrew shared the Nobel Prize in chemistry, awarded in honor of their spectacular achievements, which opened the way to a detailed understanding of the functioning of proteins. *(Courtesy Medical Research Council, Cambridge, England.)*

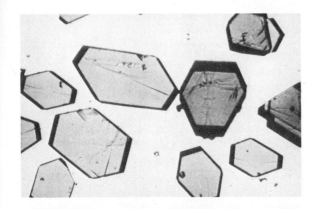

Figure 5-28 Crystals of myoglobin such as these were the starting point for the determination of the complete structure of this protein. *(Courtesy John Kendrew.)*

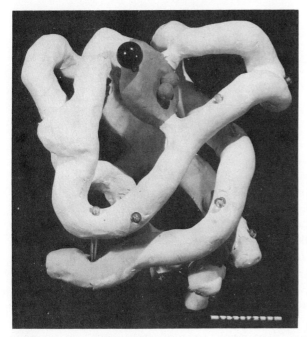

Figure 5-29 Early model of the myoglobin molecule. The twisting of the protein chain is visible, but the position of individual amino acids, as well as many other details of the structure, are missing. The darker colored object is the heme molecule, which holds on to an atom of iron in its center; an oxygen molecule, represented by the two balls, binds to the iron atom. (The shiny ball represents an atom of a heavy metal which was introduced chemically into the myoglobin, a prerequisite for solving the structure.) *(Courtesy John Kendrew.)*

By 1961, Kendrew knew the position of almost every one of the 2,600 atoms in the myoglobin molecule. In 1968, the pioneer in this field, Max Perutz—after 30 years of work—completed the structure of hemoglobin, four times bigger than myoglobin and therefore many times more difficult.

Hemoglobin and myoglobin perform similar functions—both bind oxygen. They have chemical similarities—both enclose an iron-containing heme molecule. However, whereas myoglobin consists of only one protein chain, hemoglobin is composed of four chains, two each of two

Figure 5-30 Detailed model of the structure of myoglobin. *(Courtesy John Kendrew.)*

somewhat different kinds. Each of the two types of hemoglobin chain is similar in size to a complete myoglobin molecule; each contains a heme; and each can bind one molecule of oxygen. Myoglobin and both types of hemoglobin chain have turned out to have very similar amino acid sequences and three-dimensional forms.

In 1964, Sir Lawrence Bragg said, "It will be very interesting to see how long it will be before any other laboratory produces a molecular model of a protein with the wealth of detail now firmly established for myoglobin. My guess . . . is that it will be between 5 and 10 years. . . ." Only 2 years later, in 1966, and in Bragg's own laboratory, the structure of an enzyme, lysozyme, had been worked out in as great detail. Lysozyme is found in tissues, in tears, and in egg white; it lyses, or dissolves, many bacteria by hydrolyzing one of the substances in their cell wall.

Progress has continued at an astounding rate. The complete amino acid sequence and the windings of the amino acid chain are now known for a dozen proteins. As a result, some generalizations can be made about protein structure.

Proteins Are Compact. Proteins are extremely compact molecules. In the accompanying illustrations of protein structure, only the windings of the protein backbone, the chain of peptide bonds, are shown; the amino acid residues which bristle off this backbone are omitted. If they were drawn in, it would be impossible to see anything, for the space would be entirely filled up. Proteins, it turns out, are an almost solid mass, with no space in the middle. Even a water molecule is too big to fit inside most of them.

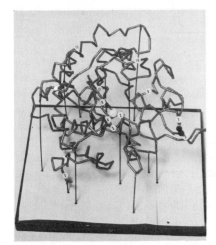 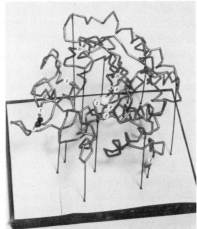

Figure 5-31 The protein chain of the proteolytic enzyme carboxypeptidase (each short rod represents an amino acid). The active site of this enzyme contains an atom of zinc, the white sphere in the model. A disulfide bond is indicated by two black spheres. As is now common practice, these stereo figures were drawn by computer. *(From J. A. Hartsuck and W. N. Lipscomb, Carboxypeptidase A, in "The Enzymes," vol. 3, 3d ed., 1971, Academic, New York, courtesy W. N. Lipscomb.)* For instructions on how to view these photographs, see fig. 3-25, p. 69.

Proteins Are Dry Inside. A second generalization about protein structure is that the inside of a protein is water-insoluble, for only water-insoluble amino acids are found there. Why should this be so? The winding protein chain is not held in place by strong ionic interactions between water-soluble amino acid residues. Rather, the three-dimensional structure is maintained by a subtle combination of two kinds of forces. Hydrogen bonds between the oxygen and nitrogen atoms of more or less distant peptide bonds maintain the alpha-helix and antiparallel-pleated-sheet structures proposed by Pauling, as well as variations of these structures. The accumulation of extremely weak attractions between the multitude of water-insoluble amino acid residues is the other major force holding the protein chain in place. This is the same attraction which holds an oil droplet together. Globular proteins, then, are like oil droplets.

The water-insoluble interior of a protein molecule repels the water in which the protein bathes, creating a dry internal environment. In some proteins, this is particularly advantageous. In hemoglobin the iron atom can be maintained in the proper state to bind oxygen because buried within the molecule it is protected from water. In the case of at least one enzyme, lysozyme, a dry environment is necessary for catalytic activity.

Proteins Are Wet Outside. Oil droplets are insoluble in water; proteins are soluble. Why? Because water-soluble amino acids form a coat around the insoluble center. This, then, is another generalization about proteins: Water-soluble amino acid residues are on the outside, on the surface of the molecule.

Why denatured proteins, such as cooked egg-white albumin, are insoluble in water is now easy to understand. It has long been known that denatured proteins have lost their normal three-dimensional conformation, becoming like a piece of cooked spaghetti. The many water-insoluble amino acid residues which were hidden inside are thereby exposed, making the protein much less water-soluble.

Dry on the inside, holding them together, and wet on the outside, making them water-soluble, this will probably turn out to describe all globular proteins. However, each protein has its own particular function to perform, and this means slight variations on the general plan. For example, within the hemoglobin molecule are two water-soluble amino acid residues. Their special function is to hold on to the iron-containing heme

Figure 5-32 The thin filament in muscle myofibrils consists of intertwined chains of molecules of the protein actin. *(a)* Electron micrograph of thin filament. *(From P. B. Moore et al., J. Mol. Biol.* **50:**279 (1970).) *(b)* Model of the structure of thin filament in which each sphere represents a molecule of actin. *(From H. E. Huxley and W. Brown, J. Mol. Biol.,* **30:**383 (1967), *courtesy H. E. Huxley.)*

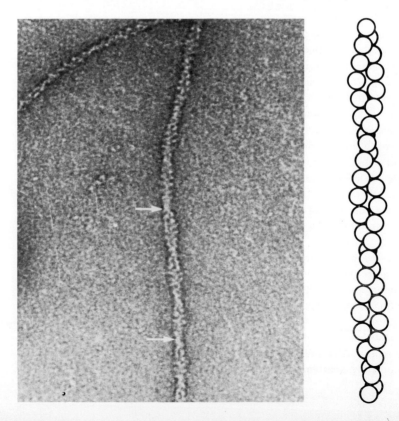

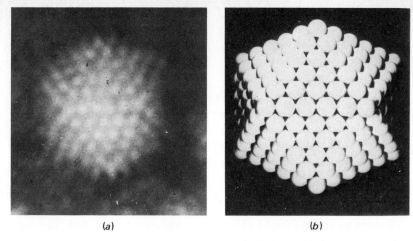

(a)   (b)

Figure 5-33 Viruses have an outer protein coat which frequently consists of a relatively simple arrangement of protein molecules. *(a)* Electron micrograph of an adenovirus, which causes upper respiratory-tract infections; *(b)* model of the structure of the adenovirus protein coat, which consists of 252 subunits called capsomers, represented in the model as spheres. Of these capsomers, 240, located on the faces and edges of the icosahedral virus, consist of six protein molecules; the remaining 12 capsomers, located at the apexes of the icosahedron, consist of five protein molecules. *(Courtesy R. W. Horne.)*

molecule. The same two amino acids serve the same function in myoglobin. Inside some enzymes have been found one or two water-soluble amino acids which serve special catalytic or structural functions.

Some Proteins Stick Together. The role of the surface amino acids can be discerned only in the case of hemoglobin. Some serve to make hemoglobin water-soluble. Others serve a different function: In hemoglobin the four chains, each folded into a ball, must stick together, and this involves surface interactions. The identical chains are bound together by interactions of water-soluble residues; the unlike chains by interactions of water-insoluble residues.

Among the 100 abnormal hemoglobins which are now known, some have been found in which a surface water-soluble amino acid which helps to solubilize the protein is replaced by another. Many of these exchanges have little effect on the functioning of hemoglobin. On the other hand, replacement of an amino acid responsible for holding chains together, like replacement of an internal amino acid, is very serious, often resulting in a nonfunctional molecule.

The functioning of many proteins depends on surface interactions. Hemoglobin is only one among those which consist of subunits, that is, folded protein chains which must stick together properly if the protein is to do its job properly. Certain enzymes with especially complex functions also consist, like hemoglobin, of subunits.

Surface interactions may cause protein molecules to cohere, forming large structural and functional units. The thin filaments of muscle myofibrils consist of two intertwined chains of actin molecules. Some viruses are spheres or cylinders of protein molecules stuck together in a precise way. Groups of enzymes sometimes cohere, forming multifunctional units. Enzymes may also be bound by surface interactions to fixed cell structures, thereby keeping them where they are needed in the cell; an example is the membrane-bound ATP-generating group of enzymes in mitochondria. The surface interactions of proteins are clearly of great importance; nevertheless, little is yet known about what makes proteins stick together.

How Enzymes Catalyze Reactions

How does an enzyme work? A substrate undergoes a reaction (hydrogen peroxide decomposes into water and oxygen gas, for example). When that reaction is catalyzed by an enzyme (such as catalase), the enzyme first combines with the substrate, which is bound to the enzyme's active site. How does this happen, and how does the enzyme catalyze the reaction? In order to find out, it has been necessary to determine not only the structure of enzymes but also the structure of enzymes combined with their substrates.

What does the enzyme's active site look like? As had been suspected, the folding of the protein creates a surface groove, or depression, which complements the shape of the substrate. The folding is so tortuous that very distant amino acids are brought together in the active site. In one enzyme, ribonuclease, amino acids 12 and 119 in the chain are found in the active site; in another, the proteolytic enzyme chymotrypsin, amino acids 16, 57, and 195 are found there (see fig. 5-4).

The amino acid residues in the active site have different roles. Some have a catalytic function. Others impart the right fit and chemically attract the various parts of the substrate molecule, holding it in place. In the hydrolytic enzyme lysozyme, amino acids 62, 63, and 108 are important in binding the substrate; amino acids 35 and 52 catalyze the hydrolysis.

The shape of the site may not be a perfect complement to the shape of the substrate. In some cases the active site deforms the substrate, forcing it out of its normal three-dimensional shape. When this happens, the new shape facilitates the chemical reaction which is to take place. At the same time, the binding of the substrate may deform the protein molecule, which then also changes shape. Hemoglobin (which is not an enzyme, for it catalyzes no chemical reaction, but which in certain respects behaves like one) is deformed when the first molecule of oxygen is bound to one of the four subunits. This makes it much easier for the next three oxygens to be bound and helps elucidate hemoglobin's sensitivity to slight variations in oxygen concentration.

In the case of the hydrolytic enzyme lysozyme, the deformation of the protein explains, at least in part, the mechanism of catalysis. When the

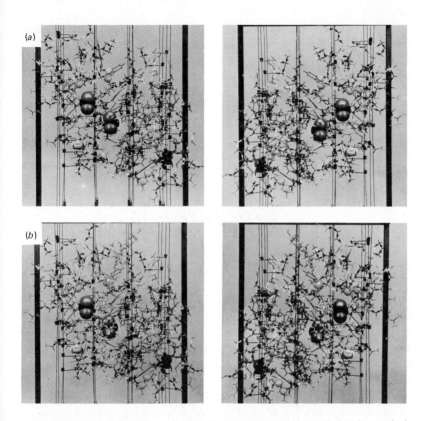

Figure 5-34 Lysozyme is an enzyme found in egg white, in tears, and elsewhere, which lyses many kinds of bacteria. It accomplishes this by hydrolyzing a component of the bacterial cell wall; this component is a polysaccharide, that is, a polymer of sugar molecules. *(a)* A model of the lysozyme molecule. The active site is a deep cleft in which the polysaccharide substrate fits. Among the amino acid residues which line the cleft are three tryptophan residues, amino acids 62, 63, and 108 in the protein chain, which bind the substrate; two acidic residues, glutamic acid 35 and aspartic acid 52, catalyze the hydrolysis (their carboxylic acid groups are greatly exaggerated in the model). *(b)* A model of lysozyme with substrate bound in the cleft, the active site. The cleft accommodates six linked sugar molecules, indicated by A, B, C, D, E, and F in the model. The bond linking sugars D and E is broken in the hydrolysis reaction. *(Courtesy D. C. Phillips.)* For instructions on how to view these photographs, see Fig. 3-25, p. 69.

substrate enters the active site, the enzyme changes shape slightly, closing down like a mouth on the substrate molecule. Two acidic amino acid residues are thereby brought very close to the bond which will be hydrolyzed; they do the catalyzing. This enzymatic hydrolysis is then a very special case of the chemist's everyday technique of adding acid to catalyze a hydrolysis (an example is the acid hydrolysis of insulin used by Sanger), but the chemist must add countless acid molecules to his solution to make it sufficiently acidic. The enzyme accomplishes the same thing with just two acidic amino acid residues. They are able to function in a neutral liquid because the protein molecule of which they are a part surrounds them with a dry microenvironment.

Like many other enzymes, lysozyme does something else which is completely beyond the chemist. Its substrate contains many bonds which can be hydrolyzed and which would be hydrolyzed in an acidic solution, but the enzyme hydrolyzes just one. This is possible because when the enzyme changes shape, closing down upon the substrate molecule, the two acidic residues are brought to bear on only one of the many hydrolyzable bonds.

Many Problems Remain

Are all substrates deformed when they enter an enzyme's active site? Are all enzymes deformed by the binding of the substrate? At present it is not possible to generalize, for the structures of too few enzymes and too few enzyme-substrate complexes are known. If such deformations turn out to be the rule, perhaps it will also turn out that they explain an extraordinary characteristic of enzymes—their efficiency. Enzyme catalysis increases reaction speeds phenomenally. Nobody is yet sure how, but enzymologists now hope within the next 10 years to fathom their fabulous catalytic power.

The effort to elucidate the structure of proteins continues. However, many proteins are too big or for other reasons are still beyond present-day x-ray crystallographic techniques. Antibodies, for example, have molecular weights of about 160,000. Despite this, progress with these

Figure 5-35 The active site of carboxypeptidase A. This proteolytic enzyme hydrolyzes the last peptide bond of proteins, releasing the C-terminal amino acid. (a) The active site of carboxypeptidase includes an atom of zinc (Zn), which is held in the protein structure by three amino acids, histidine 69 (his 69), glutamic acid 72 (glu 72), and histidine 196 (his 196); a molecule of water, not shown, is also bound to the zinc atom. One of the basic nitrogen atoms of arginine 145 is hydrogen-bonded to the oxygen in the peptide bond between amino acids 155 and 156. Note also the uptilted ring structure in tyrosine 248 (try 248). (The complete structure of this enzyme is shown in fig. 5-31.) Above and to the left is a substrate of the enzyme (drawn with black bonds), two amino acids, glycine (gly) and tyrosine (tyr) joined by a peptide bond (arrow). (b) The substrate has moved into the active site of carboxypeptidase, which can now hydrolyze the peptide bond (arrow) joining the glycine and tyrosine. The zinc atom has become bonded to the oxygen of this peptide bond (replacing the water molecule which had been bound to the zinc atom). The ring of tyrosine 248 has bent down so that its hydroxyl group is hydrogen-bonded to the nitrogen of the peptide bond. The zinc atom and this hydroxyl are thus the actual catalysts. Two basic nitrogen atoms or arginine 145 are bound to the acidic carboxyl group of the substrate's tyrosine residue; thus only a C-terminal amino acid, with its free carboxyl group, will be bound in the active site. (From D. M. Blow and T. A. Steitz, Ann. Rev. Biochem., **1970**: 63, courtesy D. M. Blow.)

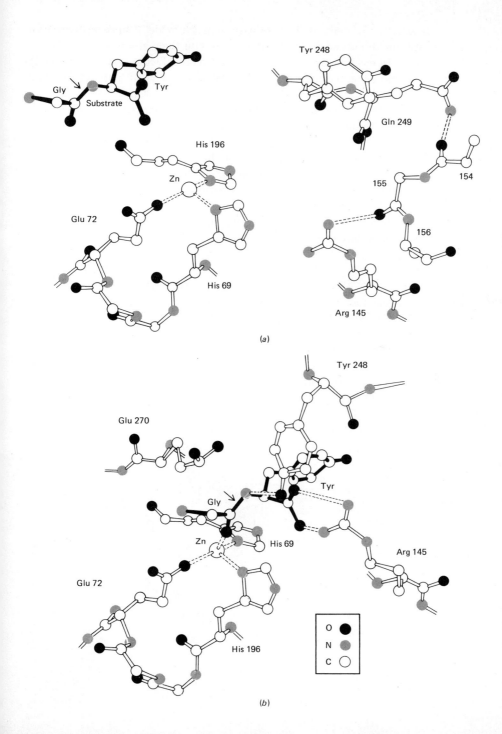

(a)

(b)

fascinating proteins will doubtlessly now be made at an ever-increasing rate, for the other grave stumbling block to their study has been overcome: Homogeneous antibodies, every molecule the same, are finally available, obtained from tissue cultures of pure lines of antibody-producing cells.

But perhaps all this work on the three-dimensional structure of proteins tells us nothing about the structure of proteins in living organisms. The x-ray crystallographic technique, which seems to give such astounding insights, can only be applied to crystallized proteins. In a cell, proteins are not crystalline, they are dissolved. Fortunately, there are reasons to believe that a crystalline protein is not very different in structure from the dissolved protein. Many enzymes have passed the most exacting test known—they can catalyze their particular reaction, though slowly, even when they are part of a crystal.

HOW ARE PROTEINS MADE?

Cells contain thousands of different proteins, each unique in its amino acid sequence and form. How are all these proteins synthesized?

The first step, the synthesis of the amino acids, is easily understood. Each amino acid is the end product of a series of enzyme-catalyzed reactions; many of the hundreds required to synthesize the twenty amino acids are known. Their synthesis is basically no different from that of a sugar, a fat, a pigment, or any other small molecule.

The final step, the folding of the protein chain into its active three-dimensional form, happens all by itself. It will even happen in a test tube. A protein can be denatured by adding huge concentrations of cer-

Figure 5-36 A normal folded protein whose three-dimensional shape is in part maintained by disulfide bonds can be transformed into a spaghettilike protein chain by appropriate substances (urea and mercaptoethanol). This open chain can undergo spontaneous reformation of disulfide bonds and refolding to regenerate the normal folded protein.

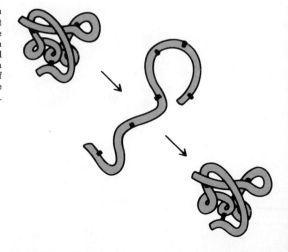

tain salts. The disulfide bonds which hold chains together or make loops in chains can be broken by the addition of other chemicals. If now the chemicals are removed very carefully, under just the right conditions, the spaghettilike protein chains reform their disulfide bonds and regain a three-dimensional structure.

Despite the many possibilities, only the correct disulfide bonds form. Despite the infinite possibilities, only the correct three-dimensional structure is remade by the folding chains. The result, then, is exactly the normal protein. Again, renatured enzymes pass the most exacting test—they have enzymatic activity. This proves that protein structure depends entirely on amino acid sequence.

And there lies the problem. How is the sequence of amino acids specified for each of thousands of proteins? How does a cell know that in a particular protein the amino acid glycine must be amino acid 294 in the chain, to be followed by a histidine, for example? This is the crucial step in protein synthesis: the specification of amino acid sequence.

All cells contain the information needed for the synthesis of their proteins. Moreover, they pass this information on to their progeny when they divide, for the daughter cells also know how to synthesize their proteins. And that information is passed on very precisely. The person who has inherited sickle-cell anemia has inherited information containing one error—in one of his hemoglobin chains the amino acid glutamic acid which should be at position 6 is replaced by the amino acid valine. The information for the synthesis of cytochrome c has been passed along from generation to generation for such a long time that it is now found, more or less unchanged, in all living organisms. From an evolutionary point of view, this protein has remained recognizably the same for over 1 billion years!

How is this possible? How is the amino acid sequence of a protein specified, and how is this information transmitted from mother cell to daughter cells during cell division? The answer to these questions, when it was discovered, provided the foundation for a chemical understanding of life and was the beginning of a new field of research, molecular biology. That answer was the outcome of a century of research in *genetics,* the study of heredity.

WHAT DO GENES DO?

Like produces like. The statuesque brunette's baby, the image of his mother, grows up tall, dark, and handsome. He may also be clever and become bald like his father, love music and have hay fever like his mother, and look at the world through blue eyes like both of them. Offspring resemble their parents, as everybody knows—though only a few inherit money, everyone inherits his nose.

GENES AND HEREDITY   The science of genetics has to its credit one of the most brilliant and consequential achievements of biology, the unraveling of the mechanism of inheritance. At first inspection, inheritance appears to be utterly confused, irregular, and haphazard. Offspring are not simply mosaics, traits of the mother and traits of the father put together in a straightforward way. Some traits disappear, and others seem to come from nowhere.

But in fact all traits come from somewhere, from parents, grandparents, great grandparents. Moreover, it has been discovered that the way they are passed on from generation to generation is described by straight-forward rules, the fundamental laws of genetics. How has the transmission of inherited characters been untangled? By studying, at least for a start, the inheritance of just one trait at a time.

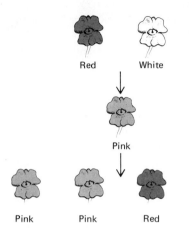

Red   White

Pink

Pink   Pink   Red   White

Figure 6-1 A red-flowered snapdragon mated to a white-flowered snapdragon gives all pink-flowered offspring. A pink-flowered snapdragon, if self-fertilized or crossed to another pink-flowered snapdragon, gives mostly pink-flowered but also some red- and some white-flowered snapdragons. *(Adapted from Paul B. Weisz, "The Science of Biology," 3d ed., McGraw-Hill, New York, 1967, by permission of McGraw-Hill.)*

A simple but telling experiment can be performed with the common garden flower the snapdragon. If a red-flowered snapdragon is mated, that is, *crossed,* with a white-flowered snapdragon, the seeds obtained from this cross grow into pink-flowered snapdragons. This hardly seems surprising, for mixing red and white gives, of course, pink.

A Genetic Experiment

If a pink-flowered plant is now crossed with another pink-flowered plant, or self-fertilized, many of the progeny will be pink-flowered snapdragons like their parents; but some will be red-flowered, and some will be white-flowered. Reds and whites? This does seem surprising. Red and white flower color had seemed to mix like paint, giving pink, but now, unlike paint, they have unmixed again.

The trait *flower color* appeared to mix or blend—white crossed with red gave pink-flowered progeny. But the genetic factors which determine flower color obviously did not mix or blend—some of the progeny of the pink-flowered plants inherited pure red, others pure white, flower color. *Inheritance is determined by elements called genes which are discrete, that is, which do not mix or blend.* This is the foundation, the basic tenet, of genetics.

Genes Do Not Mix

The pink-flowered plant, offspring of a red-flowered and a white-flowered plant, was influenced by both. The simplest explanation is that it inherited a gene for red color from one parent and a gene for white color from the other. If the pink-flowered plant has two genes for flower color, then presumably its parents and its progeny also have two genes for flower color. *Genes come in pairs, such as white white, red red, or red white.*

Genes Are Paired

The genetically *white white* white-flowered plant necessarily contributed a *white* gene to its offspring, and the *red red* red-flowered plant a *red* gene, to make seeds with one *red* and one *white* gene and thus plants with pink flowers. *One gene of a pair is inherited from each parent.*

If indeed genes come in pairs and one gene of a pair is inherited from each parent, then what kind of progeny should result from crossing two pink-flowered plants (or from their self-pollination)? These plants produce eggs half of which contain the *red* gene and half the *white* gene, and sperm also half with the *red* and half with the *white* gene. A *red* egg fertilized by a *red* sperm gives a *red red* seed and a red-flowered plant; fertilized by a *white* sperm it gives a *red white* seed and a pink-flowered plant. A *white* egg fertilized by *red* also gives *red white*; fertilized by *white* it gives *white white*, a white-flowered plant. One-fourth of the progeny will be *red red*, one-half *red white*, and one-fourth *white white*: one-fourth of the progeny will have red flowers, one-half pink flowers, and one-fourth white flowers.

One-fourth, one-half, one-fourth, 1 to 2 to 1, this is the predicted ratio among the progeny of *hybrids*, plants which are themselves the progeny

Figure 6-2 A red-flowered plant has two genes for red flower color, *red red*. A white-flowered plant has two genes for white flower color, *white white*. Their offspring receive one gene from each parent, and so all have one *red* and one *white* gene for flower color and therefore have pink flowers. *(Adapted from Paul B. Weisz, "The Science of Biology," 3d ed., McGraw-Hill, New York, 1967, by permission of McGraw-Hill.)*

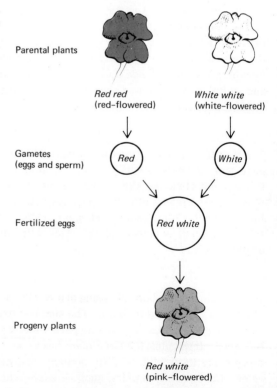

Parental plants

Red red
(red–flowered)

White white
(white–flowered)

Gametes
(eggs and sperm)

Red

White

Fertilized eggs

Red white

Progeny plants

Red white
(pink–flowered)

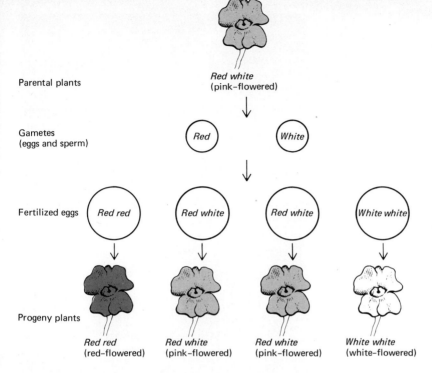

Figure 6-3 Pink-flowered plants have one *red* and one *white* gene for flower color; therefore half their gametes, eggs and sperm, receive a *red* gene; half receive a *white* gene. When such plants are self-fertilized or mated with each other, then of the eggs with a *red* gene half are fertilized by a sperm with a *red* gene, half by a sperm with a *white* gene; and of the eggs with a *white* gene, half are fertilized by a *red* sperm, half by a *white* sperm. The progeny will thus be *red red, red white,* and *white white,* that is, red-flowered, pink-flowered, and white-flowered, in the ratio of 1 to 2 to 1. (*Adapted from Paul B. Weisz, "The Science of Biology," 3d ed., McGraw-Hill, New York, 1967, by permission of McGraw-Hill.)*

of dissimilar parents (the pink-flowered plants are hybrids, the progeny of a red-flowered and a white-flowered plant). One to 2 to 1, the predicted ratio, depends on the hypotheses that a plant has two genes for each character and that it transmits one or the other of these with equal probability to each progeny. Because these hypotheses lead to such a specific prediction, they are testable. In fact, they were first conceived and put to experimental test over 100 years ago by the founder of the science of genetics, Gregor Mendel.

Over a period of 8 years, Gregor Mendel (1822–1884) conducted experiments with peas grown in the garden of the Austrian monastery in which he was a monk. Finally, in 1866 he published his results and conclusions, the basic laws of inheritance.

MENDEL AND THE LAWS OF INHERITANCE

Figure 6-4 Gregor Mendel (1822–1884),
inspired founder of the science of genetics.
Mendel discovered that the transmission of
inherited characters is determined by
independent, nonblending factors, now
called genes. *(Courtesy Radio Times
Hulton Picture Library.)*

Mendel's work is of a brilliance which makes it a model, in fact the very acme, of the scientific method: he recognized the precise nature of the problem; he invented the means of solving it; he carried out his experiments with scrupulous regard to possible sources of error; from his results he drew all possible logical conclusions; and, finally, he performed further experiments to prove his hypotheses.

The Experimental Plan

The problem Mendel defined very narrowly, so that the experimental path was simultaneously defined: He sought a "generally applicable law governing the formation and development of hybrids."* Yet Mendel was perfectly aware of the significance of such a law, which would provide "the solution of a question the importance of which cannot be overestimated in connection with the history of the evolution of organic forms."

---

*Mendel's paper was published in *Verh. Naturf. Ver. in Brunn, Abh.,* iv (1865). This and succeeding quotations are taken from the translation by W. Bateson which appeared in the *J. R. Hortic. Soc.,* 26:1 (1901), by courtesy of the Royal Horticultural Society.

What means did Mendel invent to solve the problem? "Those who survey the work in this department will arrive at the conviction that among all the numerous experiments made, not one has been carried out to such an extent and in such a way as to make it possible to determine the number of different forms under which the offspring of the hybrids appear, or to arrange these according to their separate generations, or definitely to ascertain their statistical relations."

This is the triple foundation of Mendel's work, the three exigencies which Mendel alone recognized: Discover all possible offspring of the hybrid plants; classify them according to generation; count them. What spark of genius, what penetrating insight, guided Mendel to the necessity of counting?

Which plant would he study? "The selection of the plant group which shall serve for experiments of this kind must be made with all possible care if it be desired to avoid from the outset every risk of questionable results." The chief risk was that "Accidental impregnation by foreign pollen . . . would lead to entirely erroneous conclusions." Mendel chose garden peas because they met all his requirements, including the most important—the flowers are normally self-fertilizing, but they can be artificially pollinated.

Which characteristics would he study? "Some of the characters noted do not permit of a sharp and certain separation, since the difference is of a 'more or less' nature, which is often difficult to define. Such characters could not be utilized for the separate experiments; these could only be applied to characters which stand out clearly and definitely in the plants." Tall plants had to be very tall, and short plants very short, so that they could be unambiguously differentiated and counted.

Starting with thirty-four varieties of peas, Mendel elected seven characters for study. "In the case of each of the seven crosses the hybrid-character resembles that of one of the parental forms so closely that the other either escapes observation completely or cannot be detected with certainty. . . . Henceforth in this paper those characters which are transmitted entire, or almost unchanged in the hybridisation, and therefore in themselves constitute the characters of the hybrid, are termed *dominant,* and those which become latent in the process *recessive.*" Tallness, for example, was dominant over shortness; hybrid plants were tall.

Why did Mendel choose characters in which the hybrid is essentially identical to one parent, the dominant parent (which is quite often the case), rather than intermediate between the two parents (such as the pink flowers)? His choice created a difficulty, for another year of plant breeding was required to distinguish hybrids, some of whose progeny have the recessive character, from pure dominants, all of whose progeny have the dominant character. (For example, hybrids and pure dominants are both

Table 6-1   Inheritance of Some Common Traits in Humans

TRAIT	DOMINANT	RECESSIVE
Eye characteristics	Brown, hazel, or green	Blue or gray
	Astigmatism and far-sightedness	Normal
	Normal	Nearsightedness (a less common form is dominant)
	Normal	Red-green color blindness (sex-linked)
	Long lashes	Short lashes
	Tendency to cataracts	Normal
Nose	High convex bridge	Straight or concave bridge
	Narrow bridge	Broad bridge
	Straight tip	Upturned tip
	Flaring nostrils	Narrow nostrils
Ears	Free earlobe	Attached earlobe
Other facial traits	Full lips	Thin lips
	Normal	Recessive chin
	Dimpled chin	Undimpled chin
	Dimpled cheeks	Undimpled cheeks
	High cheekbones	Normal
	Freckled	Nonfreckled
Hair	Dark	Blond
	Nonred	Red
	Kinky	Curly
	Curly	Straight
	Baldness (males)	Normal
	Normal	Baldness (females)
	White forelock	Normal
	Premature grayness	Normal
	Abundant hair on body	Sparse
	Heavy, bushy eyebrows	Normal
Hands, fingers, toes	Index finger longer than ring finger (in males)	Index finger longer than ring finger (in females)
	Second toe longer than big toe	Second toe shorter than big toe
	Hypermobility of thumb	Normal
	Right-handedness	Left-handedness
Other	Dark skin color	Light skin color
	Susceptibility to tooth decay	Normal
	Shortness	Tallness

Table 6-1 (continued)

TRAIT	DOMINANT	RECESSIVE
	A, B, AB blood groups	Group O
	Tendency to varicose veins	Normal
	Normal	Phenylketonuria
	Normal	Tendency to schizophrenia
	Normal	Congenital deafness
	Normal	Tendency to diabetes mellitus
	Normal	Hemophilia (sex-linked)
	Normal	Albinism

Note: The extent to which genes express themselves is frequently influenced by the environment, as well as by the presence of other genes. Moreover, some genes may have variable effects in a single individual—witness the individual with a dimple in only one cheek.

tall, but only hybrids give rise to some short progeny.) But dominance offered an overriding advantage: Mendel avoided the dilemma of discriminating the extremes and an intermediate type all growing together.

The first experimental step was to cross dissimilar plants to obtain hybrids. Next, Mendel could examine the first generation bred from the hybrids (by self-fertilization). What did he find? "In this generation there reappear, together with the dominant characters, also the recessive ones with their peculiarities fully developed, and this occurs in the definitely expressed average proportion of three to one, so that among each four plants of this generation three display the dominant character and one the recessive."

Results and Conclusions

Is this the expected result under the hypothesis that progeny receive one gene for each character from each parent? Let us continue.

"The dominant character can have here a *double signification*—vis. that of a parental character, or a hybrid-character. In which of the two significations it appears in each separate case can only be determined by the following generation. As a parental character it must pass over unchanged to the whole of the offspring; as a hybrid-character, on the other hand, it must maintain the same behaviour as in the first generation."

Mendel performed the indicated experiment and found that "Those forms which in the first generation exhibit the recessive character do not further vary in the second generation as regards this character; they remain constant in their offspring." Short plants give rise only to short plants.

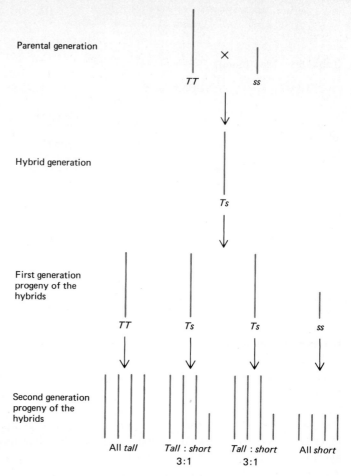

Parental generation

TT × ss

Hybrid generation

Ts

First generation
progeny of the
hybrids

TT Ts Ts ss

Second generation
progeny of the
hybrids

All *tall*   *Tall* : *short*   *Tall* : *short*   All *short*
                   3:1   3:1

Figure 6-5 Tall plants with two dominant genes for tallness TT mated with short plants with two recessive genes for shortness ss give tall hybrids Ts. Among the progeny of the hybrids are tall and short plants in the ratio of 3 to 1. Of the tall progeny, one out of three produces only tall progeny like the original tall parent. Two out of three are hybrids, for they produce progeny of which one-fourth are short. Thus the progeny of the hybrids are TT, pure tall; Ts, tall hybrids; and ss, pure short; in the predicted ratio of 1 to 2 to 1.

"It is otherwise with those which possess the dominant character in the first generation. Of these, *two*-thirds yield offspring which display the dominant and recessive characters in the proportion of 3 to 1, and thereby show exactly the same ratio as the hybrid forms, while only *one*-third remains with the dominant character constant." Thus Mendel demonstrated that the first-generation progeny of the hybrids, of which three-fourths exhibited the dominant character, were one-fourth pure dominant, one-half hybrid, and one-fourth pure recessive, 1 to 2 to 1. This ratio was obtained with all seven of the characters studied, indicating its fundamental significance.

What happened when the parental plant was hybrid for more than one character? Mendel found that among the progeny the alternatives for each character appeared in all possible combinations. Thus, if the parental plant was hybrid for height and flower color, its progeny by self-fertilization were tall, purple-flowered; short, purple-flowered; tall, white-flowered; and short, white-flowered.

Figure 6-6 Each kernel is an embryonic progeny. The purple and yellow kernels of this ear of corn, in the ratio of 3 to 1, are a striking illustration of a simple case of Mendelian inheritance. *(Courtesy "Turtox Collection," CCM General Biological, Inc.)*

"The conclusion appears logical that in the ovaries of the hybrids there are formed as many sorts of egg cells, and in the anthers as many sorts of pollen cells, as there are possible constant combination forms.* . . . It is possible to demonstrate theoretically that this hypothesis would fully suffice to account for the development of the hybrids in the separate generations, if we might at the same time assume that the various kinds of egg and pollen cells were formed in the hybrids on the average in equal numbers."

Mendel conducted many experiments. His mathematical analysis of the results revealed that *inheritance is effected by pairs of discrete, nonblending elements*, now called the *genes*, that *inheritance is equal from both parents*, that *each egg and each sperm receives one or the other gene of every pair with equal probability*, and that *the genes for the various characters get reassorted into all possible combinations*. These are the fundamental laws governing inheritance.

Mendel's contemporaries neither understood his mathematical logic nor appreciated the importance of his conclusions, and the publication of his work, though available in important libraries the world over, lay in oblivion for 35 years. Then in 1900 three biologists, botanists like Mendel, independently obtained similar results and, in studying earlier publications, rediscovered his work. Fame came to Mendel 16 years after his death.

Toward the end of the nineteenth century, tiny dye-absorbing specks were discerned in cell nuclei. They were named *chromosomes*, "color bodies." Better microscopes revealed the chromosomes as rods, sometimes bent, and of various lengths. They also disclosed the extraordinary events in which the chromosomes are the star performers.

CHROMO-SOMES, GENES, AND HEREDITY

Before a cell divides, the chromosomes, which were previously filamentous and dispersed in the cell nucleus, condense into their characteristic rodlike shapes. Each chromosome divides in two lengthwise. An elaborate machinery then appears and separates the two chromosomes, pulling them apart to opposite sides of the cell. During cell division, the cytoplasm is divided into two more or less equal parts, but the chromosomes necessitate this beautiful mechanism to ensure that each daughter cell is, in their regard, an exact duplicate of the parent.

---

*That is, possible combinations of genes.

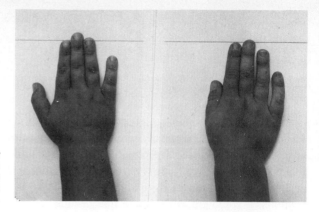

Figure 6-7 The index finger may be either longer or shorter than the ring finger, as seen in these children's hands. A longer index finger is dominant in males and recessive in females.

The germ cells, egg and sperm, result from two special cell divisions, the second of which is not preceded by chromosome division. The germ cells therefore contain only half as many chromosomes as other cells, body cells such as liver, spleen, and nerve cells. In body cells, the chromosomes are paired; that is, there are two of each kind of chromosome. The germ cells contain only one chromosome of each pair. When an egg is fertilized by a sperm, their nuclei unite, and the double, paired, number of chromosomes is reconstituted. Half the chromosomes of the fertilized egg and thence of all the body cells of the resulting individual are thus of maternal origin; half are likewise of paternal origin.

Figure 6-8 Comparison of mitosis and meiosis; the parent cell has one pair of chromosomes. In mitosis, the daughter cells receive the same chromosome complement as the parent cell; this is the pattern of chromosome segregation in body cells. In meiosis, there are formed gametes each with only one chromosome of the pair; thus, two gametes must fuse to reconstitute the chromosome complement of a body cell. The key difference between mitosis and meiosis is the way the chromosomes line up at metaphase.

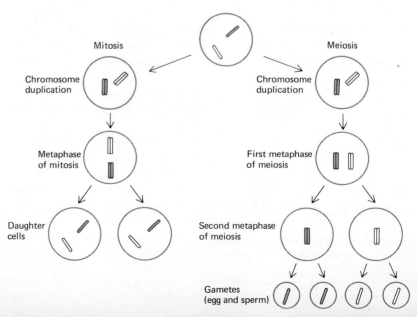

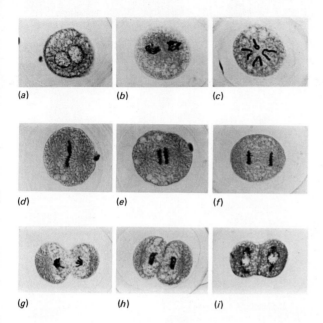

(a)   (b)   (c)

(d)   (e)   (f)

(g)   (h)   (i)

Figure 6-9 Mitosis is the name given the division of the cell nucleus that precedes cell division. It is characterized by doubling of the chromosomes, followed by an exact segregation of the identical sister chromosomes into the two daughter cells, which thereby acquire a set of chromosomes identical to that of the mother cell. The stages of mitosis are seen in these photographs of a dividing fertilized egg cell of the worm *Ascaris megalocephala*, which has only two pairs of chromosomes. *(a) Prophase:* Within the sperm nucleus and egg nucleus the chromosomes, which have already doubled, are starting to condense; the nuclear membrane has disappeared. *(b) Late prophase:* The chromosomes have condensed and are therefore now visible; each apparent chromosome is in fact a pair of parallel, identical sister chromosomes. *(c) Metaphase:* The chromosomes have aligned themselves on a single plane, called the *equatorial plane,* which divides the nucleus in two. *(d) Metaphase:* Sideways view of the equatorial plane, on either side of which is an organelle called a *centriole;* the fibers extending between the centrioles through the equatorial plane are called the *spindle* (those radiating into the cytoplasm are called the *aster*). *(e) Early anaphase:* Spindle fibers have attached to each of the sister chromosomes of every doubled chromosome and are pulling them apart to opposite sides of the nucleus. *(f) Late anaphase:* The separation of the sister chromosomes into two identical sets is complete. *(g) Early telophase:* The chromosomes have reached the opposite poles (as can be seen here, the ends of each chromosome drag along behind the point of attachment of the spindle fibers); the cell is starting to divide. *(h) Late telophase:* The two new nuclei are forming; the chromosomes are starting to uncoil. *(i) Cell Cleavage:* The two daughter cells are separated by cell membrane, and the nuclei are enclosed in a nuclear membrane; the chromosomes, no longer visible, are stretched out and filamentous. *(Courtesy Carolina Biological Supply Company.)*

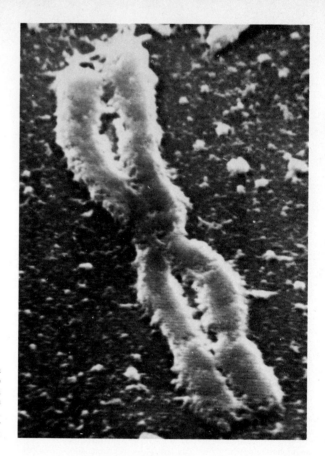

Figure 6-10 Scanning electron micrograph of a metaphase chromosome. The two sister chromosomes are joined at the region where the spindle fiber attaches and pulls them apart. (*From W. Scheid and H. Traut, Mutat. Res.* **11**:253 (1971), *courtesy of the authors.*)

All this, as well as the fact that every species is characterized by the number and form of its chromosomes, was known at the beginning of this century, but the meaning of these observations had not been penetrated.

The Genes Reside in the Chromosomes In 1900, Gregor Mendel's publication was rediscovered and received wide acclaim. In 1902, a graduate student at Columbia University, William Sutton (1876–1916), correlated Mendel's principles of heredity with the behavior of chromosomes.

Like genes, the chromosomes are paired, each cell containing two sets of chromosomes, one of paternal and one of maternal origin. Mendel had hypothesized that the germ cells contain only one of the two genes determining each character; it could actually be observed that each germ cell contains only one set of chromosomes, that is, one chromosome of each pair. Mendel had found that inheritance of each character is independent of the inheritance of others; Sutton realized that each germ cell receives either chromosome of each pair independently.

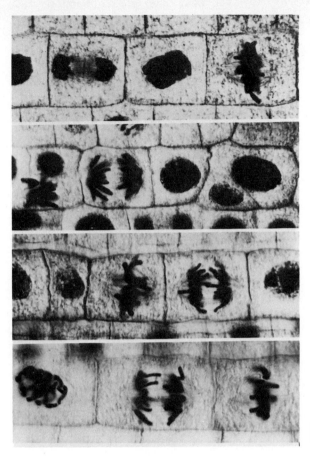

Figure 6-11 Mitosis in dividing plant cells.
(Courtesy Carolina Biological Supply Company.)

Thus Sutton discerned the parallel inheritance of genes and chromosomes and deduced the chromosome theory: *The determinants of heredity, the genes, reside in the chromosomes.*

Many years of research were required to prove beyond a doubt that the chromosomes are the bearers of the genes. The first piece of evidence was soon obtained. Sutton had posed the question whether genes and chromosomes are one and the same thing. No, he concluded, for there are relatively few chromosomes in a cell but undoubtedly hosts of genes. Each chromosome must bear many genes. Sutton suggested that genes on the same chromosome will be inherited together.

Two years later a pair of *linked* genes, genes which tend to be inherited together, was discovered. When sweet peas with red flowers and round pollen grains were crossed with sweet peas with purple flowers and long pollen grains, the offspring of the hybrids were almost all like one grandparent or the other. The genes for flower color and pollen-grain shape were linked, that is, inherited together, and therefore presumably located on the same chromosome.

Figure 6-12 Thomas Hunt Morgan (1866–1945) was awarded the Nobel Prize in medicine-physiology in 1933 for his elucidation of the mechanism of chromosomal inheritance. *(Courtesy California Institute of Technology.)*

Sex-linked Inheritance   In 1909 an embryologist, Thomas Hunt Morgan (1866–1945), skeptical about the reality of genes, embarked in genetics. Together with his students and colleagues, he not only proved that heredity is determined by genes, but he also located particular genes on their chromosomes and proved conclusively that the rules which describe the inheritance of genes are a consequence of the rules which describe the inheritance of chromosomes.

Morgan chose for study an everyday pest, the fruit fly *(Drosophila melanogaster)*, which is commonly found buzzing around rotting fruit. Unlike plants, which normally produce a new generation every year, fruit flies offered Morgan the advantage of producing a new generation every 2 weeks. But they also had a disadvantage. Different useful varieties of many plants have been developed, and their seeds are sold (thus Mendel bought his many varieties of peas in a seed store). But Morgan was the first to require different varieties of fruit flies. So he set to work raising them, examining thousands in his search for a variant. After almost a year he was rewarded by the appearance among his red-eyed flies of a male with white eyes.

Why should a white-eyed fly suddenly appear among Morgan's pure-bred red-eyed flies? Such a freak happening is called a *mutation*—the white-eyed fly was a *mutant*. Mutations are changes which, once they occur, are passed on from generation to generation. They are thus heritable changes, permanent alterations of genes. Mutations occur extremely rarely, but they have enormous importance, and not only for

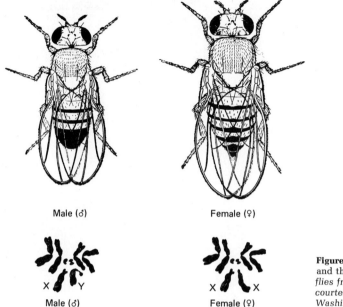

Male (♂)   Female (♀)

X   Y   X   X

Male (♂)   Female (♀)

Figure 6-13 Male and female fruit flies and their chromosomes. *(Fruit flies from T. H. Morgan, chromosomes courtesy Carnegie Institution of Washington.)*

geneticists. They are the source of the variation which serves as fodder for the Darwinian process of natural selection.

What did Morgan do with his white-eyed fly? He followed Mendel's procedure and bred it to normal, red-eyed females. The offspring were all red-eyed; red eyes were dominant. The hybrids were then inbred. In a simple Mendelian case one-fourth of the offspring would have been white-eyed and genetically pure recessive, one-half red-eyed and genetically hybrid, and one-fourth red-eyed and genetically pure dominant. Instead, Morgan found that all the female offspring had red eyes, whereas half the males had red, half white eyes. Eye color was related to the sex of the fly.

Sex-linked Inheritance and Sex Chromosomes

Female fruit flies have four pairs of chromosomes, one pair of very short ones, two pairs of long, V-shaped ones, and one pair of long, straight ones, called the X *chromosomes.* In males, three of the four pairs are the same, but there is only one long, straight X chromosome; its partner, called the Y *chromosome,* has a hook at the end. Females are thus chromosomally XX, males XY. Chromosomes are related to the sex of the fly.

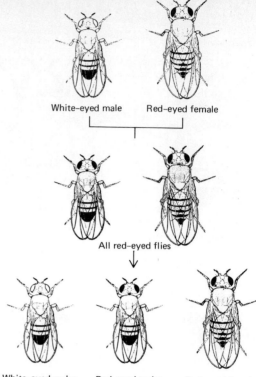

White-eyed male   Red-eyed female

All red-eyed flies

Figure 6-14 Inheritance of a sex-linked recessive gene (white eye color). *(From T. H. Morgan.)*

White-eyed males
25%

Red-eyed males
25%

Red-eyed females
50%

Figure 6-15 Sex determination in fruit flies. Males have an X and a Y chromosome, whereas females have two X chromosomes.

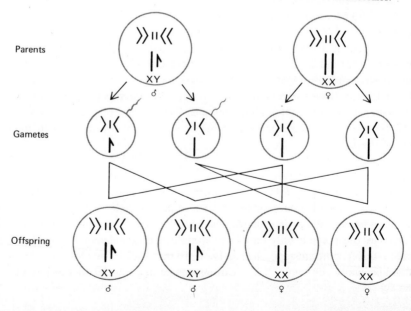

Parents

Gametes

Offspring

Surely the sex-linked inheritance of eye color is related to the sex-linked difference in chromosome complement. But how? The explanation lies in the fact that the male's Y chromosome carries almost no genes. An abnormal fly with one X and no Y chromosome is sterile because the Y chromosome is necessary for sperm formation, but otherwise the fly is a normal male. An XXY fly is a perfectly normal, fertile female, further evidence that the Y chromosome in flies has little influence.

The gene for eye color is located on the X chromosome; it has no counterpart on the Y chromosome. Since females have two X chromosomes, they have two genes for eye color. If both are for red eyes or if she is hybrid, she has red eyes; if both are for white eyes, she has white eyes. But the male has only one X chromosome and therefore only one gene for eye color. If that one is for red eyes, he has red eyes; if for white eyes, then he has white eyes. Of course he inherits that one X chromosome, and thus his one gene for eye color, from his mother.

Why did Morgan find that among the second generation offspring of his white-eyed male the females all had red eyes while the males were half red-eyed, half white-eyed? Morgan's original mutant, with a gene for white eyes on his lone X chromosome, was crossed to females with red on both X chromosomes. The female offspring were hybrids, having a gene for white eyes on the X chromosome inherited from their mutant father and for red eyes on the X chromosome inherited from their mother. The male offspring were simply ordinary red-eyed males, having inherited their lone X chromosome, and thus a lone gene for red eyes, from the mother.

Morgan then crossed these males, which he mistakenly believed to be hybrids, to their hybrid sisters. The female offspring all received their father's normal X chromosome, and thus all had red eyes (half were, of course, genetically hybrid, having received a gene for white eyes from the hybrid mother). Among the male offspring, half received the maternal X chromosome with the red-eye gene and thus had red eyes; half received the other maternal X chromosome with the white-eye gene and had white eyes. (See Fig. 6-16.)

Genetic Recombination and Chromosomal Crossing Over

From time to time, Morgan discovered other mutant flies in his collection. All were males carrying sex-linked recessive mutations. This is not surprising, for recessive mutations are the more common and if they occur elsewhere than on the X chromosome of a male, they are masked by the corresponding dominant gene on the other chromosome of the pair.

Studies of the inheritance of two different mutations on the X chromosome gave a strange result. By suitable genetic crosses, Morgan obtained female flies hybrid for two mutant genes, one on each X chromosome.

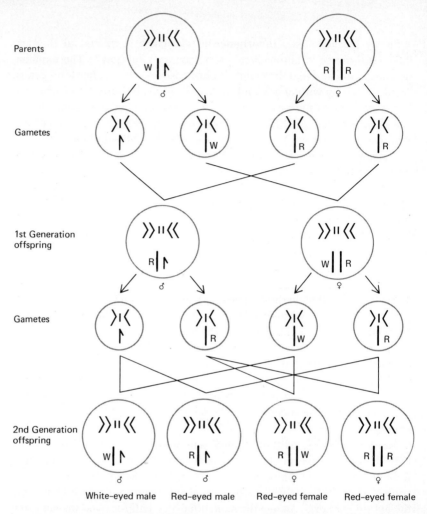

Figure 6-16 Inheritance of a sex-linked recessive gene. In the second generation, all females are red-eyed (though half are hybrids); half the males are red-eyed, and half white-eyed. This apparently non-Mendelian mode of inheritance is explained by the lack of a gene for eye color on the Y chromosome.

For example, she could have the recessive gene for white eyes on one chromosome and the recessive gene for yellow body color on the other (as opposed to the normal dominant genes for red eyes and gray body color). (See Fig. 6-17.)

Half the male offspring of such a female receive the white-eye chromosome; the other half receive the yellow-body chromosome. Half should have white eyes and gray bodies; half red eyes and yellow bodies. This was indeed what Morgan found, for the most part. But Morgan also found a few males with both white eyes and yellow bodies and whose

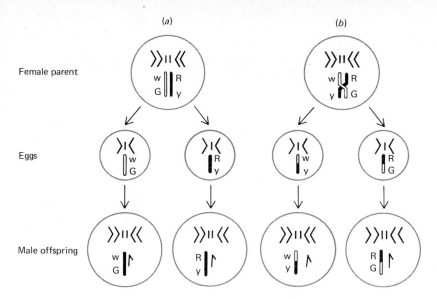

Figure 6-17 Crossing over, that is, the exchange of parts between chromosomes, results in the unlinking of linked genes. Crossing over between genes on the X chromosome can only take place in the female because only she has two X chromosomes. Its results are easily seen in the male progeny, where they are not masked by genes on a second X chromosome.

single X chromosome therefore carried both of the mutant genes. He also found some males with red eyes and gray body color and whose single X chromosome therefore had neither mutant gene. These males thus had new combinations of genes—they were *genetic recombinants.*

Genetic recombination paralleled a known chromosomal phenomenon called *crossing over.* Just prior to the two special cell divisions which result in the formation of the germ cells, the pairs of chromosomes come together, line up side by side, then twist loosely round each other. At the points where they lie crossed, physical breaks and exchanges of parts, crossing over, can occur. If two genes, such as eye-color and body-color, lie on opposite sides of a point where two chromosomes break and rejoin, then the crossover will result in genetic recombination.

Again, the pattern of gene transmission was a direct result of chromosomal behavior. Moreover, the correlation between crossing over and genetic recombination implies that each gene occupies a specific position on the chromosome, and thus the correlation constitutes strong evidence that genes have a real physical existance.

A. H. Sturtevant (1891–1970), a student and later a colleague of Morgan, conceived the idea that the frequency of recombination must be related to the distance between genes on the chromosomes. He thereby became the first genetic cartographer, mapper of genes.

The Mapping of Genes

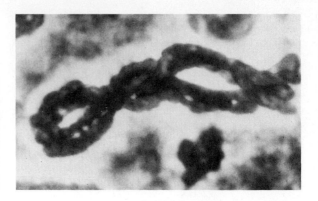

Figure 6-18 Crossing over in a grasshopper chromosome (first prophase of meiosis). The paired chromosomes are twisted round each other. Each chromosome has already doubled and consists of two sister chromosomes. Crossing over has taken place in the four regions where the chromosomes cross. *(From A. M. Winchester, "Genetics" Houghton Mifflin, Boston, 1966, courtesy of the author.)*

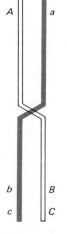

Figure 6-19 The frequency of recombination between genes is directly related to the distance separating them on the chromosome: crossing over will occur more frequently between the widely separated genes A and B than between the close genes B and C. (The maximum frequency of recombination is 50 percent. Fifty percent recombination between genes means the genes are so far apart, and crossovers between them are so frequent, that they are equally likely to end up on the same chromosome as on different chromosomes.)

Among the male progeny of females with the white-eye gene on one X chromosome and the yellow-body-color gene on the other, 1.2 percent were recombinants, having either both mutant genes or both normal genes; this is called *1.2 percent recombination*. This is a relatively low frequency of recombination, implying that these two genes lie relatively close together; the probability of a crossover between them is therefore small. On the other hand, the genes for body color and wing length recombine frequently (35.5 percent recombination). Body color and wing length must be far apart.

By determining recombination frequencies, Sturtevant was able to establish the sequence of the six sex-linked genes known in 1913. Each fell into place in a linear sequence, another correlation with chromosomes, which can be seen in a microscope to be linear with no branches or loops.

Figure 6-20 Mutant flies, progeny of males exposed to radiation. H. J. Muller (1890–1967) was awarded the Nobel Prize in medicine-physiology in 1946 for his discovery that radiation causes mutations. *(Courtesy Brookhaven National Laboratory.)*

The discovery of an aberrant fly was a mutational windfall until 1927, when H. J. Muller (1890–1967), another of Morgan's brilliant students and colleagues, caused mutations by treating flies with x-rays. (Muller at that time already sounded the first warning: Exposure of humans to x-rays may cause genetic damage to future generations.)

In flies, x-rays made possible the discovery of hundreds of genes. When these were mapped, they were found to fall into four groups, called *linkage groups*. The genes in each group are linked together; that is, they tend to be inherited together; eye color, body color, and wing length, all on the X chromosome, are linked together. But the genes in one linkage group are unlinked to the genes in the other three groups. Four linkage groups, four pairs of chromosomes. Here was powerful evidence for the theory that the chromosomes are the bearers of the genes.

Proof of the chromosome theory came from studies of giant chromosomes found in the salivary glands of fruit fly larvae. Giant chromosomes occur in some specialized cells of insects because the chromosomal material proliferates without concomitant chromosome division. In 1933, T. S. Painter discovered that the giant chromosomes each have a characteristic shape and pattern of dye-absorbing bands which he was able to correlate with genetic behavior.

GENETIC ANOMALIES AND CHROMOSOMAL DEFECTS

148

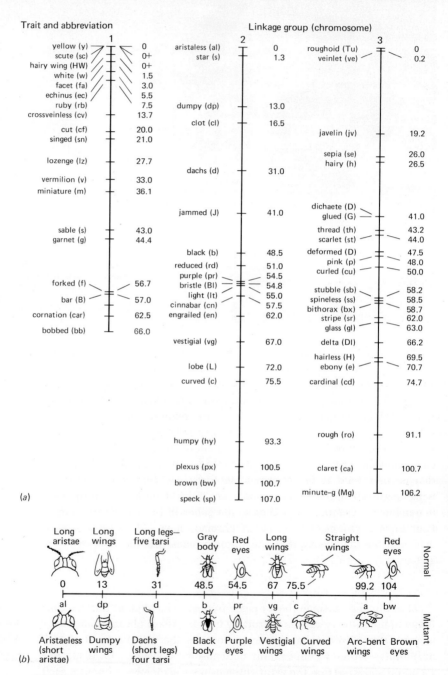

Figure 6-21 *(a)* Map of the four linkage groups, that is, the four chromosomes, of the fruit fly; *(b)* portion of chromosome 2. *(From C. B. Anfinsen, "The Molecular Basis of Evolution," Wiley, New York, 1959.)*

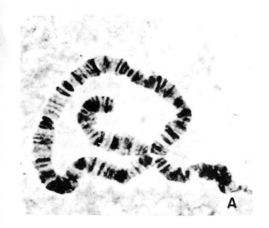

A

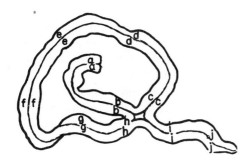

Figure 6-22 The effect of an inversion in one chromosome of a pair as seen in the giant chromosomes of the fruit fly. One chromosome has the normal sequence of genes *abcdefghij*. The other has the sequence *abhgfedcij* (the section *cdefgh* has become inverted). Because identical regions of the chromosomes are paired along their entire length, *a* with *a*, *b* with *b*, and so forth, a loop is formed in the region of the genes *cdefgh*. *(Courtesy Carnegie Institution of Washington.)*

Morgan had found that in rare variant flies a normal gene sequence *abcd* was inverted to *acbd*; examination of the giant chromosomes of a genetically *acbd* fly showed an actual physical inversion of a part of a chromosome. Genetic experiments sometimes indicated that a gene or a group of linked genes was missing; thanks to the giant chromosomes the deletion of a part of a chromosome could be seen with a microscope. Genetic data indicated the existence of chromosomal breaks and trans-locations, that is, attachment of a part of one chromosome to another; such abnormalities could now be observed.

These studies made it possible to physically locate the genes on the chromosomes; for example, inverted genes would be assigned to an inverted segment of chromosome. The beauty and success of formal genetics were thereby eloquently demonstrated—the sequence of genes established from the examination of abnormal giant chromosomes could be superimposed on the sequence of genes, the genetic maps, deduced from studies of the frequency of recombination.

The Genetics of Flies and Men

The manner of inheritance of genes by peas, deciphered by Mendel, and the manner of inheritance of chromosomes in fruit flies, worked out mainly by Morgan, Sturtevant, and others at Columbia University, also describe the inheritance of genes and chromosomes in man, mice, plants, and even bacteria and viruses—though of course there are individual peculiarities. Genetic maps have been worked out in greatest detail for flies, bacteria, molds, and viruses, for these creatures lend themselves best to experimentation. But even in humans, a species in which genetic experiments are forbidden, in which the generation time is most inconveniently long, and in which the rather large number of chromosome pairs (twenty-three) is awkward, the same phenomena are known.

A few linked genes have been discovered in humans. Most are on the X chromosome, where the gene for hemophilia, for example, is linked to color blindness (11.4 percent recombination), which is linked to another blood disorder (6.5 percent recombination). A number of other cases of linkage are known. More will surely be uncovered through studies of hybrid cells (Fig. 3-31) and through the use of brilliant fluorescent dyes which, it was discovered in 1968, give to human chromosomes a detailed banded pattern comparable to that which has been so successfully exploited in the giant chromosomes of fruit flies.

Chromosomal abnormalities such as those observed in flies are, unfortunately, also known in humans. Though it is not universally true, sex in humans is determined, as in fruit flies, by two X chromosomes in the female and an X and a Y in the male—it is thus the father, fly or human, who determines the sex of his offspring. But unlike the fly, the human Y chromosome carries genes which determine maleness (and perhaps other genes, such as a gene for hairy ears).

A person with an extra X chromosome, an XXY individual, is a male, but a sexually undeveloped, effeminate male, said to suffer from *Klinefelter's syndrome*. Even an XXXXY individual is a male. (In cats, males with an extra X chromosome are also known. Three-colored female cats

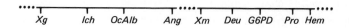

Figure 6-23 A few of the genes carried on the human X chromosome: *Xg*, blood group *Xg*; *Ich*, a skin disease called ichthyosis; *OcAlb*, ocular albinism, a form of albinism limited to the eyes; *Ang*, a skin disease, angiokeratosis; *Xm*, blood group *Xm*; *Deu*, deutan, a form of red-green color blindness; *G6PD*, glucose-6-phosphate dehydrogenase, an enzyme found in the blood; *pro*, protan, the other form of red-green color blindness; *Hem*, hemophilia A, one type of hemophilia.

are common, but white, yellow, and black males, the hybrid offspring of a yellow cat and a black cat, are extremely rare, 1 in 250,000, for the genes which determine coat colors are X-linked, and therefore such tortoiseshell males must have two X chromosomes.)

Other chromosomal disorders are known in man. Deletion of an entire chromosome is probably lethal in humans, as in other organisms. An extra chromosome, giving a total of forty-seven instead of forty-six, is associated with severe mental retardation and other serious symptoms. If the extra chromosome is number 21, then the illness is known as *Down's syndrome,* mongolian idiocy.

Eugenic Medicine

Genetics, biochemistry, and medicine have joined forces to open up a thrilling frontier which could well be called *eugenic medicine.* Still in an early stage, it may some day significantly reduce the frequency of certain defective genes in the human population by detecting fetal abnormalities at an early stage when the fetus can be aborted with a minimum of medical, legal, and moral complications. (It should be noted that every individual probably harbors a half-dozen or so harmful recessive genes, a fact which should subdue the zeal of any who dream of the ultimate elimination of such genes.)

A woman whose two brothers were victims of the form of muscular dystrophy caused by a sex-linked recessive gene needs genetic counseling before having children. So does the person whose faulty family tree

Figure 6-24 Preparing a human karyogram, an ordered arrangement of the chromosomes. A chromosome analysis starts with an enlarged photograph of a squashed metaphase cell. The pictures of the chromosomes are cut out and arranged in pairs according to size and shape. *(Courtesy World Health Organization.)*

Figure 6-25 A human karyogram, an ordered arrangement of the chromosomes. *(Courtesy Carolina Biological Supply Company.)*

suggests a high risk of transmitting hereditary disease, such as a severe inherited anemia. So do the couple who want children despite the wife's age—over 40—and therefore despite a high risk of producing an infant with Down's syndrome.

Genetic counseling and the new medical methods can already in some cases remove the risk from such genetically high-risk pregnancies. A sample of the amniotic fluid surrounding the fetus is removed by a technique called *amniocentesis.* This fluid contains a few cells of fetal origin. By means of tissue culture, these are grown into a large colony, which can be examined for enzyme levels and for chromosome complement (or *karyotype,* as it is called).

If you had been advised that half your sons would be afflicted with muscular dystrophy and if chromosome analysis of amniotic-fluid cells disclosed an X and a Y chromosome, would you decide to destroy this and eventually any other male fetuses? Here is the case history of a woman who is herself normal, although she has an abnormal chromosome complement (she has a so-called *D/G translocation,* two chromosomes attached to each other, giving her a total of only forty-five chromosomes instead of forty-six). Her abnormality will result in some of her children having Down's syndrome.

Mrs. R. K. was referred for genetic counseling because of a family history of three siblings with Down's syndrome. Chromosome analysis using peripheral blood demonstrated the presence of 45 chromosomes, XX, including a D/G translocation. Mrs. R. K. having grown up with three siblings with Down's syndrome did not wish to assume the risk of having a child with this disorder. However, she did wish to have normal children, and elected to have her pregnancy monitored. At 15 weeks of pregnancy, transabdominal amniocentesis was performed, and chromosome analysis using the cultivated amniotic fluid cells demonstrated the presence of 46 chromosomes, XY, and including the D/G translocation; a finding consistent with the diagnosis of the translocation form of Down's syndrome. Mrs. R. K. elected to terminate the pregnancy at 19 weeks, and a therapeutic abortion was performed. Three months later, Mrs. R. K. became pregnant again, and a transabdominal amniocentesis performed at 14 weeks of gestation; chromosome analysis utilizing amniotic fluid cells revealed the presence of 46 chromosomes, XX, with a normal karyotype. Mrs. R. K. delivered at term a normal female.*

Genes for flower color, genes for eye color, genes for tall or short plants, genes for tall or short men—how do genes determine every characteristic of every organism? What do genes actually do?

GENES ARE THE DETERMINANTS OF ENZYMES

In 1908 an English physician, Sir Archibald Garrod (1857–1936), hypothesized that certain diseases are inherited and are caused by the lack of an enzyme. These diseases he aptly called "inborn errors of metabolism." Thirty years passed before Garrod's brilliant conjecture, made in the infancy of genetics and biochemistry, could be proved correct: Genes (or at least many genes) are the determinants of enzymes; mutant genes are often the determinants of nonfunctional enzymes. (This explains why most mutations are recessive: A mutant gene is frequently masked by the normal gene because its nonfunctional enzyme is compensated by the functional enzyme.)

Alkaptonuria, for example, is one of the diseases cited by Garrod. It is a harmless disorder, but one which the mothers of affected babies in diapers are sure to notice, for the babies' urine turns black with time. The principles of genetics have been elucidated; metabolic pathways have been resolved; the nature of enzymes and methods for their purification and characterization have been worked out; and so this disorder is now understood with precision.

The gene defect in alkaptonuria results in the lack of one enzyme, homogentisic acid oxidase, which normally catalyzes a step in the metabolic pathway whereby an excess of the amino acid phenylalanine is oxidized to carbon dioxide and water. Homogentisic acid therefore accumulates and is excreted in the urine; it turns black on exposure to air. The missing or nonfunctional enzyme has now been identified in many inherited diseases. In several, including phenylketonuria, other enzymes in this same pathway are nonfunctional.

Homo sapiens is a particularly unhandy organism for study but also a particularly fascinating one. Man does have the advantage that his black urine is more likely to be noticed than that of a fruit fly, whose

---

*From a text on genetic counseling, edited by Dr. Arno Motulsky, in preparation. Courtesy Dr. Henry L. Nadler.

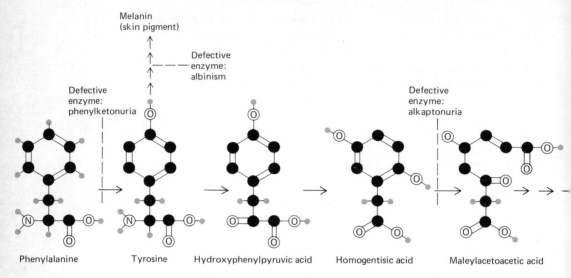

Figure 6-26 Phenylalanine may be transformed into tyrosine and thence, in two separate pathways, either into the skin pigment melanin or into molecules which enter the mitochondria and are oxidized to carbon dioxide and water with the concomitant regeneration of ATP. As indicated in the illustration, several inherited human diseases are caused by mutations affecting enzymes required in one or the other of these pathways.

mental retardation or difficult digestion may also well go unobserved. It is therefore perhaps not surprising that more is known about the effects of genes in man than in any other animal and that the first studies of the biochemical action of genes were concerned with hereditary metabolic diseases of man.

ONE GENE–ONE PROTEIN It was not with man but with the bread mold *Neurospora crassa* that the definitive experiments were performed which demonstrated that for each gene there is a corresponding enzyme—the *one gene–one enzyme hypothesis,* as this concept came to be called.

Bread mold has the advantage that during its entire life cycle only one cell ever contains a double set of chromosomes. This is the cell resulting from the union of the germ cells; it immediately divides without doubling its chromosomes, so each daughter cell and every cell thereafter contain only one of each pair of chromosomes. A single set of chromosomes means a single set of genes. Thus, recessive mutations in the bread mold are not masked by normal, dominant genes, as in organisms whose cells contain paired chromosomes.

In 1941, G. W. Beadle and E. L. Tatum set out to determine if and how genes control biochemical reactions. Their starting point was a most ingenious idea.   Previously, investigators had attempted to discover the biochemical abnormality in mutants, such as the block preventing the synthesis of red pigment in white-eyed flies.   Beadle and Tatum reversed this procedure—they invented a means of selecting bread-mold mutants which are specifically unable to carry out particular biochemical reactions.

Bread-mold, like some other organisms such as certain bacteria, is able to live on an extremely simple diet—it grows very well on inorganic salts, one vitamin (biotin), and a source of carbon such as glucose or another sugar.   From such uncomplicated beginnings it synthesizes amino acids, fats, various vitamins, and carbohydrates.   If, as was supposed, an abnormal, mutated gene gives rise to a nonfunctional or nonexistent enzyme, then it should result in an inability to synthesize at least one of these complex chemicals.   The mutant will be unable to grow on the simple salts nutrients, but it could nevertheless be grown and studied if supplied with the substance it is unable to synthesize.

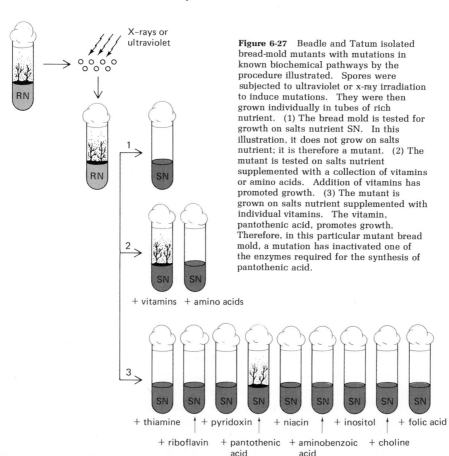

Figure 6-27   Beadle and Tatum isolated bread-mold mutants with mutations in known biochemical pathways by the procedure illustrated.   Spores were subjected to ultraviolet or x-ray irradiation to induce mutations.   They were then grown individually in tubes of rich nutrient.   (1) The bread mold is tested for growth on salts nutrient SN.   In this illustration, it does not grow on salts nutrient; it is therefore a mutant.   (2) The mutant is tested on salts nutrient supplemented with a collection of vitamins or amino acids.   Addition of vitamins has promoted growth.   (3) The mutant is grown on salts nutrient supplemented with individual vitamins.   The vitamin, pantothenic acid, promotes growth. Therefore, in this particular mutant bread mold, a mutation has inactivated one of the enzymes required for the synthesis of pantothenic acid.

Figure 6-28 George W. Beadle (1903–), together with Edward Tatum, pursued a biochemical approach to genetics, using the red bread mold *Neurospora crassa*. In 1941, they discovered that genes control the synthesis of vitamins and amino acids. From their investigations emerged the concept that genes determine the structure of enzymes. Beadle is seen here among the corn plants with which he is currently doing genetic experiments at the University of Chicago, of which he is president. *(Courtesty G. W. Beadle.)*

In practice, the Beadle and Tatum experiment was performed in this way: Mutations were induced by irradiation with x-rays or ultraviolet rays. The irradiated mold was then grown in rich nutrient containing amino acids, vitamins, and other complex substances. Mutants were detected because of their inability to grow following transfer to the simple salts nutrient, which did not supply their biochemical deficiency.

How was the particular mutation detected? By trial and error. Would the mutant grow on the simple nutrient solution supplemented with vitamins? Or supplemented with amino acids? Which one of the twenty amino acids permits growth? By trying out various supplemented nutrient solutions, the growth requirement and thus the nature of the mutation were determined.

In their first experiments, Beadle and Tatum turned up three mutant molds, each, by chance, unable to synthesize a vitamin. Within 10 years, they had collected five hundred mutants. The one gene–one enzyme hypothesis offered the simplest explanation of their finding that the growth requirement of almost every mutant could be satisfied by a single substance such as an amino acid or a vitamin.

In many cases, the mutant mold's radiation-induced inborn error of metabolism was pinpointed with even greater biochemical precision. Some mutants shared a nutritional requirement, such as a need for the same amino acid. They could be shown to be blocked, often at different steps, in the biochemical pathway terminating in the synthesis of that amino acid. In a few mutants, the lack of a particular enzyme and the presence of the other enzymes in a pathway could even be demonstrated.

Thus, mutations in the various genes give rise to distinct biochemical errors. The one gene–one enzyme hypothesis had been proved. Today it still stands with only a slight modification. Enzymes are, of course,

Figure 6-29   Edward L. Tatum (1909–   )
collaborated with Beadle in studies
of the biochemical genetics of the bread
mold.   A few years later, Tatum and
Joshua Lederberg made the remarkable
discovery of sexual reproduction in
bacteria, thereby making these handy
organisms available for genetic
experiments.   In 1958, the Nobel Prize in
medicine-physiology was awarded jointly to
Breadle, Tatum, and Lederberg.   *(Courtesy
Henrik Boudakian and the Rockefeller
University Graphic Services.)*

proteins, but not all proteins are enzymes.   The one-to-one relationship
between genes and enzymes exists between genes and all proteins:
one gene–one protein.

What is the significance of this relationship, one gene–one protein?
Proteins are long sequences of amino acids.   The particular sequence
determines the properties of the protein.   Each gene must somehow
specify the precise sequence of amino acids in a protein.   How?

WHAT ARE GENES?

Genes have three unique and astonishing properties. They double themselves cell generation after cell generation without varying: *genes replicate without changing (almost) indefinitely.* Extremely rarely, changes do occur in genes, and these changed, mutated genes then double themselves cell generation after cell generation without varying: *the rare changes, called mutations, also duplicate indefinitely.* The multitude of genes have a one-to-one correspondence with the multitude of proteins found in cells: one gene–one protein implies that in some way *genes specify the amino-acid sequences of proteins.*

The physical existence of genes could no longer be doubted once it had been proved that they are located on structures, the chromosomes, whose existence can be verified with a microscope. What are genes? What kind of substance could have such properties?

WHICH SUBSTANCE IS THE GENETIC SUBSTANCE?

In 1941, when the one gene–one enzyme hypothesis had been clearly stated and its unequivocal demonstration begun, and even 10 years later, most biologists were quite sure they knew what substance genes are made of—protein, of course. Proteins were then thought to be, and are now known to be, chemically the most complex of substances. Surely then the most complex of jobs must be performed by proteins.

In fact, there were only two candidates for the genetic material, for chromosomes consist chiefly of only two substances, protein and *DNA (deoxyribonucleic acid).* DNA had been discovered in the nineteenth century. It was known to be a polymer in which four substances, called the four *bases* A, C, G, and T (*adenine, cytosine, guanine,* and *thymine*), are linked together. Because the few samples of DNA which had been analyzed were composed of approximately equal amounts of these bases, their sequence was thought, mistakenly, to be a regular repeat such as ACGTACGTACGT . . . , on and on endlessly.

How could such a dreary molecule have an important and complex biologic role? In particular, how could a regularly repeating sequence determine the amino acid sequences of the multifarious proteins? An analogy can be made between proteins with their twenty amino acids and DNA with four bases, on the one hand, and the English alphabet with its twenty-six letters and the Morse code with three symbols, dots, dashes, and pauses, on the other hand. Sequences of dots, dashes, and pauses correspond to letters, words, and sentences. ─·· ─· ·─, dash dot dot pause dash dot pause dot dash, for example, codes for the letters DNA, but a monotonous repeat such as ─···─··─··─·· codes only for DDDD, which means nothing. In the same way, a polymeric molecule with a sequence such as ACGTACGTACGT . . . can code for nothing of interest, it can contain no information.

Yet in 1944 and again in 1952 experiments indicated that the genetic material is, in fact, DNA.

In 1928 the *Journal of Hygiene* carried an extraordinary article announcing the transformation of one type of bacterium into another. Fred Griffith, an English medical officer, was interested in the etiology of pneumonia, caused by the bacterium pneumococcus. There are many slightly different types of pneumococcus bacteria. Griffith found that during the course of this disease a patient might harbor different types. He was thus led to wonder whether one type of pneumococcus can somehow change into another.

THE TRANS-FORMATION OF BACTERIA

Griffith undertook experiments to determine if such a transformation is possible. He injected mice with a small amount of a living, noninfectious strain of pneumococci together with a large amount of dead, infectious bacteria, which he had killed by heating. Neither the noninfectious pneumococci nor the infectious, but dead, pneumococci caused pneumonia when injected separately into mice, yet when injected together, the mice died of pneumonia. Moreover, despite the fact that all the in-

Dead Bacteria Transform Live Bacteria

160

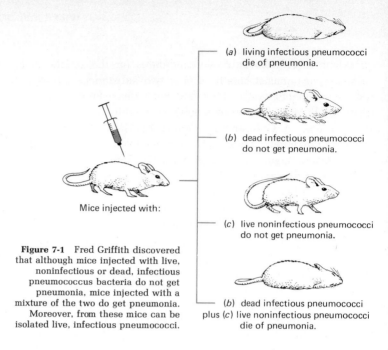

(a) living infectious pneumococci die of pneumonia.

(b) dead infectious pneumococci do not get pneumonia.

Mice injected with:

(c) live noninfectious pneumococci do not get pneumonia.

Figure 7-1 Fred Griffith discovered that although mice injected with live, noninfectious or dead, infectious pneumococcus bacteria do not get pneumonia, mice injected with a mixture of the two do get pneumonia. Moreover, from these mice can be isolated live, infectious pneumococci.

(b) dead infectious pneumococci plus (c) live noninfectious pneumococci die of pneumonia.

fectious bacteria had been killed, live infectious bacteria could be isolated from the dead mice. The dead, infectious pneumococci had thus transformed the living, noninfectious bacteria into living, infectious pneumococci.

Infectious pneumococci are enclosed in a capsule (which protects them from the disease-fighting mechanisms of the mouse). Noninfectious variants lack this capsule (and are destroyed). Thus, in Griffith's experiment, dead encapsulated pneumococci had conferred on noninfectious bacteria without capsules the ability to synthesize a capsule.

Griffith was interested in his results from a medical point of view, but a number of biologists were struck by the extraordinary possibility of inducing such a specific change in an organism. Moreover, this was a specific hereditary change, for the progeny of the transformed bacteria were also able to synthesize the new capsular material generation after generation. In a number of laboratories, Griffith's results were repeated and corroborated, and then extended.

DNA Transforms Bacteria

Griffith had made a few unsuccessful attempts to transform pneumococci in a test tube. Within a few years, in the laboratory of O. T. Avery at the Rockefeller Institute, test-tube transformation succeeded. Soon a way was found to transform pneumococci with extracts made from infectious bacteria. The extracts, a sort of bacterial juice, contained no

whole bacteria. Which chemical substance in the extract was responsible for the transformation? The way was now open to find out.

"For the past two years, first with MacLeod and now with Dr. McCarty,
I have been trying to find out what is the chemical nature of the substance
in the bacterial extract which induces this specific change," wrote O. T.
Avery to his brother, Dr. Roy C. Avery, in 1943. "Try to find in that complex mixture," he continued, "the active principle!! . . . Some job—
full of headaches and heartbreaks. But at last *perhaps* we have it."

Avery and his colleagues had isolated a substance which transformed
bacteria even when diluted 100 million times. "Potent stuff, that," as
Avery wrote. What was it? Not a protein, for it was not digested by
proteolytic enzymes. Not *RNA (ribonucleic acid),* found in ribosomes
and elsewhere, for it was not inactivated by RNase, ribonuclease, an
enzyme which digests RNA. Nor was it attacked by an enzyme which
breaks down the capsule of the infectious pneumococci; it was thus not
the capsular material itself. It did not dissolve in alcohol and ether or
in chloroform—not a lipide. The transforming substance was destroyed

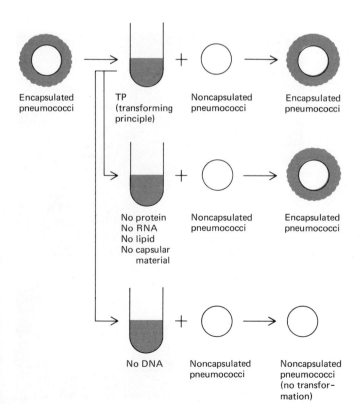

Encapsulated
pneumococci

TP
(transforming
principle)

Noncapsulated
pneumococci

Encapsulated
pneumococci

No protein
No RNA
No lipid
No capsular
material

Noncapsulated
pneumococci

Encapsulated
pneumococci

No DNA

Noncapsulated
pneumococci

Noncapsulated
pneumococci
(no transfor-
mation)

Figure 7-2 From encapsulated
pneumococci, O. T. Avery and his
collaborators isolated highly purified transforming principle, which
in very small amounts transformed
pneumococci without capsules into
pneumococci with capsules. Transforming principle treated to destroy
protein, RNA, lipides, or capsular
material was still active in transforming bacteria, but transforming
principle treated to destroy DNA
was no longer active. *Conclusion:*
The substance which transforms
nonencapsulated pneumococci into
encapsulated pneumococci is DNA.

by only one enzyme, DNase, deoxyribonuclease. DNase breaks down only DNA. The transforming substance is DNA? "Who could have guessed it?" wrote Avery.

"If we are right, and of course that is not yet proven, then it means that nucleic acids are *not* merely structurally important but functionally active substances in determining the biochemical activities and specific characteristics of cells and that by means of a known chemical substance it is possible to induce *predictable and hereditary* changes in cells. . . . But today it takes a lot of well documented evidence to convince anyone that [DNA] protein free, could possibly be endowed with such biologically active and specific properties and that is the evidence we are now trying to get. It's lots of fun to blow bubbles—but it's wiser to prick them yourself before someone else tries to."

Avery's well-documented evidence, demonstrating that the active substance which transforms pneumococci from one type into another is DNA, was published in 1944, the now-famous Avery, MacLeod, and McCarty paper. Almost 10 years passed before its importance was widely appreciated. Why? Are biologists a bit slow?

Figure 7-3 Oswalt T. Avery (1877–1955) worked for 10 years to isolate and unambiguously identify pure transforming principle. He succeeded just before his retirement from the Rockefeller Institute. Avery is seen here holding a petri dish in which are growing colonies of bacteria. *(Courtesy Roy C. Avery.)*

In 1944, this was the only evidence that genes and DNA are one and the same thing. It was thus impossible to interpret this lone piece of evidence unequivocally. Perhaps the transformation of pneumococcal types was a special phenomenon, having to do with the bacterial capsule, but unrelated to other characters and therefore unrelated to genetics in general. Perhaps transformation was mediated not by a gene, but by a virus (whatever a virus was! for little was known of viruses at that time). Most important of all, too little was known of the structure of either proteins or DNA; for this reason, knowledge of the chemical nature of genes could not elucidate the chemical basis of genetics. Interest in the structure of DNA awaited a second, and therefore convincing, demonstration of its genetic role. This demonstration came out of studies of viruses.

THE GENETIC MATERIAL OF BACTERIO-PHAGES

Bacteria are big, big enough, at least, to be stopped by certain special filters called *bacterial filters*. Toward the end of the nineteenth century, disease producers smaller than bacteria were discovered. The agent causing the plant disease tobacco mosaic passes right through a bacterial filter. Soon it was found that an animal disease, the foot-and-mouth disease of cattle, is also caused by a filterable agent, a virus. Many virus diseases affecting plants and animals are now known; human viral diseases include measles, mumps, chicken pox, smallpox, polio, rabies, and the common cold. Viruses are multifarious; each is distinguished by the disease it causes and the host it infects. In general, plant viruses infect plants, animal viruses infect animals, and insect viruses infect insects. Even bacteria suffer from viral diseases.

The Discovery of the Bacterial Viruses

In 1917, a French bacteriologist, F. d'Herelle, discovered what he called an *antimicrobe,* a killer of bacteria. To a test tube containing a nutrient solution similar to that used by Beadle and Tatum for growing bread mold, d'Herelle had added a few drops of feces from a patient recovering from dysentery. The dysentery bacteria in the feces grew for a while, but then suddenly died and *lysed,* that is, disintegrated. D'Herelle passed the contents of the tube through a bacterial filter. One drop of the resulting bacteria-free filtrate added to a fresh test tube of growing dysentery bacteria caused these also to die and lyse. (The lysis of a culture of bacteria is easily seen. A concentrated solution of bacteria is turbid or even opaque, whereas the same solution when lysed is clear except for clumps of bacterial debris.) A drop from the second tube added to a third tube again caused the bacteria to lyse, and so on, through fifty successive transfers.

D'Herelle proved that the killer, the antimicrobe, was an invisible but living creature. Only a live organism, constantly multiplying, could still be active after fifty transfers, when the original few drops of feces had been diluted away to nothing. Antimicrobes active against one strain of bacteria could, after several transfers, become killers of another strain; "adaptation is the prerogative of living organisms," wrote d'Herelle. No two strains of antimicrobes were identical, d'Herelle found; "variability," he wrote, "is an essential characteristic of life." Finally, though invisible even with the best microscopes then available (viruses can only be seen with an electron microscope), the antimicrobes could nevertheless be shown to be distinct particles like all other living creatures.

To demonstrate this last point, d'Herelle spread a few drops of a concentrated solution of bacteria together with a few drops of a solution of antimicrobes diluted 1 million times on the surface of nutrient solidified by the addition of a substance called *agar*. The multitude of bacteria grew, covering the surface with an opaque film, but that film was strewed with clear spots like little holes, called *plaques*. Each plaque, d'Herelle correctly surmised, was a colony of antimicrobes issued from one antimicrobe; the bare spaces, the plaques, had been cleared of bacteria by the growth of the antimicrobes. By counting the number of plaques and multiplying by the dilution, d'Herelle calculated the number of anti-

Figure 7-4 The electron microscope reveals the detailed structure of the phage T4. It consists of a hexagonal head and a long tail, to which are attached tail fibers. The phage attaches to a bacterium by means of these fibers. T4 and the closely related phage T2 are among the best-known organisms. Other phages have also been much studied; many have simpler structures, spheres without a tail, or rods. *(Courtesy of the Virus Laboratory, University of California at Berkeley.)*

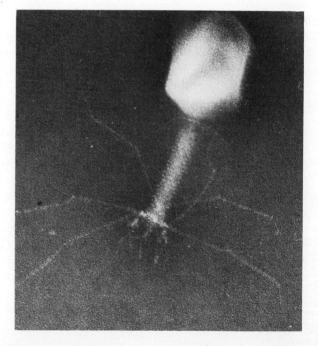

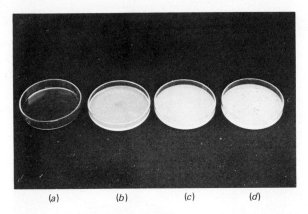

(a) (b) (c) (d)

Figure 7-5 Counting phages. *(a)* Empty petri dish. *(b)* Petri dish containing nutrient solidified with a substance called agar. *(c)* The agar surface is covered with an opaque film of bacteria, the result of spreading a relatively small number of bacteria (about 100 million) on the surface of the agar and allowing them to grow overnight, during which time they multiply many, many times. *(d)* The bacterial film, or *lawn*, is strewn with clear spots called plaques, each a colony of phages resulting from a single phage: The plate was spread with bacteria as in *(c)* and with about fifty phages; as the bacteria grew, spreading over the agar surface, each phage eventually came into contact with and infected a bacterium; its progeny then infected all bacteria growing into the area, creating a bare spot, a plaque, where no bacteria can grow. By counting the number of plaques and multiplying by the dilution, the number of phages in the original solution can be determined.

microbes in the original solution (a technique which is still used for counting viruses). Chemical substances cannot concentrate themselves in spots; antimicrobes must be living particles.

Antimicrobes only increased in numbers when mixed with live, growing bacteria. D'Herelle correctly concluded that they cannot grow alone but are obligate parasites. *Bacteriophages,* "eaters of bacteria," he called them, and so they have been called ever since—or just *phages* for short.

D'Herelle's work attracted widespread attention, for it was hoped that phages would cure bacterial infections (there were no antibiotics in those days). Though never of such direct use, they have nonetheless made a great impact. Knowledge of their life and habits has thrown light on other viruses, difficult to study because they infect the more complex cells of plants and animals, but at the same time particularly interesting to the farmer or physician. Experiments with phages have also unriddled basic cell processes, especially in genetics.

In 1939, the life cycle of a phage was outlined by Max Delbrück: The phage first attaches to a bacterium; 20 minutes later the infected bacterium bursts open, liberating about 100 phages. What happens

The Life of a Bacteriophage

Max Delbrück

Alfred D. Hershey

Figure 7-6 Max Delbrück of Caltech, Al Hershey of the Cold Spring Harbor Laboratory and Salvador Luria of M.I.T., opened up a rich vein of research with their studies of phage infection and phage genetics. They sorted out puzzling experimental results that had bedeviled earlier workers and then elucidated the nature of the infective process. The importance of their contribution to an understanding of basic cell processes was underlined in 1969 when they were jointly honored with the Nobel Prize in medicine-physiology. *(Courtesy the Nobel Foundation.)*

Salvador E. Luria

during those 20 minutes before the bacterium lyses? The search for an answer to that question became feasible after A. H. Doermann discovered in 1951 that cyanide bursts open phage-infected bacteria prematurely. Mysteriously, in the beginning of the infection he found no phages at all, not even the infecting phage, inside the bacterium. Ten minutes must pass before any phages can be detected.

What is the meaning of the disappearance of the infecting phage? In 1952, this question was answered by an important experiment, which

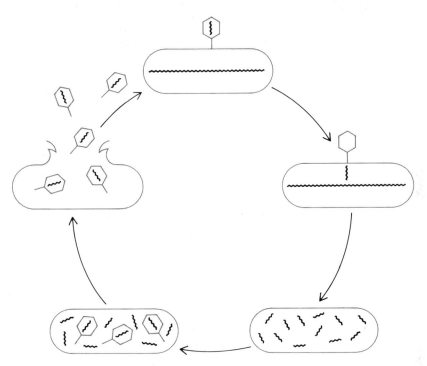

Figure 7-7 The infection of a bacterium by a phage begins with attachment of the phage particle to the bacterial cell wall. The genetic material of the phage is then injected into the host, where it multiplies (some phages cause destruction of the genetic material of the bacterium). In about 12 minutes, the bacterium contains a few fully formed progeny phage particles. After 25 to 35 minutes the bacterium lyses, liberating 100 to 200 progeny phages which can now infect other bacteria.

will be described in the next section after a little more has been said about phages and phage infection.

Early in the studies of phages came the discovery of mutants; some mutant phages infect a slightly different bacterium; others give abnormal-looking plaques, very small, very large, or encircled by a halo. If phages, like higher organisms, can suffer mutations, then, like higher organisms, they have genes. The genetic similarity between phages and other organisms became still more evident in 1946 when two of the most illustrious of the phage workers, Max Delbrück and Al Hershey, independently found genetic recombinants among the progeny of bacteria simultaneously infected with phage mutants differing in two genes. (Phages, like bacteria and some other microorganisms such as bread mold, are particularly apt for genetic experiments because they have only one set of genes on their lone chromosome, unlike peas, fruit flies, humans, and other organisms with paired genes on their paired chromosomes.)

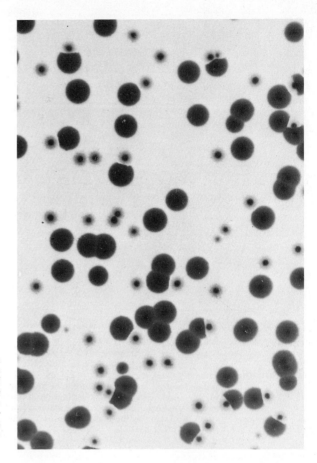

Figure 7-8 The spots in this illustration are phage plaques, colonies of phages dotting the otherwise opaque lawn of bacteria (which here appears as a white background). The small, fuzzy plaques are colonies of normal T4 phages. The larger plaques are colonies of a mutant of T4 called an *r*II mutant. *(Courtesy Seymour Benzer.)*

What happens when a phage infects a bacterium? A bacterial cell is a tiny factory, fabricating the components needed for growth and cell division. The factory operates under the direction and control of the bacterial genes, the master plan for the manufacture of bacteria. Following phage infection, the factory is taken over by the phage's genes, the phage's master plan for the manufacture of phages. The assembly lines are converted to the fabrication of phage components. What are the components of a phage? There are only two: DNA and protein. Which of these is the genetic material, the substance of which the phage genes are made, the master plan?

In 1952, A. D. Hershey, together with Martha Chase, answered that question, and in so doing explained the disappearance of the infecting phage. Hershey showed that only the phage DNA enters the bacterium. The phage protein remains outside.

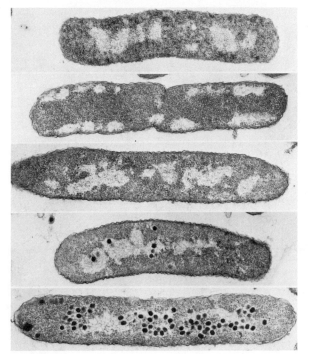

Figure 7-9 The course of a phage infection is illustrated in this series of photographs taken with an electron microscope. The top picture shows an uninfected bacterium; the clear areas are pools of bacterial genetic material. Two minutes after infection (second from top) the bacterial genetic material has been dispersed (a phage particle is seen attached to the bacterial wall toward the bottom right). Eight minutes after infection (middle picture) the bacterium is filling with phage genetic material and proteins. Twelve minutes after infection (second from bottom) the first progeny phages are seen within the bacterium. Thirty minutes after infection (bottom picture) the bacterium contains a multitude of progeny phages. *(Courtesy E. Kellenberger.)*

Only Phage DNA Enters the Bacterium

Hershey performed his classic experiment with radioactive phages grown in bacteria infected while growing in radioactive nutrient liquid. Added to this nutrient was the radioactive isotope of sulfur S^{35} or the radioactive isotope of phosphorus P^{32}. Protein contains the element sulfur; DNA does not. Therefore only the phage protein was labeled with S^{35}. On the other hand, DNA contains the element phosphorus, but phage protein does not. Only the phage DNA was labeled with P^{32}.

Hershey infected fresh bacteria growing in normal, nonradioactive nutrient with the radioactive phages. After they had attached to the bacteria, the culture was beaten in a mixer (a Waring blendor). The infected bacteria, unhurt by their thrashing, were separated from the liquid by centrifugation.

Hershey assayed both the infected bacteria and the liquid for radioactivity. He found most of the radioactive sulfur, that is, the phage protein, in the liquid and most of the radioactive phosphorus, that is, the phage DNA, in the bacteria. The beating in the mixer had stripped the phage protein off the bacteria with no ill effects on the further course of the infection. Further, Hershey purified the progeny phages resulting from this infection and found that they had inherited a large fraction of the P^{32}, but not a trace of the S^{35}, from the radioactive parental phages.

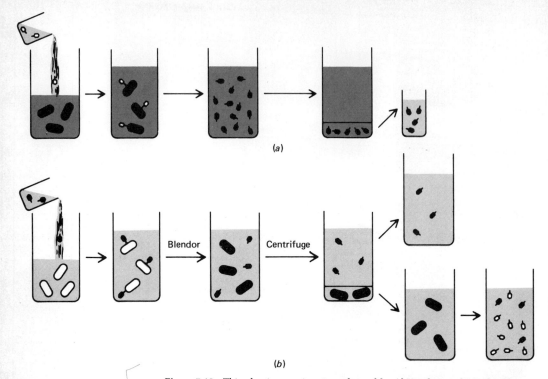

(a)

(b)

Blendor

Centrifuge

Figure 7-10 This classic experiment, performed by Al Hershey and Martha Chase, demonstrated that phage DNA and not phage protein is responsible for phage infection and the production of progeny phages. *(a)* Radioactive phages labeled with radioactive sulfur and phosphorus were first prepared: to bacteria growing in radioactive nutrient were added normal phages; the phages infected the bacteria, which subsequently liberated radioactive progeny phages; these were purified away from the radioactive nutrient by high-speed centrifugation. *(b)* Nonradioactive bacteria in nonradioactive nutrient were infected with the radioactive phages; the infected bacteria were thrashed in a Waring blendor and then centrifuged at low speed to sediment the bacteria. Analysis of the liquid after centrifugation showed that it contained almost all the radioactive sulfur; since only the phage protein contains sulfur, this meant that the liquid contained the phage protein. Analysis of the infected bacteria, and later of the progeny phages, showed that they contained much of the radioactive phosphorus; since only the phage DNA contains phosphorus, this meant that only the DNA of the parental phages had entered the bacteria and only the parental phages' DNA was transferred to progeny. *Conclusion:* The master plan of the phage, its genes, are DNA and not protein.

What is the role of the phage protein? It encloses and protects the DNA until the phage bumps into a suitable bacterial host. Protein fibers then attach the bacteriophage to the bacterial cell wall. The phage's protein coat now acts as a hypodermic syringe, injecting the DNA into the bacterium. The job of the phage protein is then done.

Only the phage DNA actually enters the bacterium. Only the DNA is needed to convert the bacterium into a phage-producing factory. Only the DNA is transmitted to progeny. Only one conclusion can be drawn— phage genes are made of DNA. And since phage genes behave like the genes of other organisms, then presumably all genes are made of DNA.

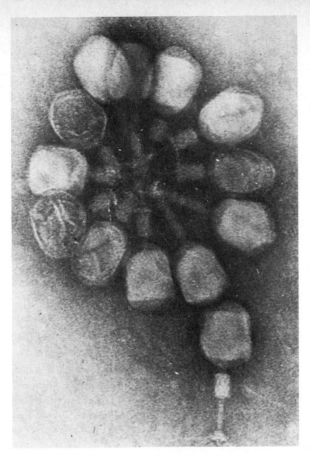

Figure 7-11 T2 phage particles attached to a fragment of bacterial cell wall. The phage DNA is contained within the hexagonal head; the enclosing head membrane and the tail, collectively called the phage *coat,* are made of protein. Two of the phages in this electron micrograph have thick tails like the phage in fig. 7-4. The tails of the others, including the lone phage at the bottom, have a thick upper and a thin lower section. This is because the outer part of the tail, the sheath, has retracted, partially revealing the inner core. Retraction of the sheath accompanies expulsion of the phage DNA. Thus, attachment of these phages to cell wall had caused them to expel their DNA as if they were injecting it into a bacterium. *(Courtesy R. W. Horne.)*

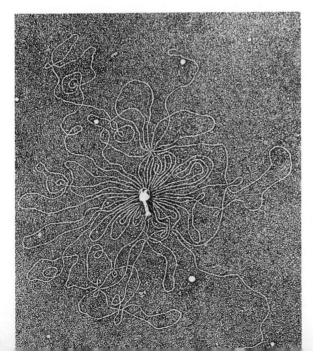

Figure 7-12 The head of this T2 phage particle has been ruptured, so the DNA it contained is displayed all around it as an enormously long fiber. Note that there are only two ends to this single gigantic DNA molecule (molecular weight 120 million). *(From A. K. Kleinschmidt et al, Biochim. Biophys. Acta,* **61:**857 (1962), *courtesy A. K. Kleinschmidt.)*

WHAT IS DNA?

By 1953, the spotlight was on DNA. Biochemists, x-ray crystallographers, and geneticists were struggling for clues to its structure.

DNA Molecules Are the Biggest

DNA was already known to be a polymer of great size. Avery had estimated that the transforming DNA he isolated from pneumococcus bacteria had a molecular weight of about 500,000, greater than that of all but a few proteins. Actually, despite Avery's gentle method of purification, the pneumococcus DNA had been smashed to pieces, and his half-million molecular weight DNA, which at the time seemed so enormous, is now known to have been a collection of fragments. Molecules whose length is 1 million times their diameter are easily broken. It suffices to stir the solution in which they are dissolved!

As better and better techniques have been devised to cope with this fragility, the molecular weight of DNA has gone up and up. The phage called T2, with which Hershey performed his famous experiment, is now known to contain a single DNA molecule of molecular weight 120 million. The bacterium which T2 infects also contains a single DNA molecule. It is fifteen times bigger—a single molecule of molecular weight about 1.5 billion! Even the largest protein molecules, in comparison with these, the biggest molecules known, are lilliputian.

DNA molecules are slender—about ten atoms across. But what they lack in diameter they make up in their quite tangible length—twenty-five bacterial DNA molecules lined up end to end would extend about 1 inch (25 mm). How can a bacterium contain a molecule which is 1,000 times its own length? Easily. The DNA's diameter and therefore also its volume are only about a five-hundredth those of the bacterium.

DNA Is a Polymer of Four Bases

DNA is a polymer of four different kinds of subunits, each consisting of a molecule of the sugar deoxyribose to which are attached a phosphate group and a base. The base may be any one of four weakly basic organic molecules, adenine (A) cytosine (C) guanine (G) and thymine (T). Neighboring subunits are linked together by a bond between the sugar of one and the phosphate of the next. Thus, DNA is a long chain of alternating sugar and phosphate groups with the four bases A, C, G, and T sticking out from the sugars.

In the early 1950s, a Columbia University biochemist, Erwin Chargaff, determined more precisely than ever before the base composition of DNA from various animals and plants and from different tissues of the same animal. He thereby disproved the theory that DNA consists of a regularly repeating series of bases, such as ACGTACGTACG . . . . The four bases, he found, do not occur in the ratio of 1 to 1 to 1 to 1. Rather,

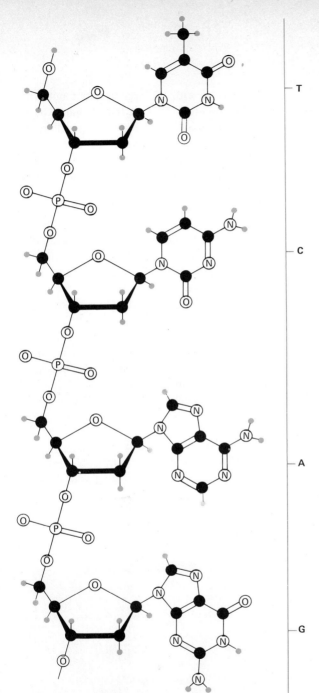

Figure 7-13 Representation of a portion of a DNA chain showing the structures of all the bases T, C, A, and G (thymine, cytosine, adenine, and guanine). The chain consists of a backbone of alternating phosphates and sugars (deoxyribose). The bases are attached to the sugars. At the left is a schematic representation.

the ratio depends on the source of the DNA. Human DNA, for example, contains about 30 percent A, no matter whether it comes from liver, sperm, or any other tissue; the avian tubercle bacillus, the agent of tuberculosis in birds, is particularly out of bounds, with only 15 percent A.

This correlation of DNA composition with the organism but not with the organ constituted further evidence that DNA is the chemical basis of inheritance. Moreover, if any sequence of bases were possible, as Chargaff's data suggested, then DNA could contain the information needed to run a cell. It would be encoded into the base sequence just as ideas are coded into the twenty-six letters of the English alphabet or the dots, dashes, and pauses of the Morse code.

Chargaff was struck by the finding that, no matter what the source of the DNA he examined, the amount of A always equaled the amount of T and the amount of G always equaled the amount of C. For example, in human DNA 30 percent of the bases are A, 30 percent T, 20 percent G, and 20 percent C; in avian tubercle bacillus DNA, 15 percent are A, 15 percent T, 35 percent G, and 35 percent C. Was this a coincidence? In fact, it was the supremely significant clue to the structure of DNA.

DNA Is Helical

Not only the biochemists but also the x-ray crystallographers were hard at work studying DNA. The three-dimensional shapes of the bases, of the sugar, and of the angles between sugar, phosphate, and bases had been fairly well worked out by 1953. Then came a snag. It is not possible to crystallize DNA, and only crystals provide really good x-ray diagrams.

For want of crystals, the x-ray crystallographer M. H. F. Wilkins studied fibers of DNA. These form readily because the long DNA molecules tend to line up side by side. The DNA molecule, Wilkins was able to deduce,

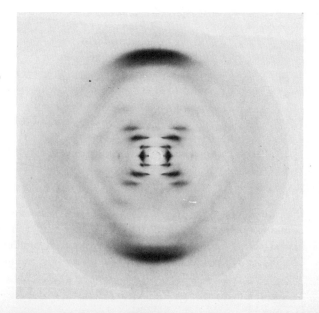

Figure 7-14 Pattern produced on a photographic plate by a beam of x-rays passed through a fiber of DNA. From such a fiber diagram, M. H. F. Wilkins was able to determine that DNA has a helical structure, and to calculate the width of the helix and the distance between turns. (*Courtesy M. H. F. Wilkins.*)

Figure 7-15 M. H. F. Wilkins (1916–   ) with the x-ray crystallographic apparatus he used to determine the structure of DNA. *(Courtesy Central Office of Information.)*

Figure 7-16 J. D. Watson (1928–   ) was a young postdoctoral fellow when he and Francis Crick (1916–   ) proposed the model of the structure of DNA now known as the Watson and Crick structure. Watson is by training a geneticist, Crick a physicist; their complementary backgrounds made them an ideal team to work out the structure of the genetic material. In 1962, Watson, Crick, and Wilkins shared the Nobel Prize in medicine-physiology in honor of their momentous discovery. *(Courtesy J. D. Watson.)*

has a helical, coiled configuration. Moreover, and very important, Wilkins could determine the overall dimensions of the helix, its diameter and the distance between turns. Any detailed model of DNA structure would have to conform to these dimensions.

Wilkins, working at King's College in London, discussed his ideas with physicist-turned-biologist Francis Crick and a young American geneticist, Jim Watson, then working with Crick in Cambridge, a few hours from London. Watson and Crick had devised a possible structure for DNA, a fascinating structure based on Chargaff's results and on the known three-dimensional shapes of the bases and the sugar. Their structure conformed perfectly to the dimensions discovered by Wilkins! In 1953, the Watson and Crick structure of DNA, published side by side with Wilkins's results, electrified biologists the world over.

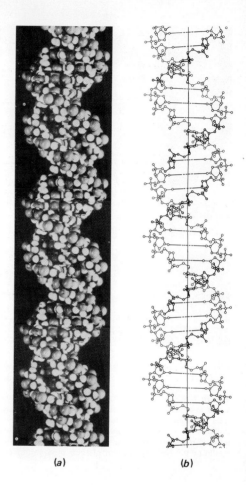

Figure 7-17 *(a)* Space-filling model of the structure of DNA; *(b)* projection of the model. The sugar-phosphate backbones twist round each other to form the famous double helix; the base pairs lie between them, perpendicular to the direction of the helix. *(Courtesy M. H. F. Wilkins.)*

(a)   *(b)*

DNA Has Two Complementary Chains

Watson and Crick proposed that DNA consists not of one chain but of two parallel chains. These are wound round each other, forming the renowned Watson and Crick double helix.

The exciting feature of the Watson and Crick structure is not its helical configuration but rather the complementary relation between the two chains: Where there is an A in one chain, then opposite it in the other there is a T; and where there is a G in one chain, then opposite it must be a C. Thus, given a particular sequence of bases in one chain, such as ACGTT, the sequence in the other chain, TGCAA, is fixed.

Because A and T, and G and C are always paired, the amounts of A and T must be equal, and the amounts of G and C must also be equal. This striking feature of DNA composition, discovered by Chargaff, was now explained.

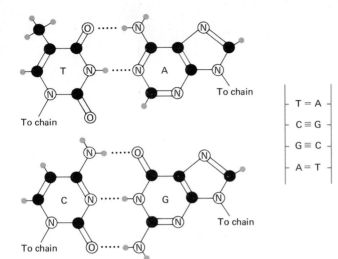

$$
\begin{array}{c}
T = A \\
C \equiv G \\
G \equiv C \\
A = T
\end{array}
$$

Figure 7-18 The two complementary strands of the double-stranded DNA molecule are held together by hydrogen bonds. T (thymine) and A (adenine) share two hydrogen bonds; C (cytosine) and G (guanine) share three hydrogen bonds. At right is a schematic representation of the double-stranded DNA structure.

Why these particular pairs and no others? Because these pairs stick together. A binds very neatly to T by a pair of hydrogen bonds, and G binds to C by three hydrogen bonds. Moreover, the base pairs lie between the sugar-phosphate backbones of the two chains like the rungs of a ladder. The A-T and G-C pairs make rungs of the same length. Other pairs would be too long or too short, distorting the ladder.

The hydrogen bonds between A-T and G-C pairs hold the two chains together. In addition, they assure correct pairing of the bases in the two chains. Thanks to them, DNA is the only known self-duplicating molecule.

In a prize understatement, Watson and Crick made the unassuming remark, "It has not escaped our notice that the specific pairing we have postulated immediately suggests a possible copying mechanism for the genetic material." What is this mechanism by which daughter cells receive an exact copy of the genetic material, the DNA, of the parent cell? The two strands of the double-stranded parent molecule separate. Next to each is synthesized its complement. Where there was one double-stranded molecule, there are now two, each identical to the parent molecule, each containing one of the parental strands. (See Fig. 7-19.)

Normally, daughter cells receive exactly the genes of the parent cell, but there are rare mutations. Normally, the two new DNA molecules are exact copies of the parent molecule, but there are rare errors. The chemistry of the bases suggests that extremely infrequently an A will

DNA AND GENETICS

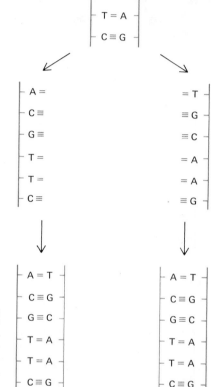

Figure 7-19 The complementarity of the bases in the two strands of DNA immediately suggested to Watson and Crick a mechanism for the replication of the genetic material: The two strands separate; the base sequence in each single strand then dictates the base sequence in its new complementary strand.

form the wrong hydrogen bonds and pair with a C or that a G will pair with a T. When such a mispaired DNA molecule replicates, the two daughter molecules will not be identical: where in one there is an A-T pair, in the other there is a G-C pair. Watson and Crick suggested that what geneticists call a mutation is, at least in some cases, the result of an error in base pairing. (See Fig. 7-20.)

What do genes do? One gene–one protein the geneticists had postulated. How does DNA determine protein structure? The sequence of bases in DNA codes for the sequence of amino acids in protein. There are only four kinds of bases in DNA, whose sequence must code for the twenty different kinds of amino acids in proteins. Clearly, a group of bases must code for each amino acid, just as a group of dots and dashes codes for each letter.

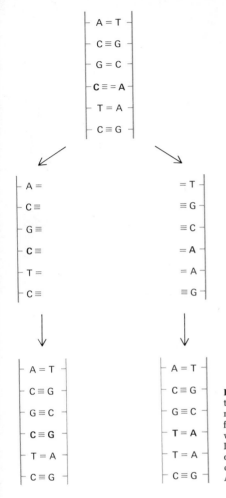

Figure 7-20 Watson and Crick proposed that some mutations may be caused by mistakes in replication. Thus, in the figure, an A has mistakenly been paired with a C instead of with a T. When this DNA replicates, the two daughter molecules will differ in one base pair: where one has a G-C base pair, the other has an A-T base pair.

The sequence of bases spells out the genetic language of the cell. How much information does the DNA of a cell contain? In each cell of your body there are forty-six chromosomes. (The DNA from all those chromosomes laid end to end would extend 2 yards!) If the sequence of bases coded for English letters instead of for amino acids, the DNA in one cell would code for about 1,000 good-sized text books. As Francis Crick has remarked, it takes a vast amount of information to make an organism that can think about itself!

The structure of DNA, the genetic material, is the key to understanding the chemistry of life. This structure, so intimately and evidently related to the functions of the genes, suggested the answers to many questions—how genes replicate, the nature of mutations, and the way in which genes determine protein structure and thereby constitute the master plan of

Figure 7-21 A segment of a DNA molecule is here magnified 7.3 million times. The intertwined chains, coiled into a helix, are visible. *(Courtesy Jack Griffith and James Bonner.)*

the cell. But these suggested answers were in fact gigantic questions, for the functions of DNA remained, and in part still remain, to be fathomed in detail and proved experimentally. Many of the major results of the explosion in biologic research set off by the discovery of the structure of DNA are described in the next chapters.

THE REPLICATION AND RECOMBINATION OF DNA

Life is characterized by growth and reproduction. A bacterial cell grows and then divides, and two new bacteria are created. A fertilized egg divides and divides and divides until, having fulfilled the complex destiny written into its chromosomes, a human being is created.

Reproduction requires that from cell to cell and from generation to generation the master plan contained in the chromosomes, the blueprint of the individual and the species, be transmitted intact. That master plan is a collection of genes; thus, when a cell divides, the daughter cells must both be furnished with a copy, an exact replica or duplicate, of each gene. How do genes duplicate? Genes are DNA. How then does DNA duplicate?

HOW DOES DNA REPLICATE?

When Watson and Crick had worked out the structure of DNA, they thought they had found the answer to that question. The two complementary strands of the parental molecule separate; each serves as the model for its complementary strand; there are then two DNA molecules where there had been only one, each identical to the original parental molecule, each containing one new and one parental strand. *Semiconservative*, the Watson-Crick replication scheme came to be called, for

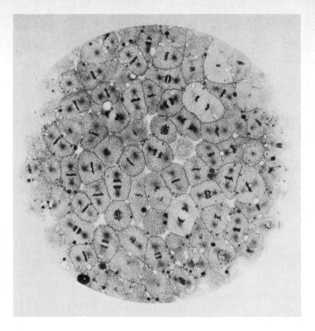

Figure 8-1 Cell multiplication, as seen in this photograph of whitefish cells, is a prerequisite of continued life on earth. Cell multiplication must be accompanied by duplication of the genes, the master plan of the cell, which are embodied in the chromosomes, seen here in various stages of mitosis. *(Courtesy "Turtox Collection," CCM General Biological, Inc.)*

the two halves of the parental molecule, the two complementary strands, are conserved separately but intact.

Does DNA in fact replicate semiconservatively? Or does it, for example, duplicate *conservatively*, one of the two daughter molecules being entirely newly synthesized, the other being simply the old parental molecule conserved intact? Or does it duplicate *dispersively*, the parental molecule being broken down into small bits, which are incorporated together with new bits into the two daughter molecules? Or does it replicate in yet another way?

The way in which DNA actually duplicates had to be determined by experiment, but inventing the experiment which could distinguish between, for example, semiconservative, conservative, and dispersive replication was far from easy.

All three schemes of replication predict that, when DNA duplicates, the daughter DNA will consist of the parental DNA plus an equal amount of new DNA. It is the distribution of the parental DNA in the daughter molecules which is different in these schemes: In the case of conservative replication, half the daughter molecules will be completely new, half will be completely old; in the cases of both semiconservative and dispersive duplication, all the daughter molecules will be half new, half old. Semiconservative and dispersive duplication can be distinguished after the daughter molecules have replicated in their turn: In semiconservative duplication, half the second-generation, granddaughter molecules will be half new, half grandparental, that is, exactly like the daughter molecules, while half will be completely new; in dispersive replication, all granddaughter molecules will be about one-fourth grandparental, three-fourths new. (See Fig. 8-2.)

In order to determine how DNA duplicates, a way had to be found to distinguish parental from newly synthesized DNA, and to separate DNA molecules according to their content of parental and new DNA. In 1957, Matt Meselson and Frank Stahl at Caltech devised the ingenious experiment that accomplished this.

Meselson and Stahl grew bacteria in a synthetic nutrient in which the salt ammonium sulfate $(NH_4)_2SO_4$ was isotopically labeled: the normal isotope of nitrogen N^{14} was replaced by the stable heavy isotope N^{15}. DNA contains carbon, oxygen, hydrogen, phosphorus, and nitrogen atoms; about 15 percent by weight is nitrogen. Replacing the nitrogen of atomic weight 14 by nitrogen of atomic weight 15 produces *heavy* DNA, whose density is almost 1 percent greater than that of normal, *light*, DNA. Meselson and Stahl examined the distribution of heavy DNA in the first- and second-generation DNA synthesized by bacteria following the bacteria's transfer from heavy N^{15} nutrient to ordinary, light, N^{14} nutrient.

THE DUPLICATION OF BACTERIAL DNA

Figure 8-2 Three possible mechanisms of DNA replication. *(a)* Watson and Crick proposed that DNA replicates *semiconservatively*: the two complementary strands of the parental molecule separate, and each serves as the model for the synthesis of a new complementary strand; daughter molecules thus consist of one old parental strand and one newly synthesized strand. *(b)* In *conservative* replication, the parental molecule is conserved intact; so both of the strands of one daughter molecule are of parental origin, while both of the strands of the other daughter molecule are newly synthesized. *(c)* In *dispersive* replication, the parental DNA is fragmented, and bits are included in both daughter molecules, together with bits of newly synthesized DNA.

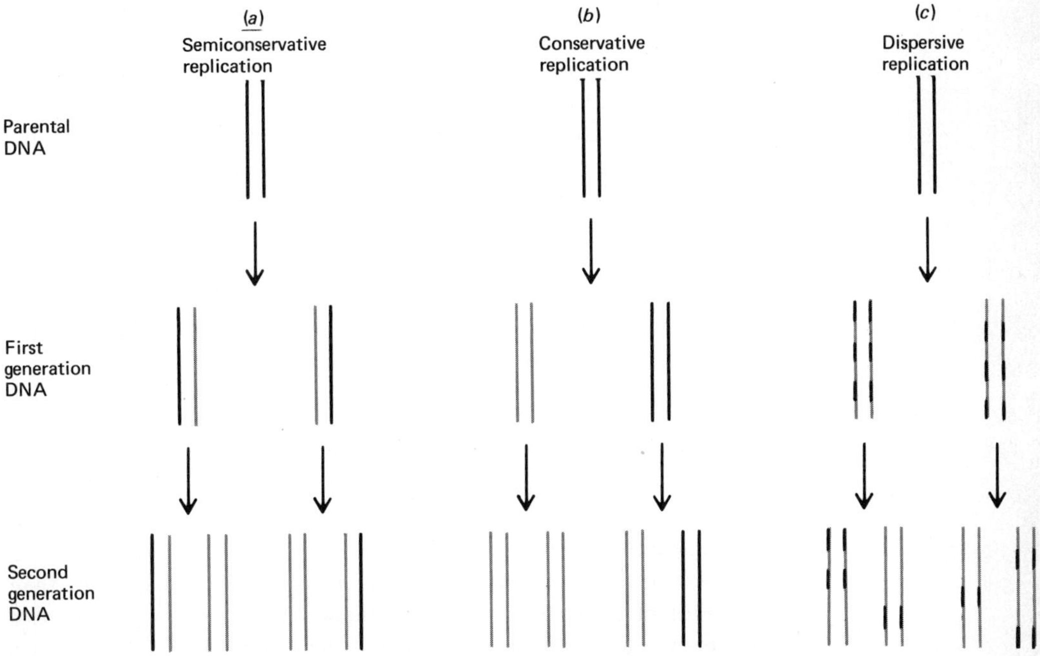

Watson and Crick's scheme of semiconservative replication predicts that when the bacteria have doubled in number in the light medium, all the heavy parental DNA will have disappeared, replaced by DNA with one heavy parental strand and one new, light strand. Such hybrid DNA would have a density intermediate between those of heavy and light DNA, a density ½ percent less than that of the heavy parental DNA (see fig. 8–2).

If replication were dispersive, the result would be the same, all heavy parental DNA being replaced by hybrid DNA of intermediate density (although in this case the hybrid DNA would consist not of one light and one heavy strand, but of strands made of intermittent heavy and light segments).

If replication were conservative, heavy parental DNA would persist, accompanied by an equal amount of completely light, newly synthesized DNA; there would thus be two species of DNA differing in density by 1 percent.

Density-gradient Centrifugation

But how can molecules which differ in density by ½ percent, or even by 1 percent, be distinguished? Meselson and Stahl, together with Jerome Vinograd, brilliantly solved that problem. They made use of an *ultra-centrifuge*. An ordinary centrifuge spins around a few thousand times per minute; this creates sufficient force to sediment large objects (such as bacteria). An ultracentrifuge spins around 50,000 or more times per minute; this creates sufficient force to sediment large molecules. DNA, for example, can be sedimented in an ultracentrifuge.

On the other hand, a salt will not sediment in an ultracentrifuge; but it will try. Meselson, Stahl, and Vinograd put to good use the fact that in trying to sediment a salt concentrates toward the bottom of the centrifuge tube. More salt at the bottom and less at the top means a solution of greater density toward the bottom and of lesser density toward the top—a salt solution, whirling around in an ultracentrifuge, forms a *density gradient*. From this was developed a way to separate DNA molecules of only very slightly different densities.

The concentration of a solution of the salt cesium chloride (CsCl, an analog of sodium chloride, NaCl, table salt) was adjusted so that its density was the same as that of DNA. When such a solution is centrifuged at high speed for some hours so that a density gradient is established, the density just at the middle of the centrifuge tube is still this original density; above this point the density is lesser, below it is greater.

If the solution contains not only cesium chloride but also DNA, then as the gradient becomes established, the DNA at the top of the tube, finding itself in a solution whose density is less than its own, sinks down toward the bottom of the tube where the density is greater; DNA at the

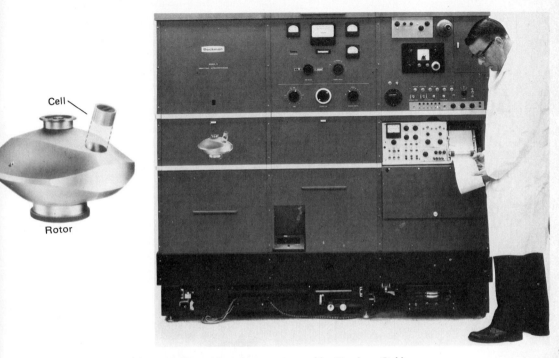

Figure 8-3 An analytic ultracentrifuge such as this one was used by Meselson, Stahl, and Vinograd in their experiments on DNA replication. The solution to be centrifuged is placed in the large hole in the cell, which is sandwiched between two glass disks (not shown). The cell fits into the hole in the rotor, that is, the centrifuge head, and the rotor hangs from a wire in the center-left compartment of the centrifuge. In an analytic centrifuge, the spinning solution can be photographed while the centrifuge is in operation; thus the actual process of sedimentation can be observed and studied. (Most of this large machine houses the motor and the vacuum and optical systems.) *(Courtesy Beckman Instruments, Inc.)*

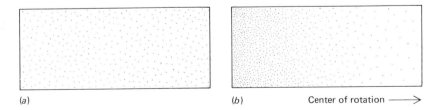

(a)   (b)   Center of rotation $\longrightarrow$

Figure 8-4 Establishment of a density gradient. *(a)* Initially, a uniform salt solution is placed in the centrifuge. *(b)* Centrifugation at high speed causes the salt to concentrate toward the bottom of the cell, creating a gradient of concentration and thus of density: the salt concentration at the center of the cell is the same as the initial concentration, whereas toward the bottom, away from the center of rotation, the concentration is greater, and toward the top it is lesser.

HOURS

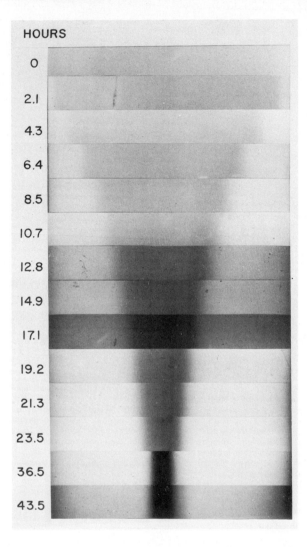

O

2.1

4.3

6.4

8.5

10.7

12.8

14.9

17.1

19.2

21.3

23.5

36.5

43.5

Figure 8-5 Banding of DNA in a cesium chloride density gradient as seen in a series of photographs of the moving centrifuge cell taken at different times. As the salt gradient forms, the DNA collects in a band at the point in the cell where the density of the solution is the same as its own, in this case the center. *(Courtesy Matt Meselson.)*

bottom of the tube, finding itself in a solution whose density is greater than its own, rises toward the top, like cream. The DNA all finally collects in a band at the middle of the tube, where the solution's density is the same as its own. DNAs of slightly different densities will collect in bands slightly higher or slightly lower in the tube.

Thus, if the cesium chloride's original density, and therefore the density at the middle of the centrifuge tube, is the same as that of heavy N^{15} DNA, then this heavy DNA will collect in a band at the middle of the tube. Light N^{14} DNA will collect slightly above the heavy DNA, toward the top of the tube, for there the density is slightly lesser. Hybrid DNA, with a density just between heavy and light, will collect just between heavy and light DNA.

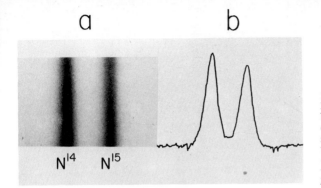

a   b

N^{14} N^{15}

Figure 8-6 Banding of heavy and light DNA. Light (N^{14}) and heavy (N^{15}) DNA band at different places in a cesium chloride density gradient. *(a)* A photograph taken of the moving cell; *(b)* a tracing of the photograph made with a densitometer makes it possible to calculate the amount of DNA in each band. *(Courtesy Matt Meselson.)*

Bacterial DNA Replicates Semiconservatively

The perfection of this new technique, called *density-gradient centrifugation,* set the stage for the experiment that proved that DNA replicates semiconservatively, as Watson and Crick had predicted 4 years previously.

Heavy DNA was extracted from bacteria grown for many generations in heavy N^{15} nutrient; this was the parental DNA, of heavy density. Other bacteria grown for many generations in heavy nutrient were transferred to normal isotope nutrient. At various times thereafter, some of the growing bacteria were removed and their DNA extracted. The DNA was analyzed in a density gradient.

Meselson and Stahl found that the longer the bacteria had grown in the light nutrient, the less heavy DNA and the more hybrid-density DNA they contained. When they had grown in light nutrient for just one generation, that is, until they had just doubled in number, all the heavy parental DNA had been replaced by hybrid-density DNA. Bacteria grown for more than one generation in light medium always contained hybrid DNA accompanied by an ever-increasing amount of completely light DNA. (See Fig. 8-7.)

"These results permit the following conclusions to be drawn regarding DNA replication under the conditions of the present experiment," wrote Meselson and Stahl in their very careful summing up.

"1. The nitrogen of a DNA molecule is divided equally between two subunits which remain intact through many generations.

"2. Following replication, each daughter molecule has received one parental subunit.

"The results of the present experiment are in exact accord with the expectations of the Watson-Crick model for DNA duplication."

UNWINDING DNA

The replication of DNA poses perplexing and largely unresolved problems, inherent in the structure of the DNA molecule. How, for example, are the two parental strands separated?

The separation of the two parental strands is a problem because they are wound round each other like the strands of a cable or a piece of twine.

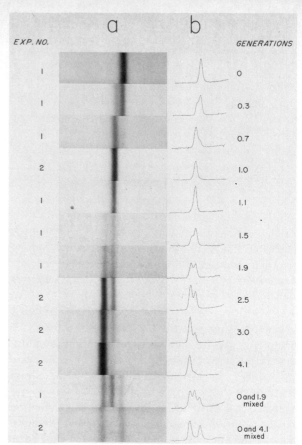

EXP. NO.	a	b	GENERATIONS
1			0
1			0.3
1			0.7
2			1.0
1			1.1
1			1.5
1			1.9
2			2.5
2			3.0
2			4.1
1			0 and 1.9 mixed
2			0 and 4.1 mixed

Figure 8-7 This experiment demonstrated that bacterial DNA replicates semiconservatively, as predicted by Watson and Crick. Bacteria were grown in heavy nutrient until time 0, when they were transferred to light nutrient. At various times thereafter, samples were removed from the growing culture; the density of the bacterial DNA, and thus its content of heavy parental DNA, was determined by centrifugation in a cesium chloride gradient. At the start of the experiment (0 generations) all the DNA was heavy *(density increases from left to right)*. When the bacteria had doubled in number in light nutrient (one generation), the heavy DNA was entirely replaced by DNA which was half parental, half newly synthesized, as evidenced by its hybrid density, midway between those of heavy and light DNA. Thereafter, the hybrid DNA remained, but it was accompanied by proportionately more and more light, completely newly synthesized DNA. *(Courtesy Matt Meselson.)*

Figure 8-8 DNA replication requires that the two strands of the parental DNA separate. Since the two strands are wound round each other, their separation makes the tail of the replicating molecule spin around.

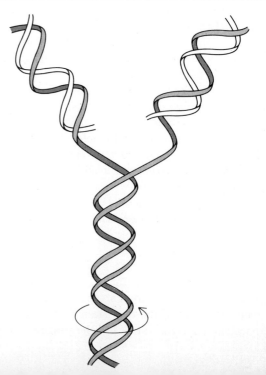

By fraying the end of a piece of twine, one can separate two strands; if they are pulled apart, the tail of the piece of twine spins round and round, one turn for each untwist of the strands. Similarly, the two DNA strands must be untwisted in order to be separated—nearing a half-million turns to untwist the DNA in a bacterium.

In the early 1970s, a new enzyme called *unwindase* was discovered in phages, in bacteria, in animal cells. It unwinds double-stranded DNA, aligning the two parental strands in preparation for their duplication. Is there also a special mechanism which during replication prevents the spinning DNA tail from flailing around? None has yet been found.

A strand of DNA has a chemical direction because of the asymmetry of the sugar molecules in the DNA backbone (going from carbon 1 of the sugar toward carbon 5 is not the same as going from carbon 5 toward carbon 1, just as going from the thumb toward the little finger is not the same as going from the little finger toward the thumb). The directions of the two complementary strands of the DNA molecule are opposite— one strand goes "up," the other goes "down." So when a DNA molecule duplicates, the two new strands must also have opposite directions: an "up" strand must be synthesized complementary to the "down" strand, a "down" strand complementary to the "up" strand.

THE ENZYMATIC SYNTHESIS OF DNA

Could one enzyme synthesize new DNA strands in both the "up" and the "down" directions? This would seem most unlikely, yet only one DNA-synthesizing enzyme has been found, and, indeed, it polymerizes the bases into DNA in only one direction.

This would pose no problem if the two parental strands separated completely before DNA replication begins; the DNA-synthesizing enzyme could then start at one end of one of the strands and at the other end of the complementary strand, thereby synthesizing both new strands in the same direction (from the arrowhead toward the tail in fig. 8-9a). In fact, the new strands are, at least usually, synthesized as the two old strands separate; so one must be synthesized "up," the other "down."

How is this accomplished? Is one new strand synthesized piecemeal as the old strands separate? This seems likely, but the answers to these questions await more knowledge about the enzymes involved in DNA synthesis. For despite intensive research, little is known about these important enzymes.

In 1956, Arthur Kornberg thought he had discovered the enzyme which synthesizes DNA. His enzyme, called *DNA polymerase,* is found in all cells; in a test tube, it polymerizes the bases, thereby synthesizing new DNA, only if some DNA is already present to serve as a model. But Kornberg's enzyme often synthesizes branched DNA and has never synthe-

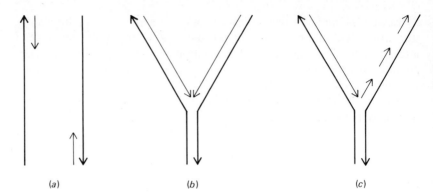

Figure 8-9 The two complementary strands of a DNA molecule have opposite chemical directions; therefore, when the molecule duplicates, the two new strands also have opposite directions. *(a)* This would pose no problem if the two strands separated completely before synthesis of the new strands begins. In that case, by starting at one end of one strand and at the opposite end of the other a single enzyme could synthesize both strands in the same chemical direction. *(b)* If the two new strands were synthesized from the ends of the old strands toward the separation point of these strands, then two enzymes would be required because one new strand would be synthesized in one direction and the other in the other direction. *(c)* In fact, there is apparently only one enzyme; so probably in most cases one new strand is synthesized in a single piece, whereas the other new strand is synthesized in the same chemical direction, but piecemeal: the parental strands separate a bit, and a piece is synthesized; the parental strands separate further, and another piece is synthesized.

sized biologically active DNA. Though a few skeptics doubted that this was really the enzyme that synthesizes DNA in cells, still nobody succeeded in finding another enzyme.

Then in 1970 John Cairns found a mutant bacterium which synthesizes none of Kornberg's DNA polymerase, yet nevertheless synthesizes DNA normally. Clearly, Kornberg's enzyme does not synthesize DNA in cells, only in test tubes. It is now supposed that, in fact, this enzyme is one of a group of enzymes that repair DNA damaged, for example, by ultraviolet or cosmic radiation.

Where, then, is the true DNA polymerase? Securely attached to the cell membrane, it would seem, where it escaped detection until the 1970s. It now appears that DNA synthesis is mediated by one enzyme or, more probably, by a group of enzymes organized as an elaborate multifunctional DNA-duplicating machine. What are the roles of the members of this replication complex? This is not yet known.

THE FORM OF DUPLICATING DNA

In 1963, John Cairns succeeded, as he put it, in catching intact bacterial DNA molecules "in the act of replication." Cairns made use of a technique called *autoradiography,* whereby DNA molecules were induced to take photographs of themselves.

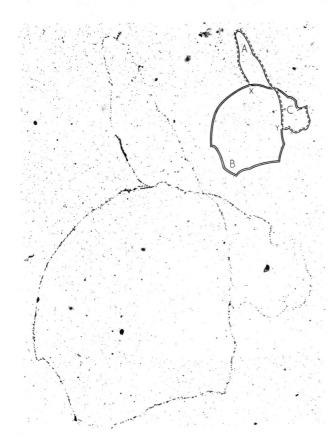

Figure 8-10 John Cairns discovered that the DNA of a bacterium is a circular molecule and that replicating circular DNA has a loop. DNA from bacteria grown in nutrient containing tritrium-labeled thymine was spread on a photographic film; disintegrating tritium atoms exposed the film, displaying the molecule as a series of black dots. (The inserted drawing indicates by a dotted line those portions which have fewer dots and therefore only one strand which contains tritium.) *(Courtesy John Cairns.)*

Cairns first prepared radioactive DNA by growing bacteria in nutrient to which had been added the DNA base thymine *(T)* labeled with tritium, the radioactive isotope of hydrogen. DNA synthesized in this nutrient contained tritium-labeled thymine. This radioactive DNA was carefully spread on a glass microscope slide which was then overlaid with photographic emulsion and stored in the dark for 2 months. During this time, the disintegrating radioactive atoms exposed tiny spots of the film. When the film was developed, the radioactive DNA molecules were displayed as strings of tiny black dots.

A linear DNA molecule caught in the act of replication would have the form of a Y. Rather, Cairns found circles with a loop. The circles measured almost ⅟₂₅ inch (1 mm) in circumference. From this, Cairns calculated that they comprise the entire bacterial chromosome, a single circular DNA molecule with a molecular weight of almost 2 billion.

Bacterial DNA: A Circle with a Loop

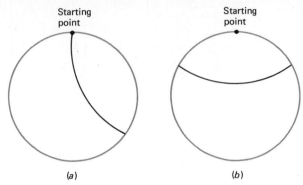

Figure 8-11 In the replication of a circular DNA molecule, either *(a)* duplication moves from the starting point around the circle in only one direction, or *(b)* it radiates in both directions from the starting point.

Cairns supposed that duplication of this giant circle, having begun at some initiation point, moves around in one direction until the starting point is again reached. It now seems more likely that duplication radiates in both directions from the initiation point.

Circular DNA and Rolling-circle Replication

In the late 1960s, thanks in large part to the development of new methods for preparing DNA for examination with the electron microscope, it was discovered that circularity is a general feature of DNA. Not only is bacterial DNA circular, but also the DNA of various phages, of several animal viruses, and of mitochondria. The DNA of a phage called *lambda* is linear when it is within a phage particle but circularizes after entering the bacterial host; for this purpose it has "sticky" ends. (See Fig. 8-12.)

At each end of the lambda DNA molecule, one strand is longer by twelve bases than the other. These single-stranded ends are complementary to each other. This allows the single-stranded bit at one end of the molecule to "stick" by base pairing to the single-stranded bit at the other end, forming a circle; a joining enzyme transforms this structure into a perfect double-stranded circle.

The Cairns pattern, a circle with a loop, seems to describe the replication of bacterial DNA, as well as the DNA of some animal viruses and phages. The replication of the DNA of some other phages and of bacterial DNA during mating seems better described by a second pattern of replication, proposed in 1968 by David Dressler and Walter Gilbert of Harvard University and baptised by them *rolling-circle* replication.

The rolling-circle model makes circularity an essential feature of DNA replication. It proposes that one strand of a replicating molecule of DNA always remains circular—it is the rolling circle. The other strand is

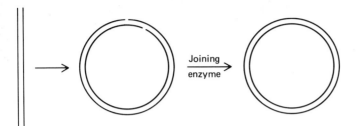

Figure 8-12 The DNA of the phage lambda is linear while it is within the phage. After injection into a bacterium, the DNA circularizes thanks to its "sticky" ends; at each end, one strand is longer than the other; these overlapping bits are complementary, so they "stick" together by base-pairing, circularizing the molecule; a joining enzyme closes the circle.

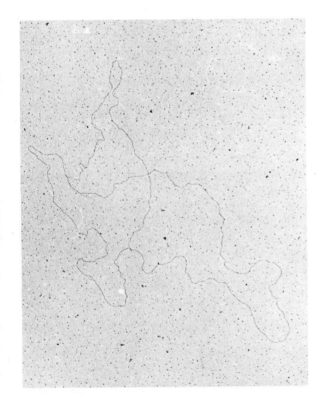

Figure 8-13 Electron micrograph of replicating lambda DNA, which has the form discovered by Cairns, a circle with a loop. *(Courtesy David Dressler.)*

broken at a specific starting place. One of the ends created by the break peels off the rolling circle and serves as a model for the synthesis of a new strand. The other end is elongated, using the bared part of the rolling circle as a model.

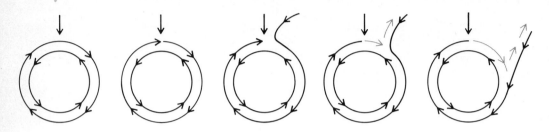

Figure 8-14 The rolling-circle model of DNA replication. One strand of the double-stranded circular DNA molecule is broken, and one end then peels off. New DNA strands are synthesized complementary to the bared section of the circle and to the peeled-off section (in this case, the DNA must be synthesized piecemeal).

The rolling-circle model of DNA replication explains some curious observations. For example, the phage φX174 contains a single-stranded, circular DNA molecule. After its entry into the host bacterium, the complementary strand is synthesized, so the DNA becomes double-stranded. This new strand is the rolling circle, from which is peeled off continuous single-stranded phage DNA, which is cut to length, circularized, and packaged inside phage protein coats. Sometimes this strand must attain rather great length before being cut into phage-length pieces, for multiple-length circles two or more times the circumference of normal φX174 circles have been observed with the electron microscope. Multiple

Figure 8-15 Replicating DNA from the phage φX174—a double-stranded rolling circle with a single-stranded tail. The single-stranded tail is continuously peeled off while new DNA, complementary to the bared rolling circle, is added on to its other end. The single-stranded DNA tail is cut to length and packaged into progeny phage particles. *(Courtesy David Dressler.)*

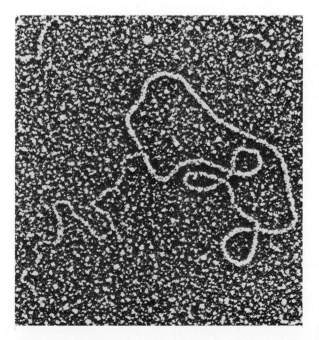

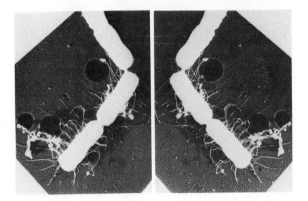

Figure 8-16 Stereo photographs of mating bacteria. The
female, in the process of dividing, is covered with filaments.
The male is identified by lambda phages, four of which
appear as bubbles attached to it by fine tails. The bacteria
are joined end to end by a tubular bridge through which
DNA passes from the male into the female. *(Courtesy T. F.
Anderson, E. L. Wollman, and F. Jacob.)* For instructions
on how to view these photographs, see Fig. 3-25, p. 69.

circles and multiple long, linear molecules have also been observed in
the case of several other phages, including lambda. Rolling-circle duplication explains these observations.

The rolling-circle model is asymmetric, in the sense that the two strands
are not equivalent—a starting point is located on only one of them. Some
predictions deduced from this asymmetry have turned out to be correct.
One of these had to do with bacterial mating. Certain bacteria mate
when a male and a female come into contact. A connecting tube forms
between them, the male's DNA then duplicates, and one copy is transferred to the female. The rolling-circle model predicts asymmetry—only
one particular strand, the one which is peeled off, should enter the female. That only one particular strand actually enters the female has been
demonstrated experimentally.

Two patterns of DNA replication already seemed like one too many when
in 1972 two more were discovered. Jerome Vinograd at Caltech untangled the complex pattern of replication of mitochondrial DNA largely
by arranging in a rational sequence the various replicating forms he
discovered with the electron microscope.

**More
Replicating
Forms**

The two strands of the circular DNA of mitochondria can be differentiated on the basis of their different densities in a cesium chloride gradient (the difference is due to their different base compositions); one strand
is called the light strand, the other the heavy strand. Replication begins

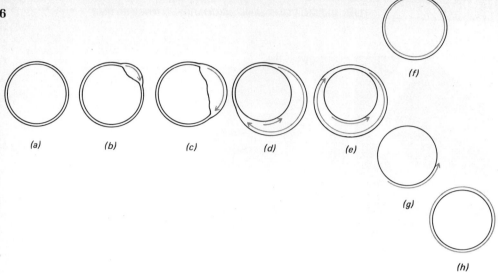

Figure 8-17 Replication of the circular DNA of mitochrondria. *(a), (b), (c)* and *(d)* Only when 60 percent of one strand has been duplicated does replication of the other strand begin. *(e)* The two daughter molecules separate (giving *[f]* and *[g]*) when one strand is still only partially duplicated. Because the two strands are duplicated in opposite directions, one enzyme would suffice to polymerize both new strands.

at a specific point on the light strand and continues around, probably in only one direction, displacing the unreplicated heavy strand. Only when about 60 percent of the light strand has been duplicated does replication of the heavy strand begin, creating a double-stranded segment in the large single-stranded loop.

Naturally, duplication of the light strand is completed long before duplication of the heavy strand. The two circles separate just before duplication of the light strand is completed, generating a double-stranded circle, progeny of the light strand, and a single-stranded circle with a double-stranded region, the partially replicated heavy strand. When its replication is completed, the heavy strand has also become a double-stranded circle.

A noncircular replicating DNA molecule was discovered, also in 1972, by David Dressler. The DNA of the phage T7, he observed with the electron microscope, replicates as a rod in which initiation of replication begins not at an end but toward the middle.

A small loop, or bubble, about 17 percent from one end of the rod, signifies the beginning of DNA duplication, the point where the two strands first separate. The bubble enlarges as replication radiates in both directions. Since duplication starts closer to one end, it reaches that end before the other, transforming the rod into a Y; when the other end has been reached, the Y becomes two rods. A second round of duplication may be initiated before the first has finished, as shown by the occasional appearance of a bubble in one arm of the Y. (See Figs. 8-19 and 8-20.)

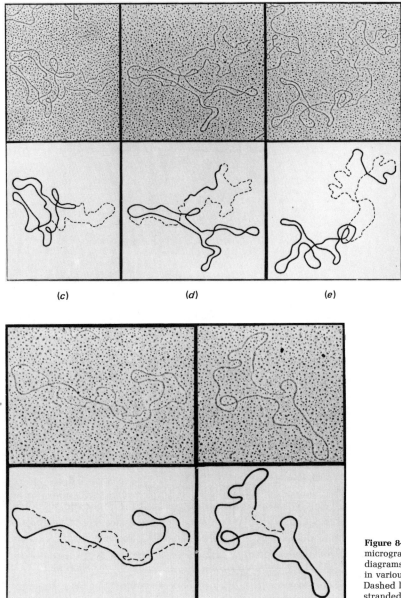

Figure 8-18 This series of electron micrographs and accompanying diagrams show mitochondrial DNA in various stages of duplication. Dashed lines indicate single-stranded segments of DNA. The lettering corresponds to Fig. 8-17. *(Courtesy Jerome Vinograd.)*

Thus, four different forms of replicating DNA have been discovered: Cairns found double-stranded circles with a double-stranded loop; Dressler and Gilbert proposed the rolling circle to account for double-stranded circles with a tail; Vinograd observed double-stranded circles which,

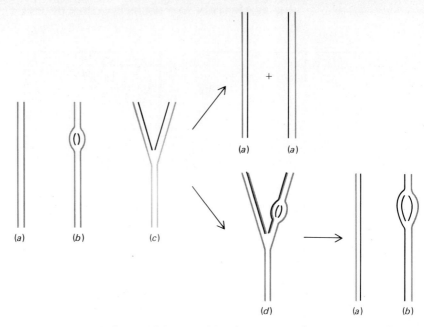

Figure 8-19 Replication of the DNA of the phage T7. *(a)* The phage DNA is a linear molecule. *(b)* Replication starts about 17 percent from one end of the molecule, forming a loop. *(c)* Enlargement of the loop transforms the rod into a Y. *(d)* Before replication is completed, yielding two rods, some molecules begin a second round of replication, as witnessed by a bubble in one arm of the Y.

during a large part of the replication cycle, have a single-stranded loop; and Dressler found rods with an internal double-stranded loop which are converted by further replication into Y's.

It would seem reasonable that such a vital and universal function as DNA replication is accomplished by a mechanism which is basically the same in all cells. Perhaps further detailed studies will reveal a fundamental similarity in these four patterns which is not as yet evident.

THE MOLECU-LAR BASIS OF GENETIC RECOMBINA-TION

Genes located on the same chromosome are usually inherited together, but not always. Crossing over of chromosomes causes an exchange of pieces and therefore an exchange of genes. An individual who on one chromosome bears genes which in his forebears were located on two chromosomes is a *genetic recombinant*.

Genetic recombination is a widespread phenomenon. We humans, for example, are all genetic recombinants, for crossing over is characteristic of the first of the two special cell divisions *(meiosis)* which give rise to the germ cells, egg and sperm. Thus, each of the twenty-three chromosomes you inherited from your mother bears, thanks to crossing over, some genes which she inherited from her mother and some which she inherited from her father; the same is of course true of your paternal chromosomes.

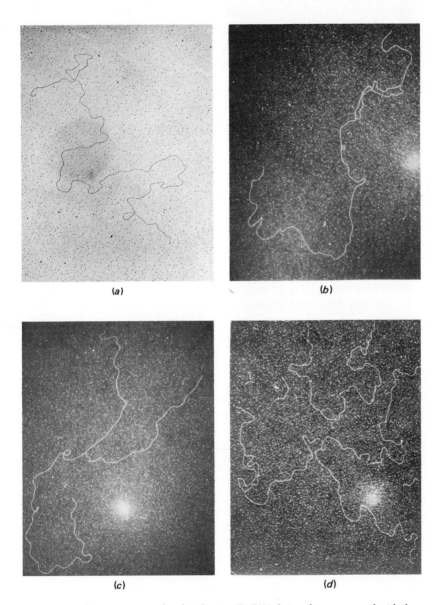

(a)

(b)

(c)

(d)

Figure 8-20 Electron micrographs of replicating T7 DNA, lettered to correspond with the stages of replication shown diagrammatically in Fig. 8-19. *(Courtesy David Dressler.)*

Genetic recombination in the fruit fly was discovered and studied by Morgan, and in the lowly bread mold by Beadle and Tatum. Genetic recombination in bacteria was the brilliant discovery of Tatum and Lederberg—it follows the transfer of DNA from a male bacterium into a female.

In 1946, the same year that bacteria were found to mate, both Max Delbrück and Al Hershey discovered genetic recombination in phages. Genetic recombination, observed in man and mold, is a characteristic of living organisms.

(The very universality of genetic recombination bespeaks its importance. Why has natural selection so favored in every plant and animal a mode of life and reproduction that allows at least occasionally for the genetic material of two individuals to come into contact and recombine? No doubt because genetic recombination increases genetic variety, maximizing the number of different types of individuals and thereby maximizing the chances of survival of the species. Not only biologists, but also philosophers and politicians may well ponder the ultimate price of uniformity: Changes in the environment can eliminate all members of a species if they are identical. The variety which Darwin recognized as the fodder of natural selection is a requisite of survival.)

Genetic recombination increases variety, for it creates new combinations of genes. How, in fact, does this happen? The task of molecular genetics has been to describe genetic recombination in terms of molecules.

MAPPING A GENE

If each gene is a segment of a continuous DNA molecule, then what separates genes one from the next? The answer is DNA itself, or, more specifically, a sequence of bases in the DNA which signifies the end of one gene and the beginning of another. Does the chemical event which results in genetic recombination recognize this special sequence of bases and thus take place only between genes, or does it occur within genes?

Genetic recombination within a gene was first observed as an extraordinarily rare event in fruit flies. Its rarity was to be expected, for the closer together the mutations, the less frequent the recombination between them, and mutations within one gene are of course necessarily extremely close together. Because of this, fruit flies were unsuitable for a study of recombination within a gene—impossible to comb them by the millions for a rare recombinant. Seymour Benzer therefore turned to the phage T4.

Finding Rare Recombinants among Phage Mutants

Benzer made use of some convenient properties of the so-called rII mutants (see fig. 7-8) of phage T4 to demonstrate that recombination commonly takes place within genes, and ultimately to map the rII gene, that is, to arrange a host of rII mutations in linear sequence.

Benzer found a way to ferret out ultrarare normal recombinants produced in crosses between two rII mutants. Although both normal and

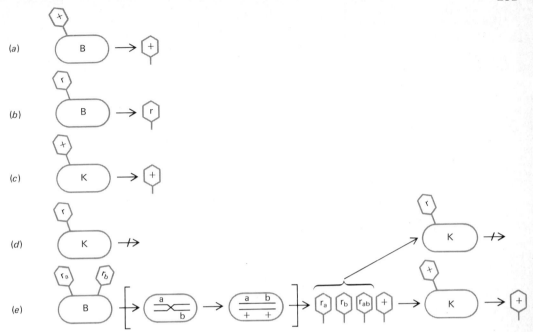

Figure 8-21 Seymour Benzer invented a technique for uncovering ultrarare recombination between phages with mutations in the same gene, the so-called rII gene; it is based on their different capacities for growth in different strains of bacteria. Thus, both normal (+) phages and r mutants can grow in strain B, but only normal phages can grow in strain K. If simultaneous infection of B bacteria by two different rII mutants r_a and r_b yields a normal phage by recombination, then this recombinant can be discovered because it alone among millions of rII progeny can grow on strain K bacteria.

rII phages grow in bacteria of strain B, Benzer discovered that only normal phages can successfully infect a slightly different strain of bacteria called K. Thus, if simultaneous infection of B with two different rII mutants yields a normal phage by recombination, then this normal recombinant can be detected because, unlike its mutant parents, it can multiply in K.

Benzer calculated that by taking advantage of the inability of rII mutants to grow in K he could detect 1 normal recombinant among 100 million rII mutants. And this would easily reveal recombination between adjacent bases in the DNA.

Benzer's first step was the isolation of thousands of rII mutants. Then came the task of characterizing them. Most of Benzer's mutants behaved as if they had a *point mutation*, a mutation involving only a tiny part of the gene. A few behaved as if they had a *deletion*, a mutation involving the loss of a segment of the gene.

Point Mutations and Deletions

Figure 8-22 Point mutations and deletions. Mutants *a* and *b* have point mutations; recombination between them gives normal phages (and also double mutants). Mutant *c* contains a deletion which includes the sites of the *a* and *b* mutations and therefore cannot give normal phages by recombination with these mutants. On the other hand, mutant *c* can give normal phages by recombination with mutant *d*, whose point mutation lies outside the deleted region *c*. The behavior of mutant *c* with regard to these point mutants defines the extend of the *c* deletion.

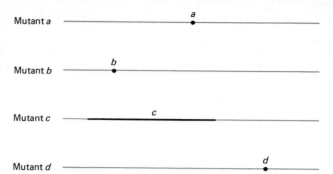

The existence of a deletion and its extent are defined by a mutant's anomalous behavior in genetic crosses: A mutant with a deletion gives no genetic recombinants when crossed with several mutants having point mutations even though these point mutants do give genetic recombinants when crossed with each other. This is because the deletion includes the sites of these point mutations. On the other hand, the deletion mutant does give recombinants when crossed with mutants having a mutation outside the deleted region.

Mapping T4 Mutants

Benzer was faced with crossing countless pairs of mutants in order to determine their frequencies of mutation and thereby map the locations of his thousands of rII mutations. Deletion mutations greatly simplified the task. Each new mutant was crossed with a reference mutant having a deletion extending into the rII region. If the cross yielded recombinants, then the new mutation lay outside the deleted region; otherwise it lay within that region. Each mutation was pinpointed by a progression of crosses with reference mutants whose deletions defined ever-narrowing regions of the rII gene.

What conclusions could be drawn from Benzer's successful mapping of several thousand rII mutants? Mapping of the genes of higher organisms, such as the fruit fly, had shown that they form a linear sequence corresponding to the linearity of the chromosome. Benzer's mutants, all within a single gene, also form a linear array, corresponding to the linearity of the DNA molecule itself. Benzer's experiments clarified the nature of the recombination event, which can separate adjacent bases in the DNA molecule. They also clarified the nature of mutations, for calculations indicated that his point mutations correspond to a change in a single base of the DNA.

Mutational Hot Spots

Benzer has turned up curious facts, as yet incompletely understood, about mutations. He has found sites which never mutate spontaneously but which can nevertheless be caused to mutate by ultraviolet light and

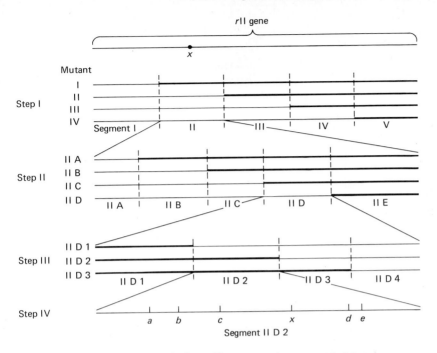

Figure 8-23 A point mutation can be located by a series of crosses with deletion mutants whose deletions terminate at different places in the rII gene. In step I, mutant x gives normal recombinants when crossed with mutants II, III, and IV, but not with mutant I, whose deletion includes the site of the x mutation; thus, the x mutation lies in segment II. In step II, mutant x is crossed with other deletion mutants whose deletions terminate in region II; it gives normal recombinants only with mutant IID, demonstrating that mutant x lies in segment IID. In step III, mutant x is located in the region IID2. It is then located with respect to other point mutations in this relatively small region.

by certain mutagenic chemicals. He has also found *hot spots,* sites which mutate with extraordinary frequency. Over 600 point mutations, one-fifth of all those mapped, are located at the hottest hot spot, while the second hottest claims half as many.

The molecular basis of the hot spots uncovered by Benzer remained obscure for a decade after the publication of his classic experiments. Then in 1972 an important clue was obtained by George Streisinger of the University of Oregon at Eugene. Streisinger had been studying the gene in T4 responsible for the synthesis of the phage enzyme lysozyme, which lyses infected cells, thereby allowing the progeny phages to escape.

Streisinger found a mutation in the lysozyme gene which reverts to normal over 100 times more frequently than other mutations—this mutation is thus an extremely hot hot spot. Streisinger determined the amino acid sequences of the abnormal segment of the mutant lysozyme molecule and of the corresponding segment of normal lysozyme. Using the genetic code described in Chap. 10, which correlates groups of bases

204

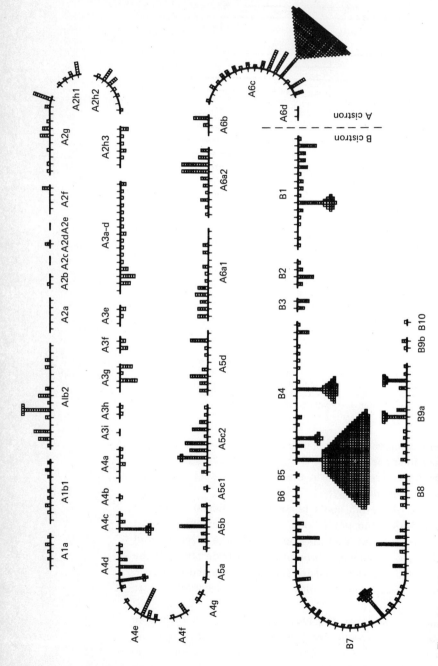

Figure 8-24 Map of mutations in the rII region of the phage T4. Each square represents one occurrence at that site. *(Courtesy Seymour Benzer.)*

with amino acids, Streisinger assigned probable base sequences to the mutant segment of DNA and to the corresponding normal DNA segment. In all likelihood, the base sequence at the mutational hot spot in the normal lysosyme gene is

A C A A A A A G T

whereas in the mutant gene it is

A C A A A A A A G T

The mutant thus has six consecutive A's (adenines) where the normal gene has five. Streisinger has evidence that several other hot spots are also associated with runs of consecutive identical bases. Presumably, when the DNA duplicates, such runs are subject to an extremely high incidence of copying error, resulting in the addition or deletion of a base.

What is the molecular event underlying genetic recombination? In 1961, Matt Meselson and Jean Weigle at Caltech demonstrated that in the case of the phage lambda recombination is due to molecular crossing over, the breakage and rejoining of DNA molecules.

BREAKAGE AND REJOINING OF DNA MOLECULES

Genetic experiments with phage had suggested two possible mechanisms of recombination, *breakage* and *copy choice*. From two tape recordings, identical except for a different defect in each, a perfect recording can be obtained by either breakage or copy choice: in breakage, the tapes are cut between their defects, and the good sections of each are spliced together; in copy choice, the good sections of each tape are recorded on a third tape. Similarly, in breakage DNA molecules are broken and rejoined, whereas in copy choice a new third molecule is made by copying parts of the old molecules. Breakage, it should be noted, gives rise to some recombinants with segments of parental DNA, copy choice only to recombinants with wholly new DNA. (See Fig. 8-25.)

Morgan had proposed in 1911 that genetic recombination is the result of breakage and rejoining of chromosomes. In 1931, J. Belling suggested the copy-choice mechanism to explain microscopical observations of chromosomes, but he abandoned it 2 years later because of irreconcilable genetic observations.

In 1949 the copy-choice mechanism was disinterred for several reasons. For example, among the progeny of phage crosses, unequal numbers of the two recombinant types were found. Was this because of experimental difficulties? Or, as was thought likely, was it because of a mechanism of recombination which, unlike breakage, does not necessarily create

Figure 8-25 Two possible mechanisms of recombination. *(a) Breakage and rejoining:* Two DNA molecules are broken at the same site, and pieces are interchanged. *(b) Copy choice:* A new DNA molecule is synthesized, copying parts of two DNA molecules.

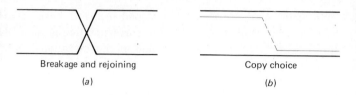

Breakage and rejoining

(a)

Copy choice

(b)

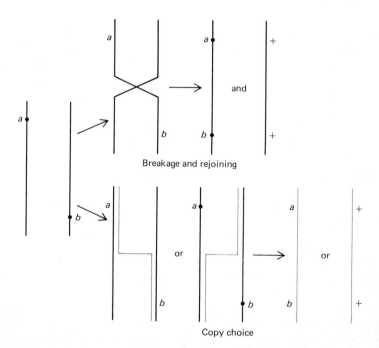

Figure 8-26 Breakage and rejoining necessarily gives rise to equal numbers of the two possible recombinants *ab* and $++$. Copy choice, on the other hand, only produces one or the other type of recombinant in each act of recombination; therefore the numbers of the two types could be unequal.

equal numbers of the recombinant types? Copy choice was also later invoked as the mechanism of integration of DNA fragments into bacterial DNA. This occurs, for example, in the transformation of pneumococcus bacteria and following the mating of bacteria. Copy choice seemed to solve certain difficulties posed by breakage, such as the possibility of an odd number of crossovers between the DNA fragment and the bacterial DNA, which would leave the bacterial DNA in two pieces.

For these and other reasons copy choice was thought the more probable mechanism of recombination, at least in phages and microorganisms, until 1961. Then Meselson and Weigle demonstrated that recombinants can contain parental DNA and therefore that breakage and rejoining is the mechanism of genetic recombination.

Meselson and Weigle performed their experiments with phage lambda (λ) labeled with the heavy, nonradioactive isotopes of nitrogen and carbon, N^{15} and C^{13}. Bacteria growing in normal, light nutrient were simultaneously infected with heavy and light phages differing not only in their density but also in two genes: the heavy phages, λ—, were a double mutant, and the light phages, $\lambda+ +$, were normal. Progeny phages were centrifuged in a density gradient to determine their density and, thus, the amount of heavy parental DNA they contained.

Figure 8-27 Density distribution of the progeny of bacteria infected with heavy λ— and light $\lambda++$ phages in light nutrient. *(a)* Some λ— progeny have a heavy density, indicating that they contain an intact, unreplicated heavy DNA molecule derived from a heavy λ— parent. Most of the parental DNA has replicated semiconservatively many times; therefore some λ— progeny contain a half-heavy DNA molecule with one strand of parental origin, while most contain entirely new synthesized DNA. *(b)* Recombinant λ—+ progeny have a density distribution similar to that of the λ— progeny: because only a crossover near one end of the DNA molecule can produce recombinants between these two genes, $\lambda+$— progeny, if they contain heavy parental DNA, have inherited either most of an unreplicated heavy DNA molecule or most of a semiconservatively replicated heavy DNA molecule. ($\lambda++$ and $\lambda+$— progeny are not shown; they all have the density of light phages because they contain entirely, or almost entirely, newly synthesized DNA.) *(Courtesy Matt Meselson.)*

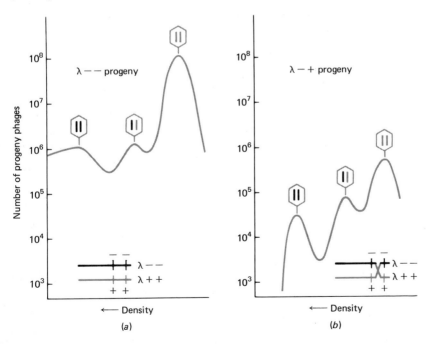

Meselson and Weigle found that some of the heavy parental DNA does not replicate; most replicates many, many times, semiconservatively. Thus, among the $\lambda--$ progeny a few contained intact heavy parental DNA, others contained DNA of hybrid density, and most contained no parental DNA and so were of light density (the $\lambda++$ progeny were, of course, all light like the $\lambda++$ parent).

What was the density of the recombinant progeny? If copy choice were the mechanism of recombination, then recombinant progeny phages could contain only light, newly synthesized DNA. If breakage were the mechanism, then some recombinant progeny could contain heavy parental DNA. In practice, because both of the genes employed lie close to one end of the λ DNA molecule, only the $\lambda-+$ recombinant progeny could inherit large amounts of heavy DNA from the heavy $\lambda--$ phages. The $\lambda+-$ recombinants could inherit only an undetectably small amount of this heavy DNA.

Indeed, Meselson and Weigle found that some of the $\lambda-+$ recombinants contained almost entirely heavy DNA, inherited without having replicated though it had undergone genetic recombination, while other $\lambda-+$ recombinants contained almost entirely hybrid DNA, inherited after having recombined and replicated semiconservatively.

The finding of recombinants with DNA from parental phage proved that genetic recombination is the result of the breakage and rejoining of DNA molecules. Furthermore, the amount of parental DNA in recombinants demonstrated that the distances between genes estimated by genetic recombination, the distances used to construct genetic maps, actually correspond to physical lengths of DNA.

Since 1961 it has been demonstrated that in bacterial transformation, in integration of DNA following mating of bacteria, and in other cases fragments of DNA are incorporated into the DNA of the recipient bacterium. Thus, these phenomena also are the result of breakage and rejoining of DNA molecules, which now appears to be the mechanism of recombination in all organisms.

THE SYNTHESIS OF PROTEIN

A formidable biochemical mystery is now largely solved; most of the jigsaw parts have been discovered and fitted together; the elaborate mechanism is unriddled: the way a living cell synthesizes a protein molecule can now be described in almost all its complexity.

The synthesis of protein differs radically from that of all other cell constituents. Small molecules such as sugars, fats, vitamins, hormones, the bases of DNA, and the amino acids of proteins are put together bit by bit and step by step from simple starting materials in a series of enzyme-catalyzed reactions. Other enzymes hook small molecules together to form polymers: sugar molecules to form starch, glycogen, and cellulose; the bases to form DNA; and the amino acids to form proteins.

Though the actual hooking together of the bases differs in no essential way from any other enzymatic reaction, nevertheless the synthesis of DNA, the self-duplicating molecule, has a unique feature: The sequence of bases in the new DNA is determined by the sequence in preexisting DNA. The synthesis of protein has a comparable feature: The sequence of amino acids is also determined by a preexisting molecule, by the sequence of bases in a segment of DNA.

But the copying of the base sequence of a DNA molecule to make a second DNA molecule is far simpler than the translation of that sequence into a protein molecule. The sequence of bases in the new DNA strand is established by immediate, firsthand comparison with the old strand— the choice of each base is determined by its chemical affinity with the corresponding base in the old strand, that is, by its forming an A-T or G-C base pair. On the other hand, because of the lack of chemical affinity between a set of three bases and the amino acid for which it codes, the sequence of amino acids must be established by an indirect, secondhand comparison with DNA. This secondhand comparison necessitates an elaborate machinery.

RNA, AN INTERMEDIATE IN PROTEIN SYNTHESIS

In 1941, J. Brachet and T. Caspersson independently recognized that cells which are synthesizing large amounts of protein are particularly rich in a substance called *RNA,* ribonucleic acid. Most RNA, it was later discovered, is localized in particles called *ribosomes.* Especially in cells very actively engaged in protein synthesis, the electron microscope reveals a multitude of ribosomes in the cytoplasm (fig. 3–19*b,* for example), where, as other evidence had demonstrated, most protein synthesis takes place.

Protein synthesis takes place, for the most part, in the cytoplasm? But the information for the structure of proteins is encoded in the base sequence of DNA which, with the exception of a small amount in mitochondria and chloroplasts, is found exclusively in the nucleus. Yet protein synthesis frequently continues for some time even after the removal

Figure 9-1 The correlation between RNA and protein synthesis is here demonstrated by autoradiographs of tissue obtained from an animal fed a radioactive amino acid; the tissue has been stained with a dye that binds to RNA. Heart muscle contains relatively little RNA (it is relatively lightly stained) and synthesizes little protein (the uptake of radioactive amino acid has been minimal, as witnessed by the scarcity of black dots corresponding to molecules of radioactive amino acid). Intestine, on the other hand, is rich in RNA (and therefore darkly stained) and active in protein synthesis (and therefore thickly studded with black dots). *(From A. Ficq and J. Brachet, Exptl. Cell Res.* **11**:135 (1956), *courtesy A. Ficq.)*

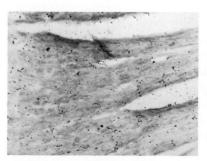
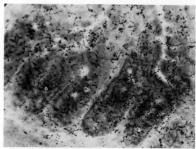

Heart   Intestine

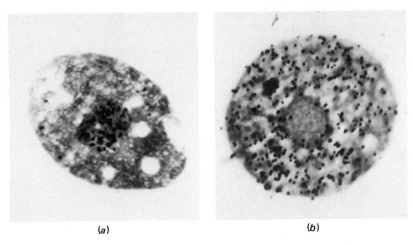

(a)   (b)

Figure 9-2 RNA is synthesized in the nucleus and then migrates to the cytoplasm, as demonstrated by this experiment. *(a)* Autoradiograph of a cell exposed to radioactive cytidine, a component of RNA, for 15 minutes. *(b)* Autoradiograph of a cell exposed to radioactive cytidine for 12 minutes followed by 88 minutes in nonradioactive cytidine. *(a)* Most of the RNA synthesized during the 15 minute exposure to radioactive cytidine is in the nucleus. *(b)* It has migrated to the cytoplasm during the 88 minutes without radioactive cytidine. *(From D. M. Prescott, Prog. Nucleic Acid Res., III:35 (1964), Courtesy of the author.)*

of a cell's nucleus.   Clearly, the information in DNA must be transferred to some other substance, the actual working model for protein synthesis.

RNA would seem peculiarly fitted for the role of working model.   In important respects it resembles DNA.   Both are polymers with a sugar-phosphate backbone; in DNA, deoxyribonucleic acid, the sugar is deoxyribose, which differs only slightly from ribose, the sugar in RNA, ribonucleic acid.   In both RNA and DNA, four different bases are attached to the backbone; three of those found in RNA, A, G, and C, are the same as those in DNA, while the fourth, U *(uracil)*, is very similar to the DNA base T.   Like T, U can form a base pair with A.   Clearly, the sequence of bases in RNA could be a copy of the sequence in DNA, with the substitution of a U for a T.   This possibility was reinforced by the finding that, like DNA itself, RNA is always synthesized in association with DNA.

Not only does RNA resemble DNA in these important respects, it also differs from DNA in a significant respect.   Unlike DNA, RNA is single-stranded.   Thus, whereas in DNA the chemically active sites of the bases are normally engaged in hydrogen bonds, forming the base pairs which hold the two strands together, in RNA these sites are available.   The bases can thus be chemically identified, the coded message read out.

Thus, in the 1950s it was supposed by many that the working model for protein synthesis is RNA, presumably ribosomal RNA.

212

Figure 9-3 DNA and RNA are similar in a fundamental respect: Both are polymers of four bases. They differ in that (1) the base T, thymine, found in DNA is replaced in RNA by the very similar base U, uracil, (2) DNA is double-stranded whereas RNA is single-stranded (although the bases in RNA can form the same base pairs as those in DNA with the substitution of U for T) and (3) the backbone of the DNA chain consists of molecules of the sugar deoxyribose linked by phosphate groups whereas in RNA the sugar is the very similar ribose.

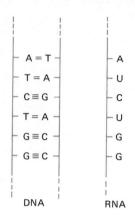

DNA   RNA

Messenger RNA, a Hypothesis

In 1960, François Jacob and Jacques Monod of the Pasteur Institute at Paris suggested that the ribosome is a nonspecific protein-synthesizing machine whose RNA does not specify an amino acid sequence. Rather, they hypothesized, any ribosome can synthesize any protein, provided it has received the necessary instructions coded into the base sequence of a special species of RNA, the *messenger*. Each gene would direct the synthesis of its own messenger RNA, which with the help of a nonspecific ribosome would direct the synthesis of that gene's particular protein.

Messenger RNA did not long remain hypothetical. In 1961, before the Jacob and Monod proposals had even appeared in print, the existence of messenger RNA had been proved.

Messenger RNA, a Fact

Infection of a bacterium by the phage T4 arrests the synthesis of bacterial proteins, bacterial RNA, and bacterial DNA, while initiating the synthesis of phage proteins, phage RNA, and phage DNA. François Jacob from Paris, Sidney Brenner of Cambridge, England, and Matt Meselson in his home territory joined forces at Caltech to demonstrate that the RNA synthesized after infection by phage T4 is the postulated messenger, transmitting information from the phage genes to nonspecific bacterial ribosomes.

The phage RNA was already known to have one prerequisite of a messenger—its base ratio closely reflects the base ratio of phage DNA, suggesting that it is a copy of that DNA.

The phage RNA has another curious property which further argued that it is a messenger: Unlike ribosomal RNA, which is stable, the phage RNA is unstable, being continually destroyed while more is synthesized.

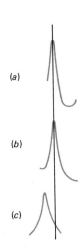

(a)

(b)

(c)

Figure 9-4   Brenner, Jacob, and Meselson demonstrated with this experiment that RNA synthesized after phage infection, which directs the synthesis of phage proteins, becomes associated with bacterial ribosomes. *Conclusion:* The phage RNA is a specific messenger RNA, whereas the ribosomes are nonspecific protein-synthesizing machines. *(a)* When centrifuged in a cesium chloride gradient, bacterial ribosomes collect at a single density (indicated by the vertical line). *(b)* Three minutes after bacteria were infected with the phage T4, a radioactive component of RNA was added to the nutrient to label the phage RNA; 2 minutes later, ribosomes were prepared from the infected bacteria and centrifuged in cesium chloride. RNA synthesized after phage infection, identified by its radioactivity, collects at the same density as bacterial ribosomes. Is this because phage infection is followed by the synthesis of phage ribosomes or of a nonribosomal RNA which becomes associated with preexisting ribosomes? *(c)* This is the same experiment as *(b)* except that before being infected the bacteria were grown in heavy, N^{15} and C^{13}-containing nutrient, so bacterial ribosomes were heavy. The bacteria were infected and simultaneously transferred to light nutrient, and after 2 minutes a radioactive precursor of RNA was added; therefore phage RNA was radioactive and of light density. Ribosomes were prepared from the infected bacteria and centrifuged in cesium chloride. The light phage RNA, identified by its radioactivity, collects at the density of heavy ribosomes, that is, at the density of ribosomes synthesized before infection. Thus, the RNA synthesized after infection, which becomes associated with bacterial ribosomes, is a messenger for the synthesis of phage proteins. *(Adapted from S. Brenner, F. Jacob, and M. Meselson, Nature, 190:576 (1961).)*

The quick postinfection switch from the synthesis of bacterial proteins to the synthesis of phage proteins indicates a rapid replacement on the ribosomes of bacterial messenger RNA by phage messenger RNA. Such a rapid replacement would suggest that messenger RNA, at least in bacteria, is unstable.

Brenner, Jacob, and Meselson performed an experiment which demonstrated (1) that after phage infection protein is synthesized by ribosomes that were present before infection—obviously, ribosomes are nonspecific —and (2) that the unstable RNA synthesized after infection becomes associated with the bacterial ribosomes and thus, presumably, endows them with the specific information needed to synthesize phage proteins. This unstable RNA synthesized after phage infection is, then, the postulated messenger.

Later in 1961 other investigators demonstrated the existence of bacterial messenger RNA, an unstable RNA which constitutes a few percent of the total RNA in uninfected bacteria. In the same year the enzyme which synthesizes messenger RNA, DNA-dependent RNA polymerase, was discovered and made to do its work in a test tube—given the four RNA bases A, U, G, and C and in the presence of DNA it catalyzes the synthesis of an RNA whose base composition reflects the base composition of the DNA. Messenger RNA, as well as DNA-dependent RNA polymerase, is found in the cells of higher organisms, in plant cells, in animal cells, in all cells.

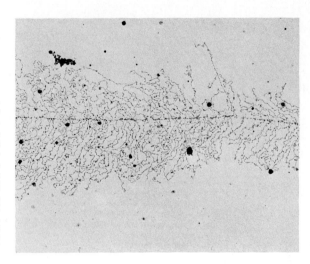

Figure 9-5 Visualization of genes in action. The electron micrograph shows a tiny segment of a so-called *lampbrush chromosome* from an immature amphibian egg cell, which is being transcribed into RNA. The main axis is the chromosome proper, composed of DNA and protein; it is dotted with molecules of RNA polymerase. From each polymerase molecule extends a thin fibril of RNA, the molecule of messenger RNA which the enzyme is in the process of synthesizing. *(From O. L. Miller and B. R. Beatty, J. Cell physiol., **74** (suppl. 1):225 (1969), Courtesy O. L. Miller, Jr., and Barbara R. Beatty.)*

Messenger RNA Is Transcribed from Only One DNA Strand

It would seem extremely unlikely that both DNA strands encode amino acid sequences. The base sequences of the two strands bear a backward base-paired relationship to each other. Thus, the sequence CCGACA in one DNA strand would be transcribed* into the RNA sequence GGCUGU, which codes for the amino acid glycine followed by the amino acid cysteine (the deciphering of the code is described in the next chapter). In the other DNA strand, the complementary sequence GGCTGT would, because of the opposite "up" and "down" chemical directions of the strands, be transcribed backward into the RNA sequence ACAGCC, coding for threonine followed by alanine.

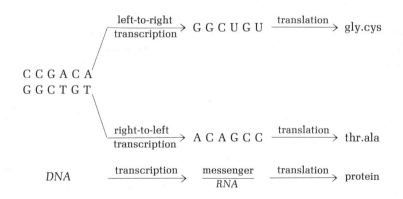

---

*The copying of a DNA base sequence into an RNA base sequence is called *transcription:* the DNA is *transcribed* into RNA. The linking together of amino acids into a sequence dictated by a sequence of bases is called *translation:* the base sequence is *translated* into an amino acid sequence, that is, into protein.

It appears reasonable that the base sequence of only one strand "makes sense," that is, codes for the amino acid sequence of a functional protein, whereas the base sequence of the complementary strand, transcribed in the opposite direction, "makes no sense," that is, does not code for a functional protein. It has, in fact, been demonstrated experimentally that only one of the DNA strands is transcribed into messenger RNA. However, every gene, that is, every segment of a DNA molecule, need not be transcribed from the same strand. In the case of the phage lambda, for example, some genes are transcribed from one strand, some from the other.

TRANSFER RNA, THE ADAPTER MOLECULE

Any number of molecules of messenger RNA can be run off a segment of DNA, providing the cell with many single-stranded working models of a gene. Messenger RNA thus makes possible large-scale synthesis of needed proteins. However, messenger RNA in no way solves the fundamental problem of protein synthesis: A sequence of bases determines a sequence of amino acids despite the lack of chemical affinity between a set of three bases, a *codon*, and the amino acid for which it codes.

In 1956, Francis Crick proposed that this problem could be solved by adapter molecules. Each adapter would attach to both an amino acid and its codon, thereby providing a link between them.

Adapter molecules were found the next year. They are relatively small molecules of RNA called *transfer* RNA, each specific for an amino acid and for the corresponding codon in messenger RNA. A molecule of transfer RNA is ready for action when it has been charged with its particular amino acid by an enzyme which recognizes both the amino acid and the transfer RNA and unites them by a covalent bond (at the expense of a molecule of ATP). Thus, for example, a specific enzyme joins the amino acid glycine to the molecule of transfer RNA with the *anticodon* GCC, the backward complement of the messenger-RNA codon for glycine GGC.

What exactly is a transfer-RNA molecule? Is it a string of perhaps a half-dozen bases, one end the anticodon, the other a handle for attaching the amino acid? That transfer-RNA molecules are very much more complex is suggested by their size—they are surprisingly large, consisting of seventy-five to eighty-five bases.

In order to probe the structure of transfer RNA, Robert Holley of Cornell University first spent 4 years isolating a large quantity of alanine transfer RNA, purifying it away from the transfer RNAs for the other amino acids. He then set to work to determine its base sequence. His method was analogous to that which Sanger had employed to determine the sequence of amino acids in insulin—he broke the transfer-RNA

molecules into smaller and smaller fragments with RNA-cleaving enzymes and then analyzed the base composition and the terminal base of each fragment. The task was simplified by the frequent unusual bases in transfer RNA, chemically modified normal RNA bases. Finally in 1965, after 3 years, Holley pieced together the sequence of the seventy-seven bases in alanine transfer RNA.

Examination of the base sequences of alanine transfer RNA and of other transfer RNAs determined subsequently has revealed an intricate structure. Transfer-RNA molecules can be folded to bring complementary regions opposite each other; these regions stick together because, like the complementary strands of DNA, they form base pairs. The most stable and therefore the most likely structure for transfer RNA is the one with the most base pairs; this structure has a cloverleaf shape with a double-stranded stem and three single-stranded loops at the ends of double-stranded regions.

All the transfer RNAs of known base sequence can be folded into the cloverleaf shape. They also have other similarities. At the end of the stem each has a single-stranded sequence CCA to which the amino acid is attached. The middle loop always includes the three bases of the anticodon. One of the other loops, the one drawn on the right, is very similar in all transfer RNAs; this loop may attach to a nonspecific site on the ribosome. What is the function of the remainder, that is, most of the

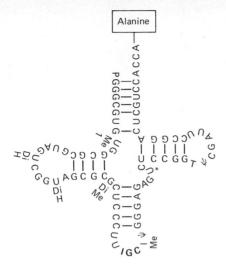

Alanine
transfer RNA

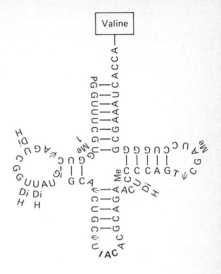

Valine
transfer RNA

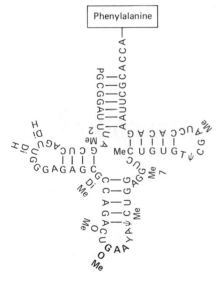

Phenylalanine
transfer RNA

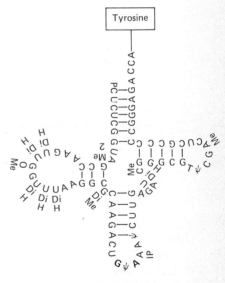

Tyrosine
transfer RNA

Figure 9-7 Four transfer RNA molecules shown in the cloverleaf configuration. Besides the four bases commonly found in RNA, A, G, C, and U, there are many modifications of these bases, such as DiMeG (dimethyl G), AcC (acetyl C) and others. The charged transfer RNA has its amino acid attached to the single-stranded AAC at the end of the "stem," as indicated. The three bases in the middle loop, in boldface, are the anticodon which binds to the codon in messenger RNA. The base sequences of more than fifteen different transfer RNA molecules are now known.

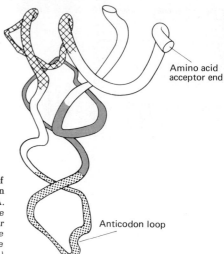

Amino acid
acceptor end

Figure 9-8 Schematic diagram of
the three-dimensional conformation
of phenylalanine transfer RNA.
(From S. H. Kim et al, Science
179:285 (1973). *Courtesy Alexander
Rich, copyright © 1973 by the
American Association for the
Advancement of Science.)*

Anticodon loop

transfer-RNA molecule? Until 1973 it was not even known how the enzymes which attach the amino acids recognize the correct transfer RNA—it had only been established that the anticodon itself is not the site of recognition.

Then x-ray crystallographers succeeded in working out the three-dimensional structure of a transfer RNA, phenylalanine transfer RNA obtained from yeast. The three-dimensional structure depends on the configuration of the floppy single-stranded regions of the cloverleaf; these are bent to give a more or less L-shaped molecule. Biochemical evidence obtained later in 1973 supports this structure, and suggests further that a key feature in recognition of a transfer RNA by its particular enzyme may be a three-point attachment to an arc formed by the angle of the L.

RIBOSOMES, PROTEIN-SYNTHESIZING MACHINES

The ribosome is the cell's protein-fabricating machine. One by one it matches up the codons of messenger RNA with the anticodons of transfer-RNA molecules charged with their amino acids and then joins the amino acids one after the next to the growing protein chain. What is this particle which coordinates messenger RNA, transfer RNAs, and a troop of other *factors*, proteins or enzymes whose roles in protein synthesis are as yet only surmised? Both the ribosome's structure and the way it functions have been so shrouded in mystery that this particle has been dubbed the "black box of protein synthesis"—a black box which is slowly being illuminated.

Figure 9-9 A bacterial ribosome (magnification $\times$ 800,000). *(Courtesy Martin Lubin.)*

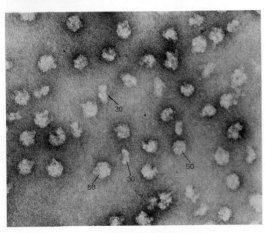

Figure 9-10 Electron micrograph of a mixture of 30S and 50S ribosomal particles prepared by dissociating intact ribosomes. Two different views of each kind of particle are indicated. A complete ribosome consisting of one 30S and one 50S subunit is shown in fig. 9-9. (magnification $\times$ 450,000). *(Courtesy Martin Lubin.)*

The ribosomes of bacteria consist of two subunits, called the 30S and 50S particles (names referring to the speed with which they sediment in an ultracentrifuge). The 30S particle, about half the size of a 50S, is composed of one large RNA molecule and about twenty different proteins; the 50S particle of one very large and one small RNA molecule and about thirty proteins. Fifty different proteins in one little ribosome! That is an elaborate piece of machinery.

HOW PROTEIN IS SYNTHESIZED

Protein synthesis is uncomplicated in outline. Molecules of transfer RNA serve as adapters, correlating amino acid sequence with base sequence. One after the next they line up in an order dictated by the base sequence of the messenger RNA, to which their anticodons are bound by base pairing. The amino acids attached to the transfer RNAs are then hooked together one after the next by peptide bonds to make a protein. Ribosomes coordinate and facilitate these operations. This is the principle underlying protein synthesis.

In practice, protein synthesis is considerably more complex, in part because a ribosome has only two sites for binding two molecules of transfer RNA. Therefore elongation of the protein chain must take place stepwise. An amino acid, while attached to a transfer-RNA molecule which is in the so-called *acceptor site,* accepts the growing protein change which becomes attached to it by a peptide bond. This transfer RNA, to which is now attached the growing protein, together with the messenger RNA, moves over to the *donor site*. The transfer RNA then donates the growing protein chain to the next amino acid, which is attached to the transfer RNA that has just entered the vacated acceptor site. Over and over this process, called *elongation*, is repeated, building an ever-longer protein molecule. It is facilitated by a number of so-called *elongation factors*, proteins of unknown function.

The initiation of protein synthesis constitutes a unique and complicated step. In bacteria, synthesis of a protein starts at an initiation codon located someplace in a molecule of messenger RNA, not necessarily at the beginning. A 30S ribosomal particle attaches there, together with several recently discovered and as yet poorly defined *initiation factors*, and a molecule of a transfer RNA bearing the special initiation amino acid *formylmethionine*, a modification of the usual amino acid methionine (the formylmethionine is subsequently removed). The initiation step is concluded when this initiation complex is joined by a 50S ribosomal particle to make a complete ribosome. The second transfer RNA can now enter the acceptor site; both the 30S and 50S particles include part of the acceptor site.

Some functions of the 30S and 50S ribosomal subunits are known. The 30S particle binds the messenger RNA, matching up the messenger RNA's codon with the incoming transfer RNA's anticodon. The 50S particle holds on to this transfer RNA and then catalyzes the linking of its amino acid to the growing protein chain, which is attached to a transfer RNA in the donor site. The 30S particle includes the donor site.

The coupling of amino acids to the growing protein comes to a halt when the ribosome reaches a termination codon. There, with the help

Figure 9-11 Schematic diagram of protein synthesis. Initiation: A 30S ribosomal particle (semilunar cap) attaches to messenger RNA at the site of an initiation triplet AUG to form complex II (this step requires initiation factor F3). Fmet transfer RNA with attached formylmethionine binds to the AUG codon (III) (requires initiation factors F1 and F2). The ribosome is now completed by addition of a 50S subunit (IV). Elongation: An incoming transfer RNA (in this case alanine transfer RNA) binds to the next codon in the messenger RNA (in this case GCU) (V); this requires factors Tu and Ts. The formylmethionine is transferred from its transfer RNA to the second amino acid, alanine (VI). The messenger RNA and the transfer RNA with attached formylmethionyl-alanine move over from the acceptor site to the vacated donor site (VII). These steps are repeated over and over, building an ever-longer protein chain. Termination: The elongation process finally produces complex VIII, in which the completed protein attached to transfer RNA occupies the donor site. As the next codon UAA signals termination of the protein, no transfer RNA enters the acceptor site. In response to a release factor, the completed protein is released and perhaps also the transfer RNA (IX). Messenger RNA may contain the information for the synthesis of several proteins; if this is the last protein, then IX decomposes into X, messenger RNA and the dissociated ribosome. *(Adapted from Ann. Rev. Biochem.* **1971:**698, *courtesy Sidney Pestka.)*

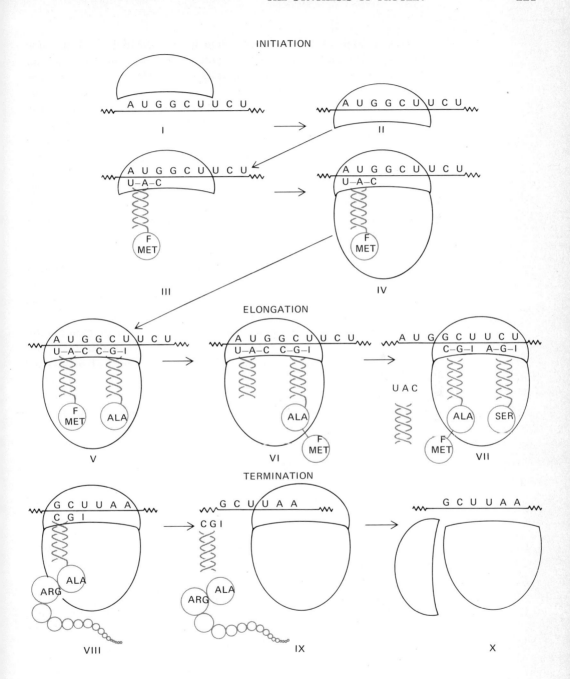

of *release factors* the completed protein is released from the last transfer RNA. The protein-synthesizing machine may then fall apart into its components, the 30S and 50S subunits of the ribosome and the messenger RNA.

This, then, is the current picture of protein synthesis in bacteria. In animal cells, protein synthesis is much the same, also being mediated by messenger RNA, transfer RNAs, and ribosomes; but the messenger RNA is more stable, the initiation amino acid is the normal amino acid, methionine, rather than formylmethionine, and the ribosomes are slightly larger and therefore surely more complex. Though more differences will inevitably be discovered, they will no doubt also be relatively minor, for it is now clear that protein is synthesized in basically the same way in all cells.

In animal cells the components of the protein-synthesizing apparatus are synthesized in the nucleus; they then migrate to the cytoplasm, where most protein synthesis takes place. Therefore, in the electron microscope protein synthesis is visualized as strings of ribosomes joined by a fine thread, the messenger RNA. (See Fig. 9-12.)

In the simpler and very much smaller bacterial cells, protein is synthesized as fast as messenger RNA is made. Beautiful pictures taken recently with the electron microscope show the strands of messenger RNA hanging off the DNA. To each strand cling many ribosomes, which have attached to the end of the messenger one after the other and are moving along toward the DNA, translating into protein the genetic message encoded in the messenger RNA. (See Fig. 9-13.)

VIRUS-HOST CELL INTER-ACTIONS

$$\text{DNA} \longrightarrow \text{RNA} \longrightarrow \text{protein}$$

This has been called the central dogma of molecular biology. It signifies that the information, that is, the sequence of bases, in DNA directs the synthesis of more DNA and of RNA; the information in RNA directs the synthesis of protein. This pathway of information transfer constitutes the chemical basis of life.

Viruses are parasites which, in one way or another, intrude into the DNA-to-RNA-to-protein chain of their host. Many viruses contain DNA; viral DNA may coexist with or supplant the DNA of the host cell. Other viruses contain RNA; novel syntheses, the synthesis of more RNA or even of DNA, are initiated by viral RNA.

DNA Viruses

How viruses insert themselves into the DNA-to-RNA-to-protein chain of the host cell is illustrated by the DNA-containing phages. Infection by these viruses may have one of two possible outcomes.

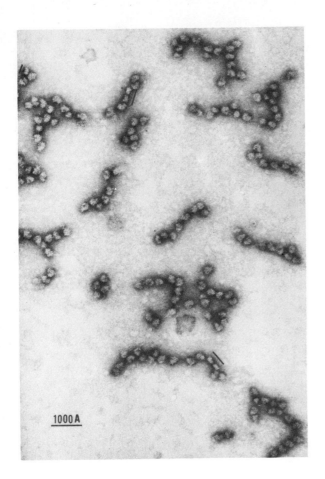

1000 A

Figure 9-12 Ribosomes from rat liver are strung along molecules of messenger RNA, which they are translating into protein. *(From G. Nomomura, G. Blobel, and D. Sabatini, J. Mol. Biol.,* **60**:303 *(1971), courtesy David Sabatini.)*

T2, like the very similar phage T4 and others, is a *virulent* phage, which provokes an active infection in its host. As has already been described (figs. 7-7 and 7-9), the injection of the DNA of T2 into a bacterial cell is followed by appropriation of the bacterium's biochemical machinery to the synthesis of viral DNA, messenger RNA, and protein, leading to the production of hundreds of phage progeny and lysis of the cell.

The phage lambda may also cause an active infection; this depends on the strain of bacteria and the conditions. Otherwise, it establishes a lasting, more or less harmless relationship with its host. In this case the lambda DNA, instead of initiating its own duplication and the synthesis of lambda proteins, becomes physically integrated into the DNA of the host, where its capacity for active infection is repressed and no progeny phages are engendered.

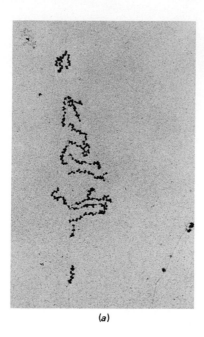 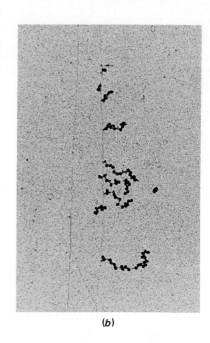

(a)   (b)

Figure 9-13 Visualization of bacterial genes in action. The
three electron micrographs show segments of bacterial chromosome where protein synthesis is taking place. The filamentous
chromosome consists of DNA and protein. Hanging off it are
threads of messenger RNA with ribosomes all along their length;
the ribosomes are undoubtedly synthesizing protein, reading off
the messenger RNA from the far end toward the chromosome.
At the site of attachment of each messenger RNA to the DNA
there is an irregularly shaped granule, a molecule of RNA
polymerase, which is synthesizing the messenger RNA.
(b) The molecule of polymerase located at the point on the
chromosome where messenger-RNA synthesis is initiated is
indicated by an arrow. Messenger-RNA molecules are
progressively longer with more ribosomes attached the farther
they are from this initiation point. The entire segment of
chromosome from the arrow to the last polyribosome is
sufficiently long to code for several proteins. An inactive stretch
of chromosome, devoid of polyribosomes, can be seen.
(c) The sample was prepared for electron micrography by
another technique, and the magnification is greater, showing the
ribosomes and RNA polymerase in greater detail.
[Magnifications: (a) × 72,000; (b) × 92,000; (c) × 306.000.]
((a) and (b) From O. L. Miller, Jr., Barbara A. Hamkalo, and C. A.
Thomas, Jr., Science, **69**:392 (1970), copyright © 1970 by the
American Association for the Advancement of Science. (c) From
O. L. Miller and Barbara A. Hamkalo, Int. Rev. Cytol., **33** (1972),
courtesy O. L. Miller, Jr.)

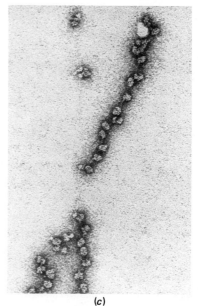

(c)

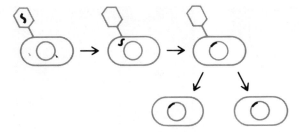

Figure 9-14 The phage lambda can establish a lasting, more or less harmless relationship with a host bacterium. In this case, the phage DNA after being injected into the bacterium is integrated into the bacterial DNA, from which it is then indistinguishable. As long as it is a part of the host DNA, it is multiplied along with this DNA and passed on to all daughter cells. Normally, its capacity for causing an active infection with the release of progeny phages is repressed.

The lambda DNA, duplicated along with the bacterial DNA of which it is simply a segment, is transmitted to all daughter cells. A lambda-carrying bacterium runs the risk that the lambda DNA will escape repression and initiate an active infection leading to the formation of progeny phages and death of the cell. Normally, about 1 bacterium in 100,000 suffers this fate although certain agents, for example ultraviolet light, provoke active infection in all cells.

Chicken pox, mumps, and rabies are due to virulent DNA viruses which cause in animal cells an active infection resembling in many ways T2's active infection in bacterial cells. However, virulent animal viruses are usually liberated progressively from infected cells instead of lysing them and bursting forth all at once like virulent phages.

The DNA-containing animal virus herpes simplex appears to parallel in a striking way the behavior of the phage lambda. Herpes simplex virus infects young children, most frequently causing a blisterlike sore which heals in 1 or 2 weeks. Later in life, a fever, emotional strain, or too much sun may trigger the eruption of a cold sore or fever blister, an active herpes simplex infection caused by viruses which have lain dormant for years.

Some viruses contain not DNA but RNA. The rodlike virus which causes the mosaic disease of tobacco, tobacco mosaic virus, or TMV, is a cylinder made of numberless protein molecules arranged in a spiral; inside the cylinder winds a molecule of RNA. In 1957, H. Fraenkel-Conrat of the University of California at Berkeley demonstrated that this RNA is the genetic material of TMV, determining the type of protein molecule making up the viral cylinder.

Tobacco Mosaic Virus, an RNA Virus

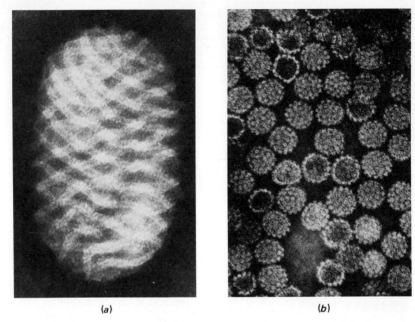

(a)   (b)

Figure 9-15 Two DNA-containing viruses whose host is man. *(a)* Orf virus causes pustular dermatitis in sheep and man; it may consist of a flexible helix wound into a cocoonlike structure. *(Courtesy R. W. Horne.)* *(b)* Papilloma virus causes warts; it has a simple spherical structure. *(Courtesy the Virus Laboratory, University of California at Berkeley.)*

Fraenkel-Conrat found that TMV treated with mild alkali or with detergent falls apart into its protein and RNA components. He purified the protein and the RNA separately; with neither alone could he cause infection of tobacco leaves. Then Fraenkel-Conrat recombined them in a slightly acidic solution. The typical rods of TMV reformed and were capable of causing the tobacco mosaic disease.

Fraenkel-Conrat next made mixed viruses whose protein and RNA had been obtained from different parents, the common TMV and the strain called HR. Tobacco leaves infected with viruses made of TMV RNA and HR protein developed the patchy yellow splotches typical of TMV infection; infected with viruses made of HR RNA and TMV protein, they developed the small, round ringspot lesions typical of HR infection. Thus, the RNA, and only the RNA, determined the type of lesion.

Most dramatic, Fraenkel-Conrat demonstrated that the protein of the progeny of a mixed virus was chemically like the protein of the parent that had donated the RNA and not like the protein of the parent that had donated the protein. The protein cylinder of the HR strain includes two

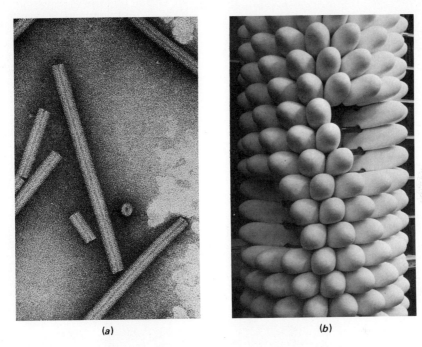

(a) (b)

Figure 9-16 This rodlike virus causes the tobacco mosaic disease. *(a)* Electron micrograph of virus particles; the rod is hollow, as can be seen in the small turned-over segment. *(Courtesy the Virus Laboratory, University of California at Berkeley.)* *(b)* Model of tobacco mosaic virus; the virus consists of a helical arrangement of identical protein subunits inside of which winds the RNA. *(Courtesy D. L. D. Caspar and A. Klug.)*

Table 9-1   Role of RNA and Protein Components of TMV

PARENTAL VIRUS		APPEARANCE OF INFECTED LEAVES	PROTEIN OF PROGENY VIRUSES
RNA	Protein		
TMV	TMV	Patchy yellow splotches	TMV protein (no histidine or methionine)
HR	HR	Small ringspot lesions	HR protein (includes histidine and methionine)
TMV	HR	Patchy yellow splotches	TMV protein (no histidine or methionine)
HR	TMV	Small ringspot lesions	HR protein (includes histidine and methionine)

(a)

(b)

(c)

Figure 19-17 Tobacco leaves infected by tobacco mosaic virus. *(a)* and *(b)* Leaves infected by tobacco mosaic virus are covered with splotchy yellow patches. *(c)* Leaves infected by the Holmes ribgrass (HR) strain of tobacco mosaic virus are speckled. [*(a)* and *(b)* Courtesy K. R. Keller and G. V. Gooding, Jr., *(c)* Courtesy Marvin Williams.]

amino acids, histidine and methionine, which are absent from the protein of TMV. The protein cylinder of progeny of a mixed virus consisting of HR RNA and TMV protein includes these amino acids, that is, it is HR protein; the progeny of mixed viruses made of TMV RNA and HR protein have neither histidine nor methionine in their protein cylinder, that is, they have TMV protein.

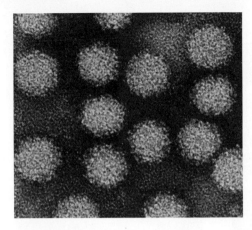

Figure 9-18 Bushy stunt virus is a spherical RNA-containing plant virus very different in appearance from the tobacco mosaic virus. *(Courtesy the Virus Laboratory, University of California at Berkeley.)*

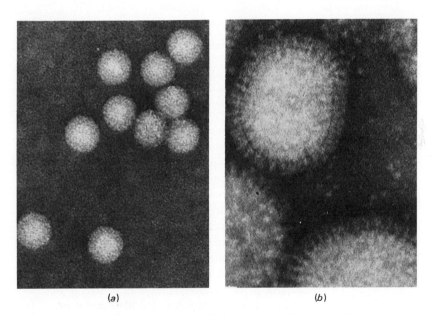

(a)   (b)

Figure 9-19 Two RNA-containing viruses which infect human beings. *(a)* Polio virus is a symmetrical sphere. *(b)* Influenza virus has a complex envelope which derives, at least in part, from the cell membrane as the virus leaves the infected cell. *(Courtesy the Virus Laboratory, University of California at Berkeley.)*

This was the clinching experiment, demonstrating that the hereditary material of TMV viruses is RNA. Just when it was finished, two German scientists, Alfred Gierer and Gerhard Schramm, succeeded in infecting tobacco leaves with purified TMV RNA uncontaminated by TMV protein. The genetic role of the viral RNA was now incontestable.

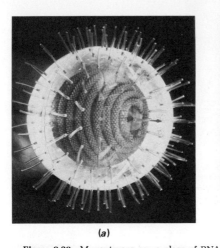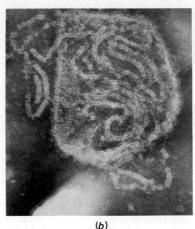

(a)   (b)

Figure 9-20 Myxoviruses are a class of RNA-containing animal viruses, one subgroup of which includes the influenza virus, the other the viruses responsible for mumps, measles, and parainfluenza (which causes severe childhood respiratory disease). *(a)* A model of the structure of myxoviruses: The virus consists of a flexible protein and RNA-containing helix wound inside a complex envelope. *(b)* Electron micrographs such as this one of a parainfluenza virus, which shows the doughnut-shaped subunits of the flexible helix, contributed to construction of the model of the structure of the myxoviruses. *(Courtesy R. W. Horne.)*

Virulent RNA Viruses

RNA is the hereditary material of many viruses. The virulent RNA-containing viruses include all the known plant viruses, some phages, and many of the disease-producing animal viruses (polio, yellow fever, influenza, and encephalitis are examples of human diseases caused by RNA viruses). The virulent RNA viruses fit themselves neatly into the DNA-to-RNA-to-protein chain of their host—the viral RNA supplants the host's messenger RNA on the ribosomes, eliciting the synthesis of viral proteins. The viral RNA is thus a messenger RNA.

Among the viral proteins is a unique enzyme, RNA-dependent RNA polymerase, which synthesizes RNA using viral RNA as a model. The first step in the duplication of the single-stranded viral RNA is the synthesis of its complement to give a double-stranded RNA molecule. This parallels the duplication of the single-stranded DNA of the virulent phage ϕ X 174, described previously, in which the first step is also the synthesis of a double-stranded intermediate. Reovirus, an animal virus, and the rice dwarf virus and wound tumor virus of plants actually contain double-stranded RNA.

Tumor Viruses

The wound tumor virus is one of a group of DNA- or RNA-containing viruses which induce tumors. A DNA virus is the agent of warts, which are benign tumors; similar benign tumors of dogs, cattle, horses, rabbits, mice, and hamsters are also caused by DNA viruses. Until the way of life of the phage lambda had been worked out, the lack of any virus in these tumors was extremely puzzling. Now it has been demonstrated in some cases that the viral DNA is inserted into the DNA of the host cell and thereby transmitted to daughter cells. The viral DNA (unlike lambda DNA) transforms the host cell into a tumor cell which grows and divides again and again in a more or less unrestrained way. How the virus brings about this transformation is obviously of enormous interest, but it is not yet known.

Most challenging to researchers are the RNA-containing viruses that induce tumors, for in animals other than human beings they are known to cause cancers and leukemia. It has not yet been possible to demonstrate unequivocally the viral origin of any human cancers. In 1970 a big advance was made in the investigation of these RNA viruses, for in that year Howard Temin of the University of Wisconsin and David Baltimore of M.I.T. uncovered a virus-specific enzyme, RNA-dependent DNA polymerase, which synthesizes DNA from a viral RNA model (an intermediate in this virus-induced synthesis of DNA from RNA is a double-stranded RNA-DNA hybrid molecule).

This finding strongly supports Temin's hypothesis, proposed in 1964, that the tumor-producing RNA viruses also behave like lambda, in that viral DNA is incorporated into the DNA of the host cell. RNA-dependent DNA polymerase has been found in cells infected by all the known malignant and benign tumor-inducing RNA viruses but not in cells infected by virulent, infection-producing RNA viruses.

RNA-dependent DNA polymerase has been found in the white blood cells of patients suffering from leukemia. This and much other evidence indicates that in humans, as in other animals, at least some cancers are of viral origin. Should this finally be proved definitively, it would, unfortunately, still leave many questions about cancer unanswered. What normally restrains cell growth and division? What events lead to the invasiveness and unrestrained growth of malignant cells? The control mechanisms operating in animal cells are still largely unknown; their eventual elucidation will surely enormously further the fight against cancer.

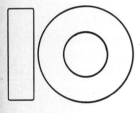

THE GENETIC CODE

In 1957, Vernon Ingram demonstrated that the hemoglobin of patients suffering from the hereditary disease sickle-cell anemia differs from normal hemoglobin by the replacement of one amino acid for another: a valine is substituted for a glutamic acid. He thereby proved that the structure of a gene determines the amino acid sequence of a protein.

How does a gene specify the structure of a protein, how does a sequence of bases encode a sequence of amino acids? How is the coded message read out? Which particular group of bases signifies each amino acid? These questions constituted the baffling *coding problem*, as it came to be called. In 1960, a solution to the coding problem seemed remote. A few years later it had been solved.

GENERAL NATURE OF THE GENETIC CODE

How many bases constitute a codon, the group of bases designating an amino acid? The four bases in DNA must code for the twenty amino acids found in proteins. If one base coded for one amino acid, then the four bases in DNA could code for only four amino acids. If a pair of bases coded for an amino acid, then the four bases could code for sixteen amino acids, still not enough (four different bases can be arranged in 4 × 4, or sixteen, different pairs: AA, AC, AG, AT, CA, CC, CG, CT, GA, GC,

GG, GT, TA, TC, TG, and TT).   Sixty-four different triplets of bases, that is, sets of three bases, can be arranged from four different bases (4 × 4 × 4), and this is more than enough to code for twenty amino acids.   Thus, the group of bases coding for an amino acid, the codon, must consist of at least three bases.

There are more than enough triplet codons.   Are most of the possible codons nonsense in that they code for no amino acid?   Or is the code *degenerate*, that is, can an amino acid be designated by more than one codon?   And how is the base sequence read off?   Is there punctuation, a "comma" such as a nonsense triplet coding for no amino acid, separating the codons from each other?

In 1961, Francis Crick, together with several colleagues, answered all these questions and thereby set the stage for the complete solution of the coding problem, the assignment of codons to amino acids.

Crick's elucidation of the general nature of the genetic code began with a mutant of the phage T4, which he called FCO.   The FCO mutation, located in the rII gene so extensively studied by Seymour Benzer, had been caused by treatment of T4 with the mutation-inducing chemical acridine.   Acridine, Crick argued (he has since been proved correct), induces mutations by causing the addition or deletion of a base (unlike other mutation-inducing chemicals, which generally cause one base to be substituted for another).

The Genetic Message Is Read from a Fixed Starting Point

Among the FCO mutants, Crick found rare phages, *revertants*, which appeared normal in that they gave rise to normal plaques (see fig. 7-5). Crick crossed these revertants with standard nonmutant phages.   Had the revertants also been nonmutant phages, then all the progeny would likewise have been nonmutants.   Instead, Crick found rII mutants among the progeny, either the original FCO mutation or another rII mutation located near FCO.   These rII mutants, obtained by genetic recombination between the revertant and the normal phage, demonstrated that the revertant actually contained two mutations rather than no mutations.

Figure 10-1   Crick found that crosses of apparently normal revertant phages with truly normal phages produced some mutant progeny, genetic recombinants, with either the original FCO mutation or another nearby mutation, also in the rII gene.   Thus, the original revertant must have had these two mutations which together made it appear normal.

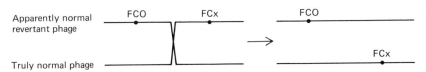

Apparently normal revertant phage   FCO   FCx   FCO

Truly normal phage   FCx

How could a second nearby mutation suppress the effect of the first? Suppose the message encoded in the base sequence of DNA is read off three bases at a time from a fixed starting point. Then if the reading starts at the wrong point, the message may be read off in the wrong groups of three. In fact, while there is only one correct way of grouping the bases into triplets, there are two wrong ways.

Similarly, the addition or deletion of a base any place in a gene will cause misreading, misgrouping, from that point on; but if a mutation, for example, the addition of a base, is either preceded or followed by another mutation, the deletion of a base, then misreading will occur only between the two mutations. The DNA will be read off in the correct groups of three after the second mutation has been passed.

This line of reasoning led Crick to give the FCO mutation the designation "plus" (though he did not, in fact, know whether it was due to the addition or deletion of a base) and to give the suppressor mutations the designation "minus."

Among the phages with a suppressor mutation, Crick looked for and found revertants. Again, they contained two rII mutations, the minus suppressor mutation and a suppressor of the suppressor, which Crick designated "plus." Finally, from the suppressors of the suppressors Crick isolated suppressors of the suppressors of the suppressors. These he designated "minus." In this way, Crick isolated eighty mutants, some plus, some minus.

Figure 10-2 If the codons which signify the amino acids consist of three bases and if the base sequence is read off triplet after triplet from a fixed starting point with nothing to indicate where one triplet ends and the next begins, then there are two incorrect ways to group the bases into triplets. (The base sequence is here simplified into a repeat of the triplet TAG.) The addition (or deletion) of a base is also followed by an incorrect grouping into triplets; the correct grouping is restored after the subsequent deletion (or addition) of another base.

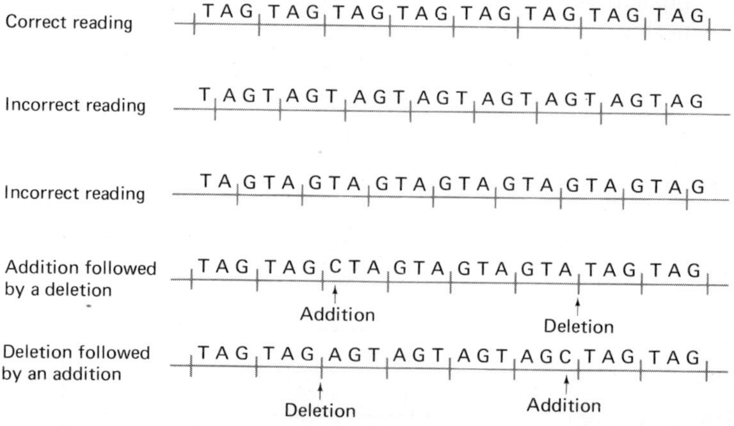

From them, Crick constructed double mutants with new pairs of mutations. Double mutants with a plus and a minus mutation frequently appeared normal, but double mutants with either two plus or two minus mutations never appeared normal. These results confirmed the hypothesis that reading of the base sequence of DNA begins at a fixed starting point and simply continues three bases at a time. Therefore disruption of the correct triplet grouping is caused, for example, by the addition of a base and is remedied, in that case, by the deletion, but not by the addition, of another base.

The Genetic Code Is Degenerate

Most double mutants having both a plus and a minus mutation appeared normal because the region of the rII gene studied by Crick is not important for the function of the rII protein. Therefore, even if a few wrong amino acids are inserted in the small bit between a plus and a minus mutation, the rII protein will be more or less functional.

But Crick found some plus-minus double mutants that did not appear normal. He concluded that the misreading generated by these pairs of mutations included nonsense triplets which do not code for an amino acid (but may signify, for example, termination of the protein).

If the twenty amino acids commonly found in proteins were designated by only twenty of the sixty-four possible triplets, then most plus-minus pairs of mutations would generate triplets which do not code for an amino acid. Since this was patently not the case, Crick concluded that the code is degenerate; that is, the amino acids can be designated by more than one triplet, or codon.

Codons Are Triplets

Finally, Crick asked the question, are there in fact three bases in a codon, or are there more? And he answered that question masterfully. He put together triple mutants having three plus mutations or three minus mutations, taking care not to generate nonsense. These triple mutants were

Figure 10-3 The addition (or deletion) of only one base gives rise to a mutant phage. The addition (or deletion) of two bases also gives rise to a mutant phage. But the addition (or deletion) of two bases also gives rise to a mutant phage. But the addition (or deletion) of three bases gives rise to a seemingly normal phage. Since the grouping into codons, which is incorrect after the first and second addition (or deletion), is again correct after the third, the codons must be triplets.

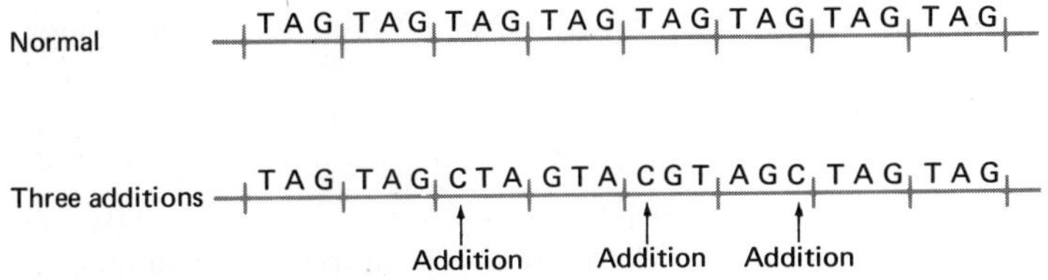

Normal   T A G | T A G | T A G | T A G | T A G | T A G | T A G | T A G

Three additions   T A G | T A G | C T A | G T A | C G T | A G C | T A G | T A G

          Addition   Addition   Addition

revertants. One plus or one minus mutation gives an *r*II mutant. Two plus or two minus mutations give a mutant. But three plus or three minus mutations give an apparently normal phage, a truly extraordinary result. Conclusion: the addition or deletion of three nearby bases restores normal reading because a codon consists of three bases.

WHICH TRIPLETS CODE FOR WHICH AMINO ACIDS?

Crick had demonstrated that a codon consists of three bases and that a base sequence is read off triplet after triplet starting from a fixed point. Brenner, Jacob, and Meselson had demonstrated that proteins are synthesized by nonspecific ribosomes which translate the base sequence of messenger RNA into an amino acid sequence. With these and a few other discoveries, plus some luck and much ingenuity, Marshall W. Nirenberg of the National Institutes of Health at Bethesda, Maryland, was able to break the code, to discover which triplets signify which amino acids.

Nirenberg made use of a system for cell-free test-tube synthesis of protein worked out over a period of several years, largely through the efforts of Paul Zamecnik and Mahlon Hoagland of Harvard University. Here are the ingredients for making protein in a test tube:

Amino acids.

Transfer RNAs.

The enzymes which attach each amino acid to its transfer RNA.

ATP to provide energy for this reaction.

Ribosomes.

GTP, a substance resembling ATP but with the base guanine G substituted for the base adenine A. GTP, it is now thought, provides the energy to move the ribosome along the messenger RNA; probably two GTP molecules are used up for every amino acid added on to the growing protein.

Cell extract, which is only now being resolved into initiation, continuation, and termination factors.

Odds and ends, such as magnesium ions.

With this mixture the Harvard group could synthesize a tiny bit of protein.

But in 1961 Nirenberg realized that an all-important ingredient was missing from the test tube—messenger RNA. When he added a messenger, RNA isolated from tobacco mosaic virus TMV, protein synthesis increased 200-fold. Then Nirenberg made the crucial discovery that ultimately cracked the code—an artificial messenger also stimulates protein synthesis. He first tried poly U, a synthetic "RNA" with only one base, uracil. Poly U was enormously active in stimulating amino acid

Figure 10-4 Marshall W. Nirenberg (1927–) is credited with cracking the genetic code; his assignment of base triplets to the amino acids was confirmed by the work of H. Gobind Khorana (1922–). Nirenberg and Khorana for their work on the genetic code and Robert W. Holley for the determination of the base sequence of a transfer RNA shared the Nobel Prize in medicine-physiology in 1968. *(Courtesy U.S. Public Health Service.)*

polymerization, but of only one amino acid, phenylalanine, which was polymerized into an artificial protein, polyphenylalanine. Nirenberg now knew the first codon—the triplet UUU in messenger RNA codes for the amino acid phenylalanine.

Nirenberg synthesized other synthetic messengers with the different bases in various ratios and in a random sequence. Each synthetic messenger directed the polymerization of only certain amino acids. By comparing the calculated frequency of each possible triplet in his messenger with the frequency with which the different amino acids were polymerized, Nirenberg was able to infer the base composition, but not the base sequence, of the triplets corresponding to many amino acids. This was progress, but still not a solution of the coding problem.

In 1965, Nirenberg made the breakthrough that cracked the code. He mixed ribosomes with transfer-RNA molecules charged with their amino acids, and with a synthetic minimessenger consisting of only three bases, that is, a single codon. When the mixture was passed through a special kind of filter, he found that the ribosomes, the triplet messenger, and a transfer RNA charged with its amino acid were retained on the filter. Each triplet caused the binding to ribosomes and, thus, retention on the filter of transfer RNA charged with only one amino acid. For example, the triplet GGC causes retention only of transfer RNA to which is attached the amino acid glycine. By this technique, Nirenberg discovered which triplets code for which amino acids. The genetic code was deciphered.

First letter	Second letter				Third letter
	U	**C**	**A**	**G**	
U	UUU ⎫ Phe UUC ⎭ UUA ⎫ Leu UUG ⎭	UCU ⎫ UCC ⎬ Ser UCA ⎪ UCG ⎭	UAU ⎫ Tyr UAC ⎭ UAA ⎫ STOP UAG ⎭ STOP	UGU ⎫ Cys UGC ⎭ UGA ⎬ STOP UGG ⎬ Try	U C A G
C	CUU ⎫ CUC ⎬ Leu CUA ⎪ CUG ⎭	CCU ⎫ CCC ⎬ Pro CCA ⎪ CCG ⎭	CAU ⎫ His CAC ⎭ CAA ⎫ Gln CAG ⎭	CGU ⎫ CGC ⎬ Arg CGA ⎪ CGG ⎭	U C A G
A	AUU ⎫ AUC ⎬ Ile AUA ⎪ AUG ⎬ Met START	ACU ⎫ ACC ⎬ Thr ACA ⎪ ACG ⎭	AAU ⎫ Asn AAC ⎭ AAA ⎫ Lys AAG ⎭	AGU ⎫ Ser AGC ⎭ AGA ⎫ Arg AGG ⎭	U C A G
G	GUU ⎫ GUC ⎬ Val GUA ⎪ GUG ⎬ Val START	GCU ⎫ GCC ⎬ Ala GCA ⎪ GCG ⎭	GAU ⎫ Asp GAC ⎭ GAA ⎫ Glu GAG ⎭	GGU ⎫ GGC ⎬ Gly GGA ⎪ GGG ⎭	U C A G

Figure 10-5 The genetic code. The first base of each triplet is indicated in the column at the left, the second base is indicated across the top, and the third base in the column at the right. The amino acids are designated by the abbreviations of their names. As can be seen, every amino acid except tryptophan (try) is coded for by two or more triplets which, in general, differ only in the third base.

The Nature of the Code

As Crick had predicted, Nirenberg found that most codons—sixty-one out of sixty-four—could be assigned to amino acids. In general, each amino acid is coded for by several codons which differ only in the third base. Phenylalanine, for example, is coded for by UUU and UUC, and glycine by GGU, GGC, GGA, and GGG.

What is the significance of the three nonsense codons UAA, UAG, and UGA which code for no amino acid? It was soon discovered that these are punctuation codons. Each is a "period," signifying that the protein chain should be terminated. Two other codons AUG and GUG can mean "start a protein here," in which case in bacteria, as has been described, they direct the binding of a transfer RNA with an attached formylmethionine; elsewhere than at the beginning of a protein chain, AUG codes for methionine, and GUG for valine.

CONFIRMING THE GENETIC CODE

Using triplet minimessengers and nitrocellulose filters, Nirenberg succeeded in matching up codons with amino acids. But had he merely worked out a false test-tube code, or had he worked out the real genetic code used by living cells to translate a sequence of bases in DNA into a sequence of amino acids in protein?

H. Gobind Khorana of the University of Wisconsin succeeded in synthesizing messengers with a regular predetermined base sequence; then he determined the amino acid sequences made by ribosomes following their directions. For example, UGUGUG . . . , read as a sequence of two alternating triplets UGU–GUG–UGU–GUG. . . , directs the synthesis of a polymer with two alternating amino acids, cysteine and valine. The sequence AUCAUCAUC . . . can be read in three different ways depending on the starting point (AUC–AUC–AUC. . . , UCA–UCA–UCA. . . , and CAU–CAU–CAU. . .); it directs the synthesis of three different homogeneous "proteins," polyisoleucine, polyserine, and polyhistidine.

Khorana, using a synthetic messenger more "natural" than a mere triplet, confirmed the triplets deduced by Nirenberg, including some doubtful ones. Still the question remained, are these the real codons in living cells?

Corroboration from Abnormal Proteins

Vernon Ingram's studies of amino acid alterations in abnormal hemoglobins provided evidence that in fact the Nirenberg triplets are the real triplets. Ingram had found that a glutamic acid in normal hemoglobin is replaced by a valine in sickle-cell hemoglobin and by a lysine in hemoglobin C, another abnormal hemoglobin. An examination of the Nirenberg code shows that both of these amino acid replacements could have arisen from a mutation which caused one base to be replaced by another. Glutamic acid is coded for by GAA and GAG; valine by GUU, GUC, GUA, and GUG; and lysine by AAA and AAG. If the RNA codon for this glutamic acid in normal hemoglobin is GAA, then an exchange of the second base could give GUA, one of the codons for valine, and an exchange of the first base could give AAA, one of the codons for lysine.

Scores of different abnormal hemoglobins have now been analyzed for their amino acid replacement by various investigators. Fraenkel-Conrat, among others, has characterized the amino acid change in the protein of numerous mutant strains of TMV. Charles Yanofsky of Stanford University has diagnosed the amino acid substitutions resulting from more than a dozen different mutations in the bacterial enzyme tryptophan synthetase. Always Nirenberg triplets differing by only one base could be assigned to the normal amino acid and to the amino acid which replaced it in the mutant.

An even more convincing confirmation of the code was achieved by George Streisinger. He compared the amino acid sequence of a segment of the phage enzyme lysozyme obtained from normal phages with the sequence of the same segment obtained from a mutant with two mutations of the type so successfully used by Crick to elucidate the nature of the code. He found the following amino acid sequences for the normal segment and for the segment containing a plus and a minus mutation:

Normal segment: lys.ser.pro.ser.leu.asn. ala.ala
Mutant segment: lys.val.his.his. leu.met.ala.ala

A comparison of these segments with the codons for the amino acids permits the construction of a unique base sequence coding for the normal protein, which by the deletion of one base followed later by the addition of another is transformed into a sequence coding for the mutant amino acid segment:

Normal sequence: AA?.AGU.CCA.UCA.CUU.AAU.GC?
Mutant sequence: AA?.GUC.CAU.CAC.UUA.AUG.GC?

It is interesting that the three amino acids that appear twice in these segments, serine, leucine, and histidine, are designated each time by a different codon, confirming the degeneracy of the genetic code.

RNA Base Sequencing Confirms the Code

The most direct and therefore spectacular confirmations of the code have been achieved since 1969—the base sequences of large segments of the RNA of several RNA phages have been worked out and correlated with the known amino acid sequences of the proteins they specify.

Frederick Sanger, utilizing techniques analogous to those he invented for determining amino acid sequences, had the first success sequencing the bases of a messenger RNA. (Why have base sequences of RNAs, but not of DNAs, been worked out? Because only in 1973 have the techniques for sequencing DNA been developed by the master sequencer, Frederick Sanger.) Using the Nirenberg code, Sanger and his colleagues demonstrated the correspondence between a fifty-seven-base segment of RNA from the phage R17 and a nineteen-amino-acid segment of the phage's coat protein; the complete amino acid sequence of the coat protein had been worked out previously by Klaus Weber of Harvard University. A number of other base sequences have since been determined, a few of which will now be described.

An ingenious technique was invented by Joan Argetsinger-Steitz to isolate RNA fragments corresponding to a specific segment of a protein, its beginning. Such RNA fragments have the great interest of including the base sequence which signals the initiation of protein synthesis. Their isolation was accomplished by mixing the phage RNA with ribosomes and formylmethionine transfer RNA under conditions which allow formation of initiation complexes at initiation sites (see fig. 9-11, "Initiation"), but do not allow protein synthesis. RNA-digesting enzymes were then added; they digested away all the RNA except the initiation sites, which were protected by the ribosomes.

Dr. Steitz used this procedure to study the RNA at the initiation sites of phage R17. R17, like several other closely related phages, directs the synthesis of only three proteins: the coat protein from which phage par-

                                    fMet Ala   Ser   Asn   Phe
AGA GCC UCA ACC GGG GUU UGA AGC *AUG* GCU UCU AAC UUU
                                    R17 Coat protein

                                    fMet Arg   Ala   Phe   Ser
CC UAG GAG GUU UGA CCU *AUG* CGA GCU UUU AGU G
                                    R 17 "A" protein

Ile   Tyr   fMet Ser   Lys   Thr   Thr   Lys
U AUC UAC UAA UAG AUG CCG GCC AUU CAA ACA UGA GGA UUA CCC *AUG* UCG AAG ACA ACA AAG
Coat protein   R17 Polymerase protein

Figure 10-6 The base sequence around the initiation point of two of the proteins of the RNA phage R17 and the complete sequence between the end of one of these proteins and the beginning of the next protein. In part these base sequences specify amino acid sequences, which are indicated above the base sequences. Synthesis of all three proteins begins with the codon AUG, which signifies "start." The end of the coat protein is designated by two successive codons UAA and UAG that signify "stop." The sequence of bases between the double "stop" and the AUG "start," which always includes another "stop" triplet, is not translated into protein and is, in fact, of unknown function.

ticles are made, another protein called the A protein, or maturation protein, and the polymerase (RNA-dependent RNA polymerase) which synthesizes phage RNA. She succeeded in determining the base sequence around the initiation points of the genes coding for all three proteins.

Independently, the base sequence at the end of the R17 coat-protein gene was determined, so the complete base sequence between the end of the coat protein and the beginning of the synthetase protein is known. In the case of another RNA phage Qβ the bit of RNA coding for the first six amino acids of its coat protein and for the ten preceding bases has been sequenced.

The RNA sequences of these RNA phages, when compared with the known amino acid sequences of their proteins, confirm the genetic code in the most direct way possible. The sequences also raise interesting questions about punctuation.

The initiation codon in these four cases is always AUG and never GUG. Is this a coincidence, or are the experiments suggesting that GUG is also an initiation codon in error? A termination codon, in every case UGA, precedes the initiation codon, separated from it by a group of from two to nine bases. Why? In the one case where the entire RNA segment corresponding to the end of one protein, the beginning of the next, and the sequence in between is known, termination is signaled by a double stop, the two successive termination codons UAA and UAG. Is this typical?

What is the purpose of the thirty bases separating the termination codons from the following initiation codon AUG? They are not translated into protein.

Base Sequence and Structure of a Gene

In 1972, a spectacular sequencing success was announced by W. Fiers and his collaborators at the University of Ghent—the base sequence of an entire gene. This gene codes for the coat protein of another RNA phage called MS2, a close relative of R17. Not only was the gene completely sequenced, but also the regions preceding and following it, which are not translated into protein, as well as the beginning of the next protein, the polymerase.

Again, the Fiers sequence, which includes forty-nine codons, confirms the genetic code. The punctuation in MS2 and, in fact, with the exception of one base the entire thirty-base sequence separating the coat protein and the polymerase, are identical in MS2 and R17, suggesting that this region is important for the functioning of the RNA.

Besides the discovery of large amounts of untranslated RNA (of the approximately 3,400 bases in the RNA of these phages, only 2,800 code for the three proteins), the most extraordinary result of the sequencing of phage RNA has been the discovery of its elaborate structure. Much evidence now suggests that the RNA chain folds back on itself, forming double-stranded regions with loops at the ends. Sanger recognized the possibility, in the fifty-seven-base segment of R17 that he sequenced, of a structure in which thirty-eight bases form hydrogen bonds with each other like the hydrogen bonds between the base pairs in DNA. The sequences worked out subsequently also lend themselves to complex, partially double-stranded structures.

Fiers has proposed a fabulous structure for the long RNA segment he has sequenced. It was devised by base-pairing as many of the bases as possible, thereby obtaining a structure with maximum stability. He constructed in this way a conformation he has aptly called the *flower* model, in which a long double-stranded "stem" is surmounted by radiating double-stranded "petals." Several lines of evidence suggest that his model is essentially correct.

In the flower model, the AUG which signifies the start of the coat protein forms the single-stranded loop at the end of a double-stranded region. On the other hand, the AUG which starts off the next protein, the polymerase, is located in the double-stranded "stem." This neatly explains a bizarre genetic phenomenon.

A mutation in which a base substitution results in the creation of a termination codon (for example, CAG → UAG) will cause protein synthesis to stop prematurely. Such a mutation at codon 6 in the coat protein

Figure 10-7 Base sequence of the coat-protein gene of the RNA phage MS2, together with the 129-amino-acid sequence it specifies, as well as the base sequence specifying the first 6 amino acids of the next protein, the polymerase. The base sequence preceding the coat-protein gene and the sequence between the end of that gene and the beginning of the polymerase gene are not translated into protein and are of unknown function. *(From W. Min Jou, G. Haegeman, M. Ysebaert, and W. Fiers. Nature, **237**:82 (1972), courtesy W. Fiers.)*

Leader (untranslated):

··· (G)· AUA· GAG· CCC· UCA· ACC· GGA· GUU· UGA· AGC· AUG·

Coat-protein coding sequence (codon · amino acid, numbered):

```
  1 GCU·Ala  UCU·Ser  AAC·Asn  UUU·Phe  ACU·Thr(5)  CAG·Gln  UUC·Phe  GUU·Val  CUC·Leu  GUC·Val(10)
    GAC·Asp  AAU·Asn  GGC·Gly  GGA·Gly  ACU·Thr(15) GGC·Gly  GAC·Asp  GUG·Val  ACU·Thr  GUC·Val(20)
    GCC·Ala  CCA·Pro  UCA·Ser  AAU·Asn  UUC·Phe(25) GCU·Ala  AAC·Asn

 28 GGU·Gly  GUC·Val  GCU·Ala(30) GAA·Glu  UGG·Trp  AUC·Ile  AGC·Ser  UCU·Ser(35) AAC·Asn  AGU·Ser
    CGU·Arg  UCA·Ser  CAG·Gln(40) GCU·Ala  UAC·Tyr  AAA·Lys  GUU·Val  ACU·Thr(45) UGU·Cys  AGC·Ser
    GUA·Val  CGU·Arg  CAG·Gln(50)

 51 UCU·Ser  UCC·Ser  GCA·Ala  CAG·Gln  AAU·Asn(55) CGC·Arg  AAA·Lys  UAC·Tyr  ACG·Thr  AUC·Ile(60)
    AAA·Lys  GUC·Val  GAG·Glu  GUG·Val  CCU·Pro(65) AAA·Lys  GUG·Val  GCA·Ala  ACU·Thr  CAG·Gln(70)
    ACA·Thr  GUU·Val  GGG·Gly  GGU·Gly  GUA·Val(75)

 76 GAG·Glu  CUU·Leu  CCU·Pro  GUA·Val  GCC·Ala(80) GCA·Ala  UGG·Trp  CGU·Arg  UCG·Ser  UAC·Tyr(85)
    UUA·Leu  AAU·Asn  AUG·Met  GAA·Glu  CUA·Leu(90) ACC·Thr  AUU·Ile  CCA·Pro  AUU·Ile  UUC·Phe(95)
    GCU·Ala  ACG·Thr  AAU·Asn  UCC·Ser  GAC·Asp(100)

101 UGC·Cys  GAG·Glu  CUC·Leu  AUU·Ile  GUU·Val(105) AAG·Lys  GCA·Ala  AUG·Met  CAA·Gln  GGU·Gly(110)
    CUC·Leu  CUA·Leu  AAA·Lys  GAU·Asp  GGA·Gly(115) AAC·Asn  CCG·Pro  AUU·Ile  CCC·Pro  UCA·Ser(120)
    GCA·Ala  AUC·Ile  GCA·Ala  GCA·Ala  AAC·Asn(125)

126 UCC·Ser  GGC·Gly  AUC·Ile  UAC·Tyr(129)  UAA·  UAG·
```

Intergenic region and start of polymerase gene:

ACG· CCG· GCC· AUU· CAA· ACA· UGA· GGA· UUA· CCC· AUG· UCG· AAG· ACA· ACA· AAG· (U)
(polymerase) Ser(1)· Lys· Thr· Thr· Lys(5)

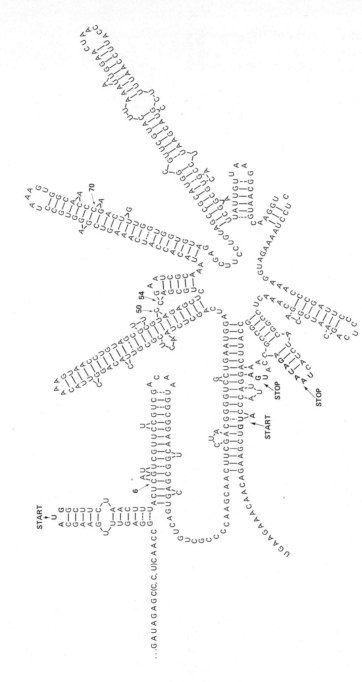

Figure 10-8 The flower model of the structure of the coat-protein gene of the phage MS2. Triplets signifying "start" and "stop" are indicated in boldface. Triplets 6, 50, 54, and 70, in each case CAG, are also indicated; these triplets are discussed in the text. *(From W. Min Jou, G. Haegeman, M. Ysebaert, and W. Fiers, Nature, **237**:82 (1972), courtesy W. Fiers.)*

not only arrests synthesis of the coat protein itself but also prevents synthesis of the next protein, the polymerase. On the other hand, the same type of mutation at codon 50, 54, or 70 arrests synthesis of only the coat protein. (See Fig. 10-8.)

The flower model suggests an explanation. When synthesis of the coat protein has reached codon 50, the double-stranded "stem" has been passed; probably this destroys the double-stranded structure, exposing the initiation codon of the polymerase gene, which had been base-paired in the intact "stem." On the other hand, if protein synthesis stops at codon 6, the "stem" remains double-stranded, and the initiation site for the polymerase remains unavailable for the attachment of ribosomes and therefore for translation into protein.

The RNA of the RNA phages has three functions: Like other messenger RNA, it codes for protein, but, unlike other messenger RNA, it must also be recognized by its polymerase and then serve as a model for the synthesis of more phage RNA. Also, it must be packaged into mature phage particles. To what extent do the fascinating features of phage RNA—its punctuation, its long stretches which do not code for protein, and its fabulous base-paired structure, reflect its special functions, and to what extent are they common to all messenger RNA? Investigators are attempting to determine the sequences of messenger RNAs which code for the hemoglobin molecule, for antibodies, and for other proteins. Only when they have succeeded will these questions be answered.

The genetic code was deduced from test-tube experiments with synthetic messengers and bacterial ribosomes. It was first confirmed in virus-infected tobacco plants and bacteria, in uninfected bacteria, and in the hemoglobin of human beings. Not only this early evidence but all evidence obtained subsequently indicates that the code is universal, the same in beast, bacterium, virus, and plant.

THE CODE IS UNIVERSAL

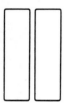

CELLULAR
CONTROL MECHANISMS

How are the hundreds, even thousands, of chemical reactions constantly going on within a living cell coordinated and regulated? The amino acids from which proteins are put together must be synthesized, but not in equal amounts. Glycine is a common amino acid, tryptophan is relatively rare; the economic running of a cell demands that relatively little tryptophan be synthesized. Moreover, if tryptophan becomes available to the cell, then its synthesis must be shut off completely. And it is, in fact, shut off instantly, as was discovered in the 1950s. Not only are the existing enzymes inhibited from making additional tryptophan, but the synthesis of more of the enzymes themselves is stopped short.

The synthesis of all substances required by a cell, such as amino acids and the bases of DNA and RNA, is controlled in the same way: If a substance becomes available in sufficient quantity, its synthesis is inhibited, and the synthesis of the enzymes in the pathway of which the substance is the end product is repressed. The synthesis of needed substances is thus regulated by two negative control systems—inhibition of enzyme activity and repression of enzyme synthesis.

Some substances, usually sugars, are broken down to provide energy. Cells prefer the sugar glucose as their energy source, but if glucose is not available, then—and only then—will they elaborate the enzymes needed to pump into the cell and metabolize whatever energy source is available. This system of control, in which the synthesis of a needed enzyme is induced by the presence of its substrate, the substance upon which it acts, was discovered at the turn of the century.

If a microorganism such as yeast is switched from a nutrient solution containing, for example, glucose to a nutrient solution containing lactose (milk sugar), the yeast stops growing for many hours. During this adaptation period a few proteins are synthesized, namely an enzyme which had not been needed to metabolize glucose but is required for the metabolism of lactose, and the proteins or enzymes which confer on the cell membrane, previously impermeable to lactose, the ability to concentrate this sugar within the cell. When this reorganization is completed, growth of the yeast resumes.

This system of apparent positive control, in which the synthesis of enzymes needed to break down a substance is induced by the presence of that substance, was much studied for half a century. Finally, in the 1950s and 1960s François Jacob and Jacques Monod of the Pasteur Institute in Paris brilliantly disentangled the elements of the control systems, demonstrating the systems' basic simplicity and showing that this seemingly positive control and negative control are actually both negative, the two sides of a single coin.

Jacob and Monod studied the effect of mutations on the expression of the three bacterial genes which control the synthesis of the three enzymes required for the breakdown of the sugar lactose. The genes, located one next to the other, make up the so-called *lactose region*. One gene codes for the enzyme beta galactosidase, which splits lactose, a double sugar, into its two component sugars, galactose and glucose. The other two genes code for acetylase, an enzyme whose function is unknown, and for

INDUCTION AND REPRESSION OF ENZYME SYNTHESIS

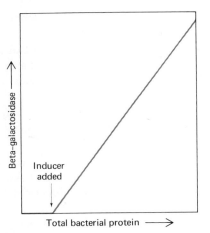

Figure 11-1 Induction of the synthesis of the enzyme beta galactosidase in a growing culture of bacteria. Before addition of inducer, no enzyme is synthesized. Instantly upon addition of inducer the synthesis of enzyme begins and continues as long as inducer is present.

Beta–galactosidase →

Inducer added

Total bacterial protein ⟶

permease, which makes possible the penetration of lactose into the bacterial cell.

A cell grown on a sugar other than lactose synthesizes negligible amounts of the three lactose enzymes—it contains, for example, only a few molecules of beta galactosidase. Grown on lactose, it contains 5,000 molecules of beta galactosidase. This is control in operation, regulating the synthesis of enzymes as a function of the presence of their substrate.

Induction: Repressor Combines with the Operator

How does lactose induce synthesis of these enzymes? An important clue was the finding that some substances chemically similar to lactose are excellent inducers although they are not substrates of the enzymes whose synthesis they induce. The conclusion is that the enzymes themselves are not involved in their own induction.

Jacob and Monod proposed and then proved the existence of two distinct genetic systems. One system comprises the *structural* genes, each responsible for the structure of an enzyme or other protein (the three structural genes of the lactose region specify the amino acid sequences of the three enzymes, beta galactosidase, permease, and acetylase). The other genetic system comprises the *regulatory* genes, responsible for turning the structural genes "on" and "off" so that proteins are or are not synthesized.

If in fact there are regulatory genes as distinct from structural genes, then, reasoned Jacob and Monod, there must be mutants with normal structural genes but with mutations in regulatory genes. These would lead either to the synthesis of enzymes even in the absence of an inducer or to the lack of synthesis of enzymes even in the presence of inducer. Moreover, a single mutation in a regulatory gene could affect the expression of several related structural genes, such as the three genes of the lactose region. Knowing what they were looking for, Jacob and Monod found the postulated mutants.

The so-called *constitutive* mutants are constitutionally unable to stop synthesizing the enzymes of the lactose region. They need no inducer for all-out production—6 to 7 percent of their total protein is the enzyme beta galactosidase.

Jacob and Monod mapped the mutation leading to this uncontrolled synthesis of the lactose enzymes. It was located just beyond the three structural genes. The findings that this single mutation results in unrestrained synthesis of all three lactose enzymes and that the mutated gene is physically distinct from the lactose structural genes confirmed the hypothesis of an independent regulatory gene, a gene which directs the synthesis of a special regulatory substance.

François Jacob

André Lwoff

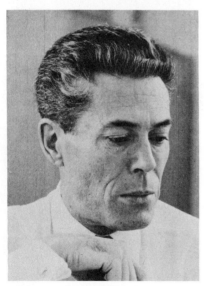

Jacques Monod

Figure 11-2 Francois Jacob, André Lwoff, and Jacques Monod of the Pasteur Institute, Paris, shared the Nobel Prize in medicine-physiology in 1965 for their brilliant resolution of control mechanisms in bacteria. *(Courtesy the Pasteur Institute.)*

In the mutant, the regulatory substance must be absent or defective because of the mutation. Thus, it is in the *absence* of the regulatory substance that enzyme is synthesized. The regulatory substance must then be a *repressor*, preventing enzyme synthesis in the absence of inducer. Jacob and Monod suggested that the repressor does this by preventing transcription of messenger RNA from the structural genes. But

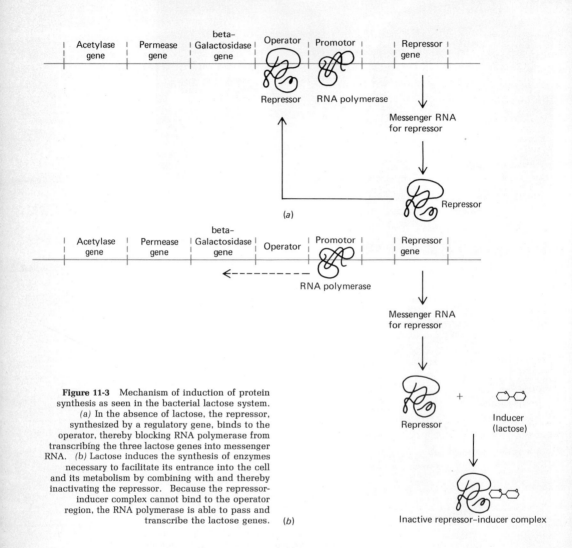

(a)

(b)

Figure 11-3 Mechanism of induction of protein synthesis as seen in the bacterial lactose system. (a) In the absence of lactose, the repressor, synthesized by a regulatory gene, binds to the operator, thereby blocking RNA polymerase from transcribing the three lactose genes into messenger RNA. (b) Lactose induces the synthesis of enzymes necessary to facilitate its entrance into the cell and its metabolism by combining with and thereby inactivating the repressor. Because the repressor-inducer complex cannot bind to the operator region, the RNA polymerase is able to pass and transcribe the lactose genes.

when inducer, in this case lactose, is present, it combines with the repressor and inactivates it, rendering it incapable of preventing the synthesis of messenger RNA.

Where does the repressor act? Obviously it must act someplace. Jacob and Monod named the site of its action the *operator*. The operator, as they correctly surmised, is a segment of DNA adjacent to the structural genes. On the other side of the operator from the structural genes is a segment of DNA called the *promotor*, discovered in 1968, to which the messenger-RNA-synthesizing enzyme, DNA-dependent RNA polymerase, attaches. Thus, in order to transcribe the structural genes into messenger RNA, the polymerase must pass the operator region. In the absence of repressor, the polymerase passes and transcribes all the structural genes controlled by the operator into one long molecule of messenger RNA; but if a molecule of repressor is sitting on the operator, then access to the structural genes is blocked, and they cannot be transcribed.

The scheme of regulation described above explains the mechanism for controlling the synthesis of enzymes which degrade substances such as lactose. Naturally, such enzymes are needed only when the substance they degrade is present; otherwise their synthesis is repressed.

Repression: Repressor–End-product Complex Combines with the Operator

On the other hand, enzymes which fabricate needed substances such as amino acids are only required when the substance they synthesize, their end product, is absent. The presence of the end product represses the synthesis of such enzymes.

The mechanism of this repression differs from that of induction in only one particular: In the case of induction, the repressor alone combines with the operator, whereas the repressor-inducer complex does not, so protein synthesis proceeds *only in the presence of inducer;* in the case of repression, it is the repressor–end-product complex which combines with the operator, whereas the repressor alone does not, so protein synthesis proceeds *only in the absence of end product.* Thus, induction and repression, though producing opposite regulatory effects, are basically the same—both are negative control systems in which under proper conditions the synthesis of enzymes is repressed. (See 11-4.)

Induction and repression can be combined to delicately adjust rates of enzyme synthesis, as in the metabolic pathway in which a substance called mandelate is broken down to acetate and succinate:

$$\text{Mandelate A} \xrightarrow{a} \text{benzoyl formate B} \xrightarrow{b} \text{C} \xrightarrow{c} \text{D} \xrightarrow{d} \xrightarrow{e} \xrightarrow{f} \xrightarrow{g} \xrightarrow{h} \text{acetate} + \text{succinate I}$$

In the first reaction, mandelate (A) is converted to benzoyl formate (B) by enzyme a; in the second reaction, B is converted to C by enzyme b; and so on for the remaining reactions.

The synthesis of the enzymes in this pathway, enzymes a to h, is controlled by three operators. Operator 1 controls the first three enzymes a, b, and c, whose synthesis is induced by substance A, mandelate, and repressed by substance D, their end product; operator 2 controls the synthesis of enzyme d, which is induced by D and repressed by E and I; the third operator controls the synthesis of the remaining enzymes e to h, which are induced by E and repressed by I. No doubt there are metabolic pathways whose control is even more intricate!

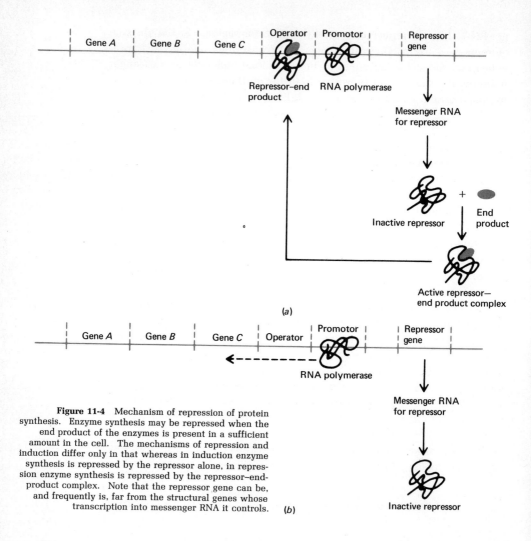

Figure 11-4   Mechanism of repression of protein synthesis.   Enzyme synthesis may be repressed when the end product of the enzymes is present in a sufficient amount in the cell.   The mechanisms of repression and induction differ only in that whereas in induction enzyme synthesis is repressed by the repressor alone, in repression enzyme synthesis is repressed by the repressor–end-product complex.   Note that the repressor gene can be, and frequently is, far from the structural genes whose transcription into messenger RNA it controls.

Isolation of Repressors   Genetic experiments provided most of the information which enabled Jacob and Monod to develop and substantiate the theory that protein synthesis is controlled by repressors which, in the absence of inducer or in the presence of end product, combine with an operator to prevent transcription of structural genes.   Their brilliant achievement was crowned 5 years later by a striking biochemical confirmation, the isolation of two repressors.

In order to purify repressor away from other substances, a way had to be found to identify it.   By what property could a repressor be identified?   Two different ideas were behind the isolation of the two repressors.

Walter Gilbert, a professor at Harvard, reasoned that the lactose repressor should be identifiable by its affinity for an inducer of the lactose enzymes. He chose the best inducer known, IPTG (isopropylthiogalactoside), on the assumption that it induces best because it attaches best to the repressor.

Gilbert placed a cellophane bag containing a concentrated extract of bacteria in a solution of IPTG. Large molecules such as protein molecules cannot pass through cellophane and are retained inside the bag. IPTG, a small molecule, passes freely, so the concentration of IPTG inside and outside the bag should equalize (see Chap. 3). Actually, Gilbert found that the concentration of IPTG inside the bag became slightly greater than the concentration outside—a large molecule trapped in the bag, the repressor, was binding some of it.

The purification of the repressor was now in the bag. Classical techniques for purifying proteins could be used, testing each fraction for the presence of repressor by assaying its ability to attract extra IPTG into the cellophane bag.

Meanwhile Mark Ptashne, also of Harvard, was working to isolate the repressor of the phage lambda. When lambda DNA enters a cell, as has already been described, there may ensue either an active infection producing progeny phages and the death of the cell, or incorporation of the phage DNA into the bacterial DNA, where it is passively and harmlessly duplicated along with the bacterial DNA. What determines the outcome of an attack by lambda? A repressor.

Figure 11-5 Isolation of the repressor of the lactose genes was based on its ability to concentrate inducer. *(a)* A concentrated extract of bacterial cells containing repressor enclosed in a cellophane bag is placed in a solution of IPTG, an excellent synthetic inducer of the *lactose* genes. IPTG, a small molecule, enters the cellophane bag freely; protein molecules are too big to pass out through the cellophane's microscopic pores. *(b)* IPTG has entered the bag. Its final concentration inside is slightly greater than outside because a small amount is bound to repressor molecules trapped in the bag. Gilbert worked for months before finding a way to concentrate the bacterial extract sufficiently for the difference in IPTG concentration inside and outside to be detectable. Once he had succeeded, the purification of the repressor molecule, using standard techniques of protein purification and this technique for assaying the repressor, was straightforward.

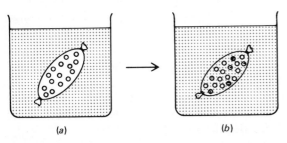

(a)   (b)

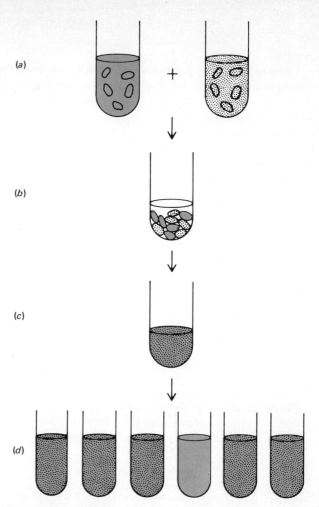

(a)

(b)

(c)

(d)

Figure 11-6 Technique for isolating lambda repressor. *(a)* Bacteria which had been treated so that 5 to 10 percent of the protein they synthesized was lambda repressor were grown in nutrient containing the radioactive isotope of hydrogen tritium H³ (indicated by shading). Other bacteria, identical except that they were not synthesizing lambda repressor, were grown in nutrient containing radioactive carbon, C¹⁴ (indicated by stippling). *(b)* The bacteria were combined and concentrated, and *(c)* an extract prepared from them. *(d)* The many different kinds of proteins in the extract were separated by a chromatography technique related to paper chromatography. All the fractions but one contained both H³ and C¹⁴. This one fraction, which contained only H³, was the lambda repressor, the only protein synthesized by the H³-labeled bacteria but not by the C¹⁴-labeled bacteria.

A lambda regulatory gene called cI is responsible for the synthesis of this repressor, which prevents transcription of the lambda genes needed for the production of progeny phages. When the lambda DNA is incorporated into the DNA of a bacterium, it is maintained in an inactive state by the continuous synthesis of repressor.

Ptashne succeeded in isolating the repressor because he created a situation in which the repressor made up a large part, 5 to 10 percent, of all the protein synthesized by lambda-infected bacteria. He grew these repressor-synthesizing bacteria in nutrient containing amino acids labeled with radioactive hydrogen H³ (tritium); protein synthesized after infection, including of course the repressor, was thus labeled with H³. Other bacteria, identical except that they were not synthesizing lambda repressor, were grown in nutrient containing amino acids labeled with radioactive carbon C¹⁴; the protein synthesized by these bacteria, which included no repressor, was thus labeled with C¹⁴.

Ptashne mixed the H^3- and C^{14}-labeled bacteria together and then proceeded to fractionate the proteins in the mixture. Almost all the fractions contained both H^3 and C^{14}, but one fraction contained only H^3— this was the lambda repressor.

Thus, in two entirely different ways the lactose and lambda repressors were isolated. Gilbert's and Ptashne's successes proved what previously had been surmised, that repressors are proteins. In fact, they are large proteins, the lactose repressor consisting of four subunits of molecular weight 38,000 each and the lambda repressor also consisting of four subunits, of molecular weight 28,000 each.

Moreover, experiments with purified repressors proved the Jacob and Monod hypothesis that a repressor combines directly with DNA, the segment of DNA they named the operator. Gilbert and Ptashne found that the lambda repressor binds to lambda DNA but to no other DNA, while the lactose repressor binds only to DNA which includes the lactose genes and detaches from such DNA on the addition of inducer.

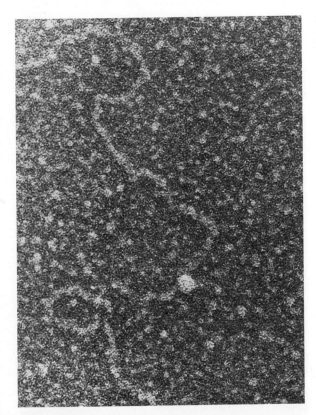

Figure 11-7 Electron micrograph of the lambda repressor bound to DNA, presumably the lambda operator. *(Courtesy Jack Griffith.)*

How a Repressor Binds to DNA

In 1972, Benno Müller-Hill, who had collaborated with Gilbert in the isolation of the lactose repressor, together with several colleagues, proposed a fascinating model for the binding of the lactose repressor to a particular sequence of bases in DNA, the operator.

They first isolated a large number of repressor mutants. Mapping their mutations disclosed that all those located at one end of the gene, corresponding to the N-terminal end of the protein, destroyed the repressor's capacity to bind to the operator. They concluded that the N-terminal end of the repressor includes the DNA-binding site. Moreover, all these mutations were clustered in a region coding for only the first fifty amino acids of the protein.

Next they determined the amino acid sequence of these first fifty amino acids. By "playing," as they put it, with a model of the DNA double helix and a model of these amino acids in their most likely three-dimensional configuration, that of Pauling's alpha helix, they discovered that the region from amino acid 17 to amino acid 33 fits into the deep groove of the DNA helix, binding to both the phosphates of the DNA backbone and to the bases. Binding to the phosphates would make the repressor stick to the DNA. Binding to the bases would make it stick to only one specific sequence of bases.

Figure 11-8 Model of the lactose repressor interacting with DNA. *(From K. Adler et al., Nature,* **237**:*322 (1972), courtesy B. Müller-Hill.)*

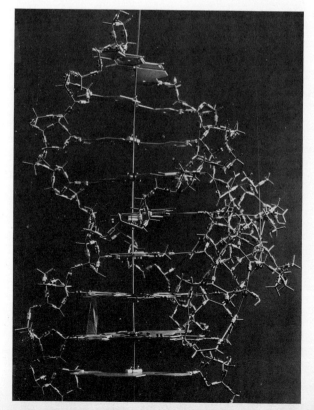

C,A——T——A——G,T——C,A
G,T——A——T——C,A——G,T
   1   2   3   4   5

Figure 11-9 Proposed sequence of five bases in DNA recognized by the lactose repressor. The base pairs at positions 2 and 3, a T-A and an A-T base pair, are unambiguous. The Müller-Hill model of the repressor cannot, however, differentiate between two possibilities at positions 1, 4, and 5: at position 1 could be either a C-G or a T-A base pair; at position 4 could be a G-C or a T-A base pair; and at position 5 could be either a C-G or an A-T base pair. Because the *lactose* repressor consists of four identical subunits, this sequence of five bases is presumably repeated four times, with a separation of several bases between repeats.

If the Müller-Hill model is correct, then it will be the first case of a protein whose binding site is a protrusion and not a cleft or groove, as is the case for all the enzymes whose three-dimensional structures are known. But the most exciting feature of this model is that from it Müller-Hill and his colleagues have predicted the sequence of eight base pairs in the DNA which are recognized by the protruding end of the repressor. These eight base pairs would presumably be repeated four times, so that each of the four subunits of the repressor molecule would recognize the same DNA sequence.

Is the Müller-Hill model correct? Is this the way a protein recognizes a base sequence? Is the sequence of bases in DNA suggested by Müller-Hill and his colleagues actually the sequence found in the operator? The experiments which will answer these questions have not yet been performed.

POSITIVE CONTROL OF PROTEIN SYNTHESIS

Repression and induction regulate the rate of synthesis of proteins by negative control: repressor (or in induction repressor combined with end product) prevents transcription of genes into messenger RNA; only in the absence of repressor can messenger RNA and ultimately protein synthesis proceed. But repression and induction are not the only mechanisms of regulation of protein synthesis. Even in the simplest organisms there are additional mechanisms of control.

When bacteria are infected by phages lambda or T4, the orderly succession of events leading to the production of progeny depends on sequential control mechanisms, which are as yet only partially understood. The initial synthesis of so-called *early* proteins is a prerequisite for duplication of the phage DNA, and only after DNA synthesis is under way does synthesis of the *late* proteins, which include the structural proteins from which progeny phages are put together, begin.

The control systems operating in the phage lambda, worked out chiefly by René Thomas at the University of Brussels, are nearest to complete

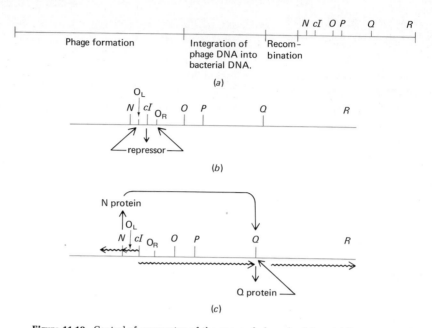

Figure 11-10 Control of expression of the genes of phage lambda. *(a)* Genetic map of lambda showing the regions of the DNA responsible for the formation of progeny phage particles, for integration of the phage DNA into the DNA of the bacterial host (see fig. 9-14), for genetic recombination, for regulation (genes *N*, *cI*, *O*, *P*, and *Q*), and for lysozyme, the enzyme which lyses the infected cell, liberating progeny phages. *(b)* An enlargement of the region responsible for regulation showing how synthesis of progeny phages is repressed: The product of the gene *cI* is a repressor which binds to two operators, O_L just to its left and O_R just to its right; this prevents transcription into messenger RNA of all genes except *cI*, which codes for the repressor itself. *(c)* Enlargement of the region responsible for regulation, showing the complex system of positive controls regulating the synthesis of progeny phages: In the absence of the *cI* repressor, that is, in an active infection, transcription of the DNA radiates from the *cI* gene, left on one DNA strand and right on the other; to the right, transcription stops at gene *Q*; to the left, transcription of gene *N* results in synthesis of a protein, the N protein, which modifies the RNA polymerase and thereby makes possible transcription of gene *Q*; the Q protein then initiates a powerful wave of transcription which goes to the right and includes the genes required for phage formation (shown to the left of *Q* in the genetic map above but located to its right during infection, when the DNA circularizes).

elucidation. They include not only the negative control system whereby synthesis of messenger RNA is repressed by the lambda repressor but also active positive control whereby synthesis of messenger RNA depends on an activator.

The lambda repressor, product of the gene *cI* located toward one end of the lambda DNA molecule, can combine with two nearby operators, one on either side of *cI*; in this case, all messenger-RNA synthesis, excepting that needed for the synthesis of repressor itself, is repressed.

In the absence of lambda repressor, that is, in an active infection, messenger-RNA synthesis proceeds outward from the two operators, leftward on one DNA strand and rightward on the other.

But messenger-RNA synthesis proceeds only a short distance because an activator is required for its continuation. This activator is the product of a gene called N, located near and to the left of cI. The N protein, the product of the N gene, seems to combine with the RNA polymerase which synthesizes messenger RNA, conferring on it the possibility of continuing on toward the ends of the DNA. But this modified RNA polymerase too comes to a halt before reaching one end. The product of gene Q is required for transcription of the last genes.

Positive control has been recognized not only in phages but also in the expression of several groups of bacterial genes—it was discovered simultaneously in lambda by René Thomas and in bacteria by Ellis Englesberg. As more cases are discovered and their complexities understood, positive control will surely take its place beside negative control, the two interacting to regulate the rates of protein synthesis.

Repression, induction, and positive control regulate the rate at which proteins are synthesized. Feedback inhibition, on the other hand, controls the activity of the enzymes themselves. For example, the amino acid threonine is converted in five sequential steps to the amino acid isoleucine. When a sufficient quantity of isoleucine is present in the **FEEDBACK INHIBITION REGULATES ENZYME ACTIVITY**

Figure 11-11 Feedback inhibition. The first step in the biosynthesis of the amino acid isoleucine from the amino acid threonine is the conversion of threonine to alpha-ketobutyric acid, a reaction catalyzed by the enzyme threonine deaminase (TD). When isoleucine is present in the cell in sufficient quantity, it reacts with threonine deaminase and inhibits its enzymatic activity, thereby preventing its own further synthesis.

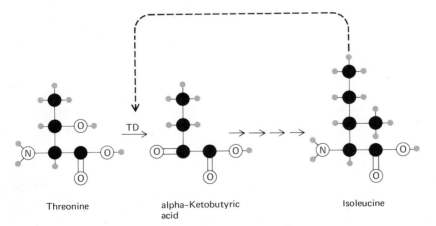

Threonine   alpha–Ketobutyric   Isoleucine
                              acid

cell, it inhibits the activity of the first enzyme in the sequence, threonine deaminase, and thereby shuts off its own synthesis.

(Feedback inhibition is a common mechanism of control outside cells as well as inside. For example, when a toilet is flushed, the water reservoir refills to the proper level thanks to a system of feedback inhibition: The reservoir's water inlet is normally blocked by a stopper attached to a float; as the water level descends after flushing, this float descends, the stopper is displaced, and water flows into the reservoir; when the reservoir has refilled, the float is again high, so the stopper again blocks the water inlet. With this most ancient of all mechanical systems of feedback inhibition, an inflow of water shuts itself off through the intermediary of a float when the desired water level has been reached. Similarly, through the intermediary of a thermostat heat turns off the room's heating system, and through the intermediary of a complex nervous system a full stomach turns off the hunger signal which led to the stomach being filled.)

Feedback inhibition, sometimes by more than one substance, may be combined with repression of enzyme synthesis to achieve fine control of complex biochemical pathways. For example, isoleucine is only one of the end products of a branched pathway which leads to the synthesis of four amino acids, lysine, threonine, methionine, and isoleucine, starting from the amino acid aspartic acid. The first enzyme in the series,

Figure 11-12 Biochemical pathway from the amino acid aspartic acid to the amino acids lysine, isoleucine, threonine, and methionine, showing feedback inhibition of enzyme activity and repression of enzyme synthesis (dashed lines extend from the various end products to the enzymes they control, either by inhibiting enzyme activity or by repressing enzyme synthesis).

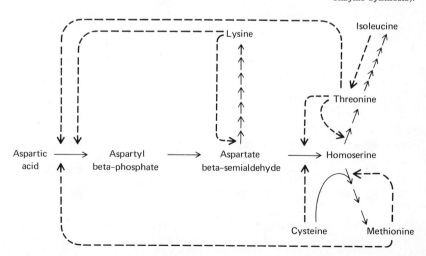

aspartokinase, catalyzes the conversion of aspartic acid to aspartoyl beta-phosphate, a precursor of all four amino acids. If only one of these four controlled aspartokinase's output of aspartoyl beta-phosphate, then an excess of this amino acid would cause a shortage of the other three. The control of this key enzyme must be multiple.

In some bacteria, multiple control is accomplished by having three distinct enzymes for this one step, each specified by a different gene and controlled by the concentration of a different amino acid: the activity of one species of aspartokinase is inhibited by threonine; the activity of the second species is inhibited by lysine which also represses its synthesis; while synthesis of the third is repressed by methionine. In other bacteria, there is probably only one species of aspartokinase whose activity is not inhibited by any single amino acid but only by the concerted action of lysine and threonine, and whose synthesis is partially repressed by methionine.

REGULATION AND ALLOSTERIC PROTEINS

How does lactose, by combining with the lactose repressor, abolish the repressor's ability to attach to the lactose operator? Surely not by preventing the repressor from binding to DNA by getting in the way—lactose, a small sugar molecule, could not possibly be bound to the same site on the repressor which binds the much bigger and chemically very different operator, a segment of DNA perhaps eight bases long. How does isoleucine inhibit the enzyme threonine deaminase? Isoleucine cannot prevent threonine, the enzyme's substrate, from entering the enzyme's active site simply by occupying that site itself, for threonine and isoleucine bear little resemblance to each other apart from both being amino acids. The active site could not attract and bind them both.

The chemical independence of the regulated system and of the regulatory signal—inducer, end product, or inhibitor—is a fundamental feature of regulatory mechanisms. It makes possible delicacy and latitude in the regulation of a multitude of interacting chemical reactions. It also provides the clue to the mechanism of action of regulatory signals.

In the 1960s, Jacob, Monod, and Jean-Pierre Changeux proposed that regulatory proteins such as enzymes subject to regulation by feedback inhibition have at least two distinct binding sites and can exist in two three-dimensional shapes, or conformations. They baptized such proteins *allosteric*, meaning "having two sites."

A regulatory enzyme such as threonine deaminase has a binding site for the substrate, threonine, and another for the inhibitor, isoleucine. In its catalytically active conformation, the substrate site has the right shape to bind threonine, but the inhibitor site is deformed and cannot

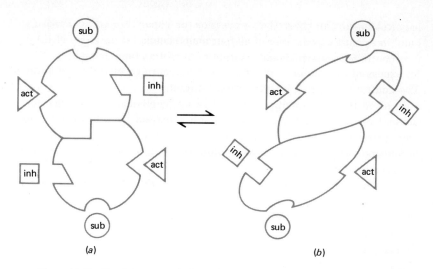

Figure 11-13 Regulatory control of an allosteric enzyme (such enzymes are thought to consist necessarily of several identical subunits, two in this case). In the active form *(a)*, the enzyme can bind substrate (sub) and activator (act) but cannot bind an inhibitor (inh). In the other, inactive, form *(b)*, the enzyme can bind inhibitor but cannot bind substrate or activator.

bind isoleucine. In the absence of inhibitor, most enzyme is in this conformation, which is stabilized by binding of the substrate.

In the enzyme's inactive conformation, the inhibitor site has the right shape to bind isoleucine, but the substrate site is deformed and cannot bind threonine. In the presence of isoleucine, most enzyme is in this conformation because it is stabilized by the binding of the inhibitor.

Not only can enzyme activity be inhibited, it can also be enhanced by interaction with a small regulatory molecule. In this case, binding of the regulator, the activator, to its allosteric site stabilizes and therefore favors the active conformation of the enzyme.

Repressors probably function in a similar way. In the case of induction, binding of the inducer, for example, lactose, would favor the inactive conformation of the repressor in which it is unable to bind to the operator. In the case of induction, binding of the inducer would favor the active form of the repressor in which it binds to the operator and prevents transcription of the DNA.

Probably most regulatory proteins are subject to more than one kind of regulation—inhibition by one or more end products, activation by a substance formed by degradation of the end product or by a substance from another biochemical pathway, for example (thereby guaranteeing appropriate relative amounts of substances such as amino acids), or by a precursor of the substrate, or even by the substrate itself. Each small molecule acting as a regulator is bound to its own site in one or the other of the two (active and inactive) enzyme conformations.

The delicacy of these complex controls is further enhanced by differences in binding strength. For example, if an activator is strongly bound to its site whereas an inhibitor is only weakly bound to its site, then a relatively small amount of activator will have a great effect despite the presence of a relatively large amount of inhibitor.

How are regulatory states intermediate between active and inactive, "on" and "off," attained? Each individual protein molecule at any instant in time is in either the active or inactive conformation, it is true. But the fraction of protein molecules in each conformation depends on the concentration of inhibitor or activator, or in the case of multiple regulation on the relative concentrations of inhibitors and activators. To take a simple case, only a great abundance of isoleucine will inhibit all molecules of threonine deaminase. An intermediate concentration will inhibit only a fraction of the enzyme molecules, and this fraction will fluctuate as the concentration of isoleucine fluctuates.

CONTROL BY CHEMICAL MODIFICATION OF ENZYMES

The regulatory mechanisms described above were discovered and have been demonstrated beyond a doubt in bacteria. Though probably the same sort of mechanisms exist in the cells of higher organisms, proof is sadly lacking because the clinching genetic experiments are not yet feasible in these cells.

But bacteria and viruses do not always carry the day. Another regulatory mechanism, control by chemical modification of enzymes, was discovered and has been studied chiefly in animal tissues, and has only recently attracted attention in bacteria, where its importance is now also acknowledged.

Several kinds of chemical modification are known. An enzyme may be turned "on" by joining two sulfhydryl groups ——S——H to form a disulfide bond ——S——S—— and "off" by re-forming the sulfhydryl groups, or vice versa. Other enzymes are turned "on" and "off" by the attachment and detachment of a phosphate—the active enzyme is in some cases the phosphorylated protein and in other cases the unphosphorylated protein. The "on-off" reaction can be the attachment and detachment of adenosine, part of the cell's energy "money," ATP. In general, such chemical modifications are mediated by two regulatory modifying enzymes, one to do and the other to undo.

The uniqueness of control by chemical modification lies in the stability of the two forms of the enzyme. This permits the "on" or "off" state of an enzyme, perhaps in some instances the entire metabolic pattern of a cell, to be maintained even after the regulatory signal which triggered the chemical modification is no longer present.

Certain hormones exert their effect, at least in part, by promoting the chemical modification of proteins in their target cells. One effect of insulin is the activation by dephosphorylation of an enzyme, glycogen synthetase, which polymerizes glucose to form glycogen (which serves in animals as a glucose reserve). One of the manifold effects of the stress hormone adrenalin is to trigger chemical modifications that activate enzymes which break down glycogen into glucose; this raises the level of sugar in the blood, providing a quick emergency source of energy. The regulatory signals which reverse these hormone-induced chemical modifications have not yet been discovered.

MUCH REMAINS UNKNOWN ABOUT CONTROL MECHANISMS

Induction, repression, and positive control of enzyme synthesis, and inhibition and activation of enzyme activity by allosteric effects and by chemical modifications, these are not the whole story of regulation. In particular, the complex organization of higher organisms may well entail control mechanisms vastly more elaborate than those found in bacteria and viruses. Yet because of still unresolved technical problems and because of the mechanisms' very complexity, little is known with certainty, and, as will be seen, the mechanisms of regulation and coordination in animal cells remain a major and most tantalizing mystery.

THE MOLECULAR BIOLOGY OF TOMORROW

Many questions have been asked in this book and many problems described. Some questions have been answered. Others are being answered, at least in bacteria. In fact, a complete description of the molecular biologists's little pet, the bacterium *Escherichia coli,* will no doubt be achieved in the not-so-far-off future. An understanding of the cells of higher organisms is another story altogether.

What goes on inside the cells of higher organisms? At the most fundamental level, all cells are very similar. Their genetic material is DNA, probably duplicated in about the same as yet obscure way. The genetic information in DNA, its sequence of bases, is transcribed into messenger RNA. Protein is synthesized by means of this messenger RNA with the help of transfer RNAs, ribosomes, and various special factors, in almost the same way and using exactly the same code in all cells. The regulatory mechanisms which control the rate of protein synthesis and the activity of enzymes in bacterial cells may or may not exist in animal cells: much evidence suggests that they do; it would be most surprising if they do not.

But the cells of higher organisms, plant or animal, differ in striking ways from bacterial cells, and these differences must inevitably be associated with molecular interactions unknown in bacteria. The cells of higher organisms contain a nucleus, separated from the rest of the

THE COMPLEX CELLS OF HIGHER ORGANISMS

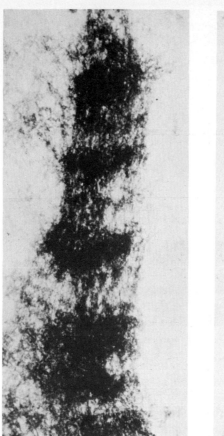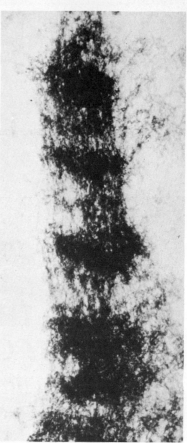

Figure 12-1 Stereo pair of photographs made with an ultrahigh-voltage electron microscope at 1 million volts showing part of a giant chromosome of the fruit fly. The chromosome is seen to be a cylindrical structure consisting of segments where thin filaments (essentially DNA and protein) run fairly straight and segments where filaments are folded into dense masses (magnification × 14,000). *(From Hans Ris, J. de Microscopie,* **8:**761 (1969), *courtesy Hans Ris.)* For instructions on how to view these photographs, see fig. 3-25, p. 69.

cell by the nuclear membrane and containing the master plans of the organism, its DNA, organized as chromosomes (whose structure is largely unknown). In addition, the cells of higher organisms are much larger than bacteria—mitochondria, of which a cell may contain many thousands, are themselves about the size of bacteria.

The very size of animal cells poses as yet unresolved problems of structure and transport of materials. A conspicuous example is a nerve cell whose nucleus, located in the spinal cord, contains the genetic information for synthesizing special enzymes needed at the extremities, which may be several feet away. Surely the messenger RNA, or the enzyme itself if it is synthesized near the nucleus, must in some way be expedited on its long journey to the end of the cell.

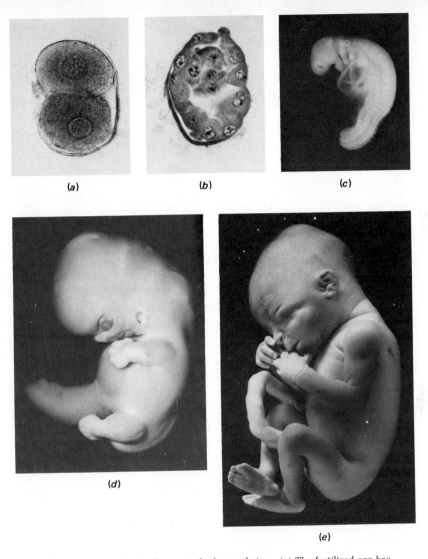

(a) (b) (c)

(d)

(e)

Figure 12-2 Stages in the development of a human being. *(a)* The fertilized egg has divided for the first time. *(b)* This 4-day-old embryo, consisting of fifty-eight cells, is differentiated into an outer layer, an inner cell mass, and a cavity. *(c)* Eyes, ears, lungs, and arms can be discerned in this 26-day embryo. *(d)* At 37 days of age, the embryo is clearly destined to become a human being. *(e)* At 19 weeks, the fetus appears to be a perfect, though tiny (11-inch-long, or 170-mm-long), baby. *(Courtesy Carnegie Institution of Washington.)*

The cells of higher animals (and of the less studied higher plants) differ from bacteria not only in having a more complex internal structure. They also have a different way of life, being specialized members of a multicellular organism. How do cells become specialized? What mechanism organizes and coordinates the specialized cells into organs and tissues? These questions are almost as baffling now as the mechanism of inheri-

HOW DO CELLS BECOME SPECIALIZED?

tance was before the work of Mendel. Their immensity can be appreciated when it is remembered that a human being in all its complexity, with
functioning and interrelated liver, heart, muscles, nervous system, starts
out as one unspecialized cell, the fertilized egg.

How is this accomplished? Embryologists have been trying to find out
since the invention of the microscope. Their work provides a description of the process.

**Determination
Precedes
Specialization**

The first step leading to the specialization of a cell is the determination
of its future role, whether it will be a liver, muscle, or nerve cell. This
is determined at an early stage in embryonic life, a result of the cell's
location in the embryo. For example, early in the development of the
salamander, when it looks like little more than a lump, a bit of skin from
the future forelimb area can be transplanted to the flank of another
embryo. There, much later and despite its inappropriate location it will
develop into a forelimb, an extra arm growing out of the side of the salamander. Clearly, the fate of that bit of skin had long since been irrevo-
cably determined.

Figure 12-3 Limb transplantation in
the salamander. A bit of tissue
destined to become a limb is transplanted from one early embryo to the
flank of another. This embryo de-
velops into a five-limbed salamander.
*(Courtesy V. Hamburger and "Encyclo-
paedia Britannica.")*

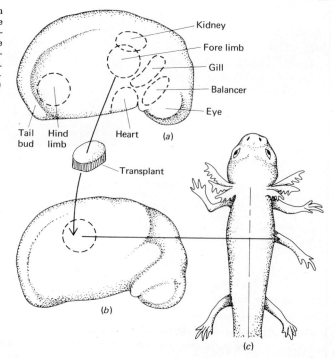

The molecular biologist asks, "What is the initial step in specialization, the chemical event, or the series of events, which determines the fate of a cell?" So far he has no answer.

Some time after the future role of a cell is determined, the cell, or its daughters or granddaughters, takes up its specialized functions: Red blood cells synthesize hemoglobin; a hormone-producing or milk-producing cell synthesizes its special product plus the apparatus needed to export that product from the cell; a nerve cell synthesizes the enzymes, structural proteins, and effectors needed to receive, propagate, and transmit nerve impulses. In general, each cell synthesizes the particular proteins required for the performance of its particular job. **Specialization Requires Control of Protein Synthesis**

What control mechanisms determine which proteins a specialized cell synthesizes? The 1970s may well see this question answered, at least in part, for the first years have produced what appear to be important clues. Control mechanisms operating in phage-infected bacteria may also exist in animal cells, playing an important role in specialization.

As has already been described, positive control in the phage lambda is probably mediated in part by modification of RNA polymerase: the modified enzyme apparently recognizes previously unrecognizable promotor sites and is thus able to transcribe into messenger RNA previously inaccessible genes. In animal cells also it is possible that the RNA polymerase from one type of specialized cell will efficiently synthesize messenger RNA with DNA from that type of cell, but not from another. Thus, different kinds of specialized cells may have their own particular RNA polymerase which recognizes and transcribes into messenger RNA only the genes coding for the proteins which that type of cell must synthesize.

At another level of protein synthesis, cell specificity may also exist. It was first discovered that following infection by the phage T4 bacterial ribosomes are modified so that with bacterial messenger RNA they synthesize protein only poorly whereas with phage messenger RNA they synthesize protein well. This is apparently because phage infection results in a new set of the initiation factors necessary for the first step in protein synthesis, attachment of ribosomes to initiation codons; the phage's initiation factors work well only with phage messenger RNA.

In animal cells also, different types of cells may have different types of initiation factors. For example, there is some evidence that messenger RNA specifying the muscle protein myosin is not translated into protein by ribosomes from red blood cells unless the ribosomes are supplied with initiation factors from muscle cells.

Clearly, specialized RNA polymerase and specialized initiation factors could go a long way toward enabling specialized cells to synthesize only their own particular sets of proteins.

Specialized Cells Form Organs

Cells which are determined to have a particular function will, as they grow and multiply, become more and more specialized and group themselves into a recognizable and, finally, mature organ. Embryologists have discovered that this process proceeds with uncanny accuracy. A striking example is the growth back to the visual centers of the brain of the thousands of nerve fibers arising in the retina of the eye.

In order for an animal to see accurately, the optic nerves must each join to the appropriate nerves in the brain so that a visual image projected on the retina becomes a corresponding pattern of nerve impulses projected on the brain. Each nerve fiber somehow connects up to exactly the right spot. This has been demonstrated by rotating the eyeball of a fish or salamander embryo long before the optic nerve has grown back to the brain (and by rotating the eyeball of an adult animal after severing the optic nerve). Though the optic nerve may look like a tangled mass as it grows back to the brain, nevertheless each of its thousands of fibers finds its right place in the brain—so the poor animal sees perfectly well and in fine detail, but because the eyeball has been rotated, upside down and backward!

What chemical clues enable each fiber of the optic nerve to find its way home? What chemical clues had enabled the formation of the beautiful eyeball itself, with its many interrelated parts, the cornea with five distinct layers, the lens multilayered like an onion, the retina with more

Figure 12-4 This frog has a white patch on its back because when it was a tadpole, white belly skin was grafted there. When the frog's white patch is tickled, he scratches his belly not his back. This inappropriate behavior indicates an uncanny matching up of a specific part of the central nervous system with its appropriate tissue. *(From R. E. Baker, Nature, 236:235 (1972), courtesy Robert Baker.)*

than a score of different kinds of specialized cells organized into ten layers? In what way is the structure of any organ realized? Not known. How does a single cell, the fertilized egg, develop into functional organs made up of a multitude of specialized cells and articulated into a coordinated organism? The molecular basis of development is still a profound mystery.

How do we think? How do we remember, make decisions, solve problems? How, in sum, do the brain and spinal cord, together with the peripheral nervous system, perform their role of regulating and integrating body functions and of relating the individual to the outside world? At no level is the functioning of the brain well understood, either in lower animals or in man.

**HOW DO
WE THINK?**

The psychologist is unable to answer in detail his questions about behavior. How does an animal integrate information coming in from the outside world through its sensory organs? How does it decide on a course of action related to that information? How does an animal remember, and what is the difference between short-term and long-term memory? How does it learn, so that future behavior is modified by new information? How—perhaps the most characteristic function of the human brain, shared by only a few of the higher animals and then only to a much lesser extent—does an animal imagine, does it enact in its mind's eye the future, constructing in its head the problem to be solved and there working out its solution? It is this ability, closely related to the ability to speak, which enables man to successfully go to the hunt or the laboratory, employing the tools he has himself created. It is a by-product of this ability which endows man with a consciousness of his own existence, the projection of himself into his dreams, his aspirations, and, for better or for worse, his goals.

The neurophysiologist studies not behavior but the physiology of the nervous system. He tries, for example, to map the brain, to determine which of its parts are responsible for which of its manifold functions. In some cases he has had great success. Nerve impulses coming in from the sense organs go to precisely mapped areas of the brain; commands going out to the muscles depart from other equally well-mapped areas. The sensation of pleasure arises in the pleasure center; a monkey with an electrode implanted there will again and again push the button which causes an electric current to excite the nerves in that area.

But the brain is still largely unmapped, and many of its most interesting functions are only vaguely localized. Where are plans made? Important question, for without a plan, a program of action, not even the simplest voluntary motion can be accomplished. Where are memories stored?

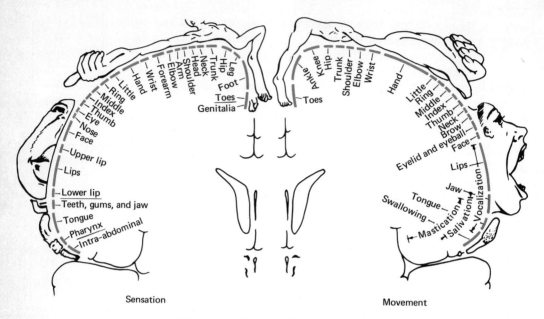

Sensation

Movement

Figure 12-5 Maps of the areas of the cerebral cortex of man devoted to sensation and movement (though drawn side by side, the part of the cerebral cortex devoted to movement in reality lies in front of the part devoted to sensation). Note that in the hand, for example, more importance is accorded movement than sensation, whereas in the lips the reverse is true. *(Reprinted with the permission of the Macmillan Company from W. Penfield and T. Rasmussen, "The Cerebral Cortex of Man," Macmillan, New York, 1950.)*

Apparently memory storage is diffuse, for rather extensive brain damage or disruption may affect memory only minimally.

This question is challenging both the neurophysiologist and computer engineer: How are the interconnections, of which there may be hundreds per cell, organized among the perhaps 100,000 million nerve cells of the human central nervous system? In an attempt to tackle this question, some neurophysiologists are probing the nervous systems of lowly creatures like crayfish, crabs, or mollusks, which have countable numbers of nerve cells. They have found that the nerve cells themselves have a complex behavior: A single cell can when excited emit either a fast or slow discharge and can either excite or inhibit other nerve cells.

In addition, single cells can affect whole sets of muscles. In the central nervous system of the crayfish, for example, electric stimulation of different *single* nerve cells causes contraction of different *groups* of muscles, leading to flexing, extension, or other movements of the stomach and tail. Reflex reactions in humans may well involve similar inborn circuitry, but learning clearly implies the setting up of new nerve pathways.

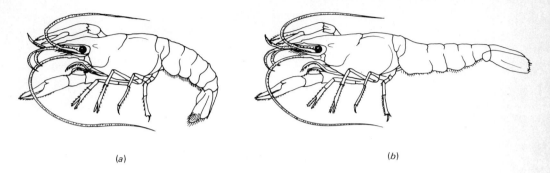

(a)   (b)

Figure 12-6 Stimulation of a single nerve cell in the central nervous system of the crayfish can elicit a complex response. (a) Before stimulation the abdomen is curled under. (b) Stimulation causes extension which involves all segments of the abdomen.

Using his machine, which compared to the human nervous system has so few and so simple components, the computer engineer tries to imitate the mighty human brain. To a certain extent he has succeeded, for computers can solve many of the classic problems of intelligence tests. Machines are as yet far from being geniuses, but the modest intelligence which has been achieved supports the idea that the organization of interconnected subunits underlies the ability to reason, to make decisions, to think.

Finally, at a molecular level how does the nervous system work? How, for a start, does a nerve impulse travel along a nerve fiber? This question has to some extent been answered: Very briefly, an advancing change in permeability moves rapidly along the cell membrane, permitting sodium ions to enter the cell; the interior of the cell thus becomes progressively electrically positive, the exterior negative. The molecular basis of this change in permeability, on which propagation of the nerve impulse depends, is unknown.

How does the nerve impulse jump from one nerve cell to another? Nerve cells are not in intimate contact. The tiny space between them, across which the impulse must jump, is called the *synapse*. Some of the chemicals—acetylcholine and norepinephrine—involved in transmission across the synapse are known. The highly complex structure of nerve cells at the synapse is attracting a great deal of attention and is slowly being worked out.

Why is the synapse so fascinating? All the higher brain functions—remembering, learning, that is, modifying preexisting patterns of response, problem solving, and judgment making—may well depend on unknown chemical processes which permanently facilitate or inhibit the passage of electric impulses across synapses. The result would be

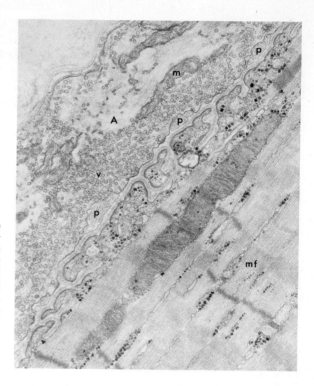

Figure 12-7 The junction between muscle and a nerve cell is very complex. A nerve-cell ending, or axon (A), is here shown in contact with muscle (mf), the banded tissue in the lower right. (P indicates parts of another cell, a Schwann cell.) Stimulation of the nerve causes rupture of the synaptic vesicles (V) which release transmitter substances into the space separating the nerve and muscle, thereby stimulating the muscle. *(From B. Ceccarelli, W. P. Hulburt, and A. Mauro, J. Cell Biol., 1972, courtesy Bruno Ceccarelli and David Sabatini.)*

a modification of the communications between particular nerve cells and a permanent change in the way the brain responds to particular stimuli.

To us humans, probably the most fascinating of all biologic phenomena is our own brain. At every level we would like to know how it works. At every level we are still confronted by profound mystery.

WHY MOLECULAR BIOLOGY?

Why any kind of scientific investigation?

Because the human being is more curious than the cat and demands answers to his questions. Because conquering the unknown is thrilling. Because knowledge is deeply satisfying.

Knowledge also brings practical bonuses. The bonuses of molecular biology lie in the field of medicine, and some of its contributions have been mentioned. In fact, modern medicine and molecular biology are inseparable. Upon the assay of particular enzymes in the blood, for example, depends the diagnosis of many diseases and the monitoring of the progress of others, such as the course of recovery from a heart attack.

Molecular biology has provided the facts needed to understand the cause of many diseases and sometimes to make possible their diagnosis, their cure, or their prevention. Molecular biology may soon provide the tools to fight virus diseases—since 1970, synthetic RNA has been tested for its effectiveness in inducing formation of a substance called *interferon*, a protein which is normally synthesized only by virus-infected cells and which protects healthy cells from viral infection. Of course the great hope is that molecular biology will, in probing the secrets of cell and organism, uncover the nature of cancer, making possible its prevention, cure, or control.

But the ultimate contributions of a new and brilliantly developing field of science cannot be foretold. Scientific discoveries which answer philosophical questions today may change our lives tomorrow. Could the great eighteenth- and nineteenth-century investigators of the fundamental laws of electricity have foreseen that their scientific discoveries would one day move and light the world?

SUGGESTED READINGS

Asimov, Isaac: "A Short History of Chemistry," Educational Services, Inc., Washington, 1965.

Berrill, N. J.: "Developmental Biology," McGraw-Hill Book Co., New York, 1971.

Brock, Thomas D. (ed.): "Milestones in Microbiology," Prentice-Hall, Englewood Cliffs, N.J., 1961. Includes original papers by Leeuwenhoek, Pasteur, Jenner, d'Herelle, and others.

Crick, Francis: "Of Molecules and Men," University of Washington Press, Seattle, 1966.

Darwin, Charles: "On the Origin of the Species by Means of Natural Selection, or the Preservation of Favoured Races in the Struggle for Life," available from several publishers. Fascinating, highly recommended reading.

Dickerson, R. E., and Irvin Geis: "The Structure and Action of Proteins," Harper & Row, New York, 1969.

"Encyclopaedia Britannica" includes many excellent chemical and biologic articles.

Gamow, George: "The Atom and Its Nucleus," Prentice-Hall, Englewood Cliffs, N.J. 1961.

Pauling, Linus: "College Chemistry," 3d ed., Freeman, San Francisco, 1964. Includes an excellent, interesting explanation of the fundamentals of chemistry.

Peters, James A. (ed.): "Classic Papers in Genetics," Prentice-Hall, Englewood Cliffs, N.J. 1959. Includes original papers of Mendel, Morgan, and others.

Scientific American magazine. Many past Scientific American articles on subjects dealt with in this book can be obtained individually as offprints from W. H. Freeman and Company, 660 Market Street, San Francisco, California 94104; a catalog is supplied on request. Scientific American is most highly recommended to those who wish to keep abreast of advances in molecular biology.

Stent, Gunther S. (ed.): "Papers on Bacterial Viruses," 2d ed., Little, Brown, Boston, 1965. Includes original papers by D'Herelle, Delbrück, Hershey, Benzer, and others; difficult but interesting.

Stern, Curt, and Eva R. Sherwood (eds.): "The Origin of Genetics, a Mendel Source Book," Freeman, San Francisco, 1966. A collection of original documents concerning the birth of genetics, and including a new translation of Mendel's brilliant paper.

Sturtevant, A. H.: "A History of Genetics," Harper & Row, New York, 1965. Written by an eyewitness, student and colleague of T. H. Morgan.

Swanson, C. P.: "The Cell," 3d ed., Prentice-Hall, Englewood Cliffs, N.J. 1969.

Taylor, J. Herbert (ed.): "Selected Papers on Molecular Genetics," Academic, New York, 1965. Includes original papers by Pauling, Ingram, Hershey and Chase, Watson and Crick, and Meselson and Stahl, among others; difficult but interesting reading.

Toner, Peter G., and Katherine E. Carr: "Cell Structure," 2d ed., Churchill Livingstone, Edinburgh, 1971. Includes excellent electron micrographs of cells and organelles.

Winchester, Albert M.: "Genetics," Houghton Mifflin, Boston, 1966. Text of classical genetics with emphasis on human genetics.

INDEX

6 3 4 1   1